DURCH STARTEN

ENGLISCH GRAMMATIK

5 bis 9

COACHINGBUCH

Verfasser: Franz Zach

Diesem Buch ist ein Lösungsheft zu den Übungen beigelegt.

Entspricht der Rechtschreibreform 2006

Bibliografische Information der Deutschen Bibliothek:
Die Deutsche Bibliothek verzeichnet diese Publikation in der Deutschen Nationalbibliografie; detaillierte bibliografische Daten sind im Internet über http://dnb.ddb.de abrufbar.

VERITAS-VERLAG, Linz

6. Auflage 2015

www.durchstarten.at
Lektorat: Klaus Kopinitsch
Grafische Gestaltung: Gottfried Moritz
Illustrationen: Helmut »Dino« Breneis
Herstellung: Julia Dresch
Gedruckt in Österreich auf umweltfreundlich hergestelltem Papier

ISBN 978-3-7058-7130-4

VERITAS

Gemeinsam besser lernen

Inhaltsverzeichnis

HELLO! Welcome to English Grammar!

Das Buch, das du jetzt in Händen hältst, fasst den Inhalt der erfolgreichen Reihe **Durchstarten Englisch** für die **5. bis 8. Schulstufe** zusammen. Es enthält alles, was du nach vier Lernjahren wissen und können solltest, und sogar noch ein bisschen mehr: Du sollst das Buch ja auch noch später als **Nachschlagewerk** oder zum **Auffrischen deiner Kenntnisse** verwenden! **„Englisch Grammatik"** bietet dir also eine leicht verständliche und übersichtliche Zusammenstellung der wichtigsten Kapitel der englischen Sprachlehre und eignet sich so als zuverlässiger Begleiter für alle, die gerade mit dem Erlernen der englischen Sprache beschäftigt sind. Zugleich ist das Buch auch ein ideales Mittel zum Beseitigen von „Lücken" für Schülerinnen und Schüler der Oberstufe.

Der **alphabetische Aufbau** des Buches – von *"The Adjective"* bis *"Word Order"* – und die Einteilung der Seiten – links die „Theorie", rechts die praktischen Übungsbeispiele aus der modernen Umgangssprache – erleichtern dir die Arbeit mit dem Buch. „Schwierige" Punkte der englischen Grammatik werden dabei ausführlicher erklärt, und wo es ratsam erscheint, findest du auch Hinweise auf „Fallen" für Lernende mit deutscher Muttersprache.

Der Abschnitt ***"Additional Exercises"*** ab Seite 150 fasst größere, zusammengehörende Bereiche zusammen und enthält weitere Übungsaufgaben. Einen Hinweis darauf findest du bei den jeweiligen Übungen.

Um dir das Üben zu erleichtern, findest du im beiliegenden **Lösungsheft** noch ein ausführliches **Vokabelverzeichnis** – für alle (Not-)Fälle!

Autor und Verlag wünschen dir vergnügliches und erfolgreiches Arbeiten mit dem Buch und viel Spaß beim Erlernen und Verfestigen der englischen Grammatik! Und vergiss nicht – so schwierig kann Englisch ja auch wieder nicht sein; immerhin wird es in Großbritannien, den USA und vielen anderen Ländern schon von kleinen Kindern gesprochen!

1. KAPITEL	*THE ADJECTIVE* – DAS EIGENSCHAFTSWORT

Das Adjektiv (Eigenschaftswort) teilt uns mit, **wie etwas oder jemand ist**. Adjektive beschreiben somit die **Eigenschaft** von Personen, Tieren und Dingen.

A STELLUNG DES ADJEKTIVS IM SATZ

1 Das Adjektiv steht

- entweder **vor dem Nomen**, das es beschreibt:

  *a **sad story***
  *an **interesting question***
  wonderful holidays

- oder **nach bestimmten Verben**, welche Eigenschaften oder Zustände beschreiben:

  *You **look sad** today!*
  *This soup **tastes interesting**.*
  *Frank, you **are wonderful**!*

2 Zur Gruppe der „bestimmten Verben" zählen:

- alle Formen von ***to be***: ***am – is – are***; ***was – were***; ***will be***; …
- die Verben ***feel, look, smell, seem, sound*** und ***taste***
- die Verben ***get*** und ***become***, wenn sie „werden" bedeuten

Alle anderen Verben verlangen ein Adverb. Siehe Abschnitte 2A und 2D, Seiten 16 und 20.

3 Diese Adjektive stehen nie vor einem Nomen:

- ***ill*** (krank) und ***well*** (gesund)

  *Uncle Edgar doesn't look very **well**, does he? I hope he's not **ill**.*

Sage daher nicht …		sondern …
an ill man	►	*a **sick** man*
a well man	►	*a **healthy** man*

A 1 **Welche Adjektive gehören in welchen Satz (in der gegebenen Reihenfolge)? Entscheide und setze ein!**

exciting – great – true – dangerous – heroic – long – hard – safe – happy

pretty – beautiful – long – dark – lovely – outstanding – gifted – big – angry – nice

easy – young – hard – much – strict – happy – okay – great – good

ill – happy – difficult – good – well – sick – right

excellent – wonderful – good – old – new – exotic – fantastic – favourite

1. Joe didn't write the English test on Wednesday because he was ... and had to stay in bed. He was quite ... about it because it was a ... test and Joe isn't so ... at English. Now he has more time to study, but he still isn't ... . His doctor said, "A ... child should not worry about school!", and I think he's ... .
2. My dad always says that it wasn't ... to be ... when he was a kid. School was ... work, people didn't have ... money, and most parents were very ... . So I'm really ... to live in our days. School is ..., I have enough money, and my parents are ... – most of the time. I feel ...!
3. "Apollo 13" is an *exciting* film with some ... actors. It is based on a ... story: the ... accidents on the way to the moon and the ... fight of the people in the space ship and on the ground to save the crew. For three ... days, they worked very ... to repair the damage, and it worked! In the end, the men were ... and everybody was ... .
4. Grandma is an ... cook. Her roasts and her pies are ... and her soups are very ..., too. She uses very ... recipes from her grandmother's time, but she also tries out some ... ones from time to time. Last Saturday, for example, she made roast lamb with ... spices and wild rice, and it tasted ...! I think it will become my ... dish!
5. Melanie is a very ... girl. She has ... green eyes, ... hair and a ... smile. She is an ... student and a very ... singer and dancer. But she has a ... problem – she gets ... very often, and then she isn't very ... .

B VERWENDUNGEN DES ADJEKTIVS

Das Adjektiv kann **wie ein Nomen** mit dem Artikel verwendet werden.

- Wenn man eine **ganze Gruppe** meint:

  The rich *and* ***the beautiful****.* ▶ **Die Reichen** und **die Schönen**.
  The old *need our help.* ▶ **Die Alten** brauchen unsere Hilfe.

- Einige Adjektive stehen im **Plural** (Mehrzahl), wenn sie eine Gruppe bezeichnen:

  *the white**s**, the black**s**, the native**s*** ▶ die Weißen, die Schwarzen, die Einheimischen

- Auf die gleiche Art verwendet man Adjektive, welche die **Herkunft** (die Nationalität) angeben und auf ***-ese***, ***-ch*** oder ***-sh*** enden:

  the Chinese, the French, the Irish ▶ die Chinesen, die Franzosen, die Iren

C ADJEKTIVE IN VERBINDUNG MIT *ONE* UND *ONES*

Oft tritt das Adjektiv mit dem Ersatz- oder Füllwort ***one/ones*** auf. Das **Ersatzwort** steht dabei **anstelle eines Nomens**, das man nicht wiederholen will.

The old house belongs to my grandparents, the ***new one*** *is ours.*
Would you like the black trainers or the ***red ones****?*

D REIHENFOLGE BEI MEHREREN ADJEKTIVEN

- Wenn **mehr als ein Adjektiv** zur näheren Beschreibung eines Nomens verwendet wird, gilt die folgende Reihenfolge:

  „subjektiv" vor „objektiv" oder **„Meinung vor Tatsache"**

a	***lovely***	***old***	*lady*
an	***expensive***	***new***	*church*
some	***nice***	***young***	*people*

- Wenn **mehrere „objektive" Adjektive** zur Beschreibung des Nomens verwendet werden, gilt diese Reihenfolge:

	Größe	Alter	Farbe	Herkunft	Material	(Nomen)
a	***small***		***blue***		***glass***	***ball***
an		***old***		***Greek***	***bronze***	***statue***
some	***big***	***new***		***American***	***leather***	***boots***

B 2 Finde die passenden Gruppenbezeichnungen.

1. Both (*die Iren*) and (*die Waliser*) speak a Celtic language.
2. (*die Jungen*) can still learn a lot from (*den Alten*).
3. (*die Briten*), (*die Franzosen*) and (*die Niederländer*) had colonies in Asia.
4. They say that at Halloween, (*die Toten*) come back for one night.
5. (*die Reichen*) live in luxury, but (*die Armen*) don't have enough to eat.
6. What's the English name of the western "Zwei glorreiche Halunken"? – I think it's "(*die Guten, die Bösen und die Hässlichen*)", although there are three and not two.
7. (*die Chinesen*) and (*die Japaner*) eat with chop sticks.
8. In the USA, (*die Weißen*) still earn more money than (*die Schwarzen*).
9. There are special schools for (*die Blinden*) in our town.
10. Mother Teresa took care of (*die Kranken*) in the streets of Kolkata, India.

C 3 Bilde Sätze mit *one/ones* (1–5) oder setze *one/ones* sinnvoll ein (6–10).

example: *pink T-shirt – green T-shirt – I like better* ▶
I like the pink T-shirt better than the green one.

1. new cars – more expensive – old cars
2. old wines – taste better – young wines
3. please give me – blue sweater – not black sweater
4. easier to ski – short skis – long skis
5. as a young man – Dad – drove – cheap cars – now – has – expensive car
6. Tom is crazy! He prefers difficult tests to easy tests.
7. Mum, I need new jeans. – Why? What's wrong with the old jeans?
8. Why did you buy a new PC? – The old PC was too slow for me.
9. There are only some cheap pictures left. The expensive pictures have all been sold.
10. Which dress should I wear? The old dress or the new dress? – I think you look better in the old dress.

Additional exercise Seite 150

D 4 Bringe die angegebenen Adjektive in die richtige Reihenfolge.

1. Italian wine – expensive, old
2. wooden chairs – new, black
3. a metal box – red, small, Japanese
4. blue jeans – old, dirty
5. a leather suitcase – big, new
6. a car – American, pink, old, big
7. a garden gnome – funny, plastic, new
8. soup – Chinese, hot, excellent
9. a girl – dark-haired, Greek, pretty
10. songs – wonderful, old, Austrian
11. a film – new, French, excellent
12. wine – Italian, red, cheap

Additional exercise Seite 150

E STEIGERUNG – *COMPARISON OF THE ADJECTIVE*

Adjektive ermöglichen uns, Dinge und Menschen miteinander zu **vergleichen**. Dazu benötigen wir die **Steigerungsstufen**.

positive Grundstufe	***comparative*** Mehrstufe 1. Steigerungsstufe	***superlative*** Meiststufe 2. Steigerungsstufe
strong	*stronger*	*(the) strongest*
difficult	*more difficult*	*(the) most difficult*
good	*better*	*(the) best*

Englische Adjektive bilden die Steigerung auf drei verschiedene Weisen:

1 Die „einfache" Steigerung mit *-(e)r und -(e)st* betrifft:

- **einsilbige** Adjektive

strong	*stronger*	*(the) strongest*
deep	*deeper*	*(the) deepest*
slow	*slower*	*(the) slowest*

- **zweisilbige** auf ***-le***, ***-er***, ***-y*** und ***-ow***

noble	*nobler*	*(the) noblest*
clever	*cleverer*	*(the) cleverest*
pretty	*prettier*	*(the) prettiest*
shallow	*shallower*	*(the) shallowest*

- **zweisilbige**, die auf der **zweiten Silbe betont** werden

polite	*politer*	*(the) politest*

Rechtschreibung:

- **einfacher Konsonant** nach einfachem Vokal ▶ **Verdoppelung:** *hot* *hotter* *hottest*
- ***-y* nach Konsonant** ▶ ***-i*:** *heavy* *heavier* *heaviest*

2 Die „zusammengesetzte" Steigerung mit *more* und *most* betrifft:

- **alle drei- und mehrsilbigen** Adjektive

dangerous	***more*** *dangerous*	*(the)* ***most*** *dangerous*
extraordinary	***more*** *extraordinary*	*(the)* ***most*** *extraordinary*

- **alle anderen zweisilbigen** Adjektive

useful	***more*** *useful*	*(the)* ***most*** *useful*
famous	***more*** *famous*	*(the)* ***most*** *famous*

3 Die „unregelmäßige" Steigerung betrifft die folgenden Adjektive:

positive	*comparative*	*superlative*	deutsche Bedeutung
good	*better*	*best*	gut
bad	*worse*	*worst*	schlecht, böse
evil	*worse*	*worst*	böse, bösartig
well	*better*	*best*	gesund
ill	*worse*	*worst*	krank
many	*more*	*most*	viele
much	*more*	*most*	viel
little	*less*	*least*	wenig
little	*smaller*	*smallest*	klein
late	*later*	*latest*	(spät, zB Uhrzeit)
	(the) latter	*(the) last*	letzterer – (der) letzte
near	*nearer*	*nearest* *(the) next*	nahe, nächst(gelegen) (der) Nächste (in der Reihe)
far	*farther* *further*	*farthest*	weit (weg, entfernt) weitere (Fragen, Bitten ...)
old	*older* *elder*	*older* *eldest*	alt (normale Bedeutung) älter, (der) älteste ... (nur bei Familienmitgliedern und nur vor dem Nomen)

E 5 **Setze die richtigen (Steigerungs-)Stufen der angegebenen Adjektive ein.**

1. What is the (*expensive*) car that you can buy at the moment? – I'm not sure, but I think it's a Lamborghini or a Bugatti. Both are (*expensive*) than a Bentley or a Rolls-Royce.
2. Our new house is a lot (*large*) than our old one, and it's (*comfortable*), too, because there are not so (*many*) stairs to climb.
3. Jessica is one of the (*pretty*) girls in the world, I think. She is even (*pretty*) than her sister Melanie. – That's true. But the (*late*) is (*nice*), isn't she?
4. I can't drive because I'm not (*old*) enough. But Alice, my (*old*) sister, has got a car; she can drive us. She is six years (*old*) than I.
5. How's Joe? – He's still (*ill*), but he looks (*well*) than yesterday.
6. What's the (*far*) you have ever been away from home? – Hawaii, I think.
7. Have you heard of the explosion? – Yes, we have, and now we are waiting for (*far*) news.
8. My dad is always the (*early*) to arrive in the morning and the (*late*) to leave in the evening.

Additional exercise Seite 151

F VERGLEICHE

Vergleiche können verschieden aussehen. Das lässt sich leicht feststellen, wenn man A mit B vergleicht.

- A ist **so** (nett, gut, breit) **wie** B; A ist **nicht so** (nett ...) **wie** B.
- A ist (netter, besser, breiter) **als** B.
- A oder B ist **der/die/das** (netteste, beste, breiteste).

Auf Englisch sieht das so aus:

positive	*comparative*	*superlative*
as *(nice, good ...)* ***as*** ***not so*** *(nice, good ...)* ***as*** ***not as*** *(nice, good ...)* ***as*** *(nice, good ...)* ***as***	*(nicer, better ...)* ***than*** *(more ..., less ...)* ***than***	***the*** *(nicest, best ...)* ***the*** *(most ..., least ...)*

G „ZUNEHMENDE" STEIGERUNG

Auf Deutsch hilft uns dabei das Wort „immer":

Der Regen wird **immer stärker**. ▶ The rain is getting ***heavier and heavier***.

Lisa wird **immer aufregender**. ▶ *Lisa is getting* ***more and more exciting***.

- „einfache" *(-er, -est)* und „unregelmäßige" Steigerung ▶ Wiederholung der **Mehrstufe**
- „zusammengesetze" Steigerung *(more, most)* ▶ Wiederholung von ***more***

H VERGLEICH MIT „JE – DESTO"

Dafür benötigst du den bestimmten Artikel ***the*** **und die Mehrstufe** ***(comparative)***.

Je größer, **desto** besser. ▶ ***The bigger***, ***the better.***

Je länger du zuwartest, **desto** schlimmer wird alles. ▶ ***The longer*** *you wait,* ***the worse*** *everything gets.*

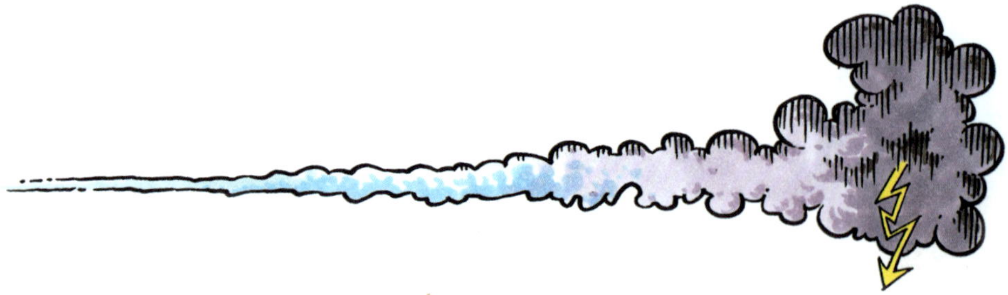

F 6 **Denke logisch und bilde die richtigen Vergleiche.**

example: *Pluto is farther from Earth than any other planet.*

1. You look worried, Tina. What's the matter? – Well, my new motor scooter needs (*much*) ... petrol than I thought, and now I have (*little*) ... money than I should have.
2. Which subject do you like (*good*) ... this year, Kevin? – I hate them all! To me, one subject is (*horrible*) ... as the other.
3. Of all the new people in my class, I like Gloria (*little*) ... . I think she is the (*horrible*) ... person in the world.
4. I'm five centimetres (*tall*) ... than my (*old*) ... brother, although he is a year (*old*) ... than I.
5. The laptop was (*expensive*) ... than I thought, so I have some money left for a USB stick or a mouse.
6. Some people say "The Return of the King" was the (*good*) ... part of the "Lord of the Rings" trilogy, but I think the first part was much (*good*) ... .
7. My dad is 1.75 m, and I'm 1.75 m. So I'm (*tall*) ... him, and very soon I'll be (*tall*) ... than him.
8. Aunt Helen feels (*ill*) ... today than yesterday. I think she should see a doctor (*soon*) ... possible.
9. The tsunami of December 26, 2004, killed (*many*) ... than 200,000 people. It was the (*terrible*) ... natural disaster ever.

Additional exercise Seite 151

G 7 **Bilde die „zunehmende" Steigerung mit den folgenden Beispielen.**

1. I think I'm getting (*good*) at tennis! – That's because you practise so much.
2. After the TV documentary, (*many*) people wanted to help.
3. The night got (*dark*) and the noises outside got (*frightening*).
4. What's the matter with Suzie? She is getting (*arrogant*), don't you think?
5. That's strange! I buy (*few*) things, but I spend (*much*) money.
6. My friends find computer games (*interesting*), but I don't.
7. I tried to catch the letter, but the wind blew it (*far*) away.
8. When I was young, I loved pizza. But now I like it (*little*).
9. The maths test is next week, but I'm getting (*nervous*) every day.

Additional exercise Seite 152

H 8 **Übersetze die folgenden „je – desto"-Sätze in gutes Englisch.**

1. Je höher der Berg, desto dünner die Luft.
2. Je älter ich werde, desto mehr weiß ich.
3. Je stärker der Gegner (*opponent*), desto spannender das Spiel.
4. Je mehr ich darüber nachdenke, desto weniger gefällt mir der Gedanke.
5. Je früher wir beginnen, desto früher sind wir fertig.
6. Je länger du wartest, desto schwieriger wird die Entscheidung (*decision*).
7. Je härter der Kampf, desto größer die Ehre.
8. Je mehr du übst, desto besser wirst du.
9. Je weniger Leute davon wissen, desto besser für uns.

Additional exercise Seite 152

2. KAPITEL *THE ADVERB* – DAS UMSTANDSWORT

Das Adverb (Umstandswort) dient zur **näheren Beschreibung eines Verbs**, eines Adjektivs oder eines anderen Adverbs. Manchmal bezieht es sich auf einen ganzen Satz.

Ein Adverb gibt an:

■ **wie** etwas geschieht	▶ Art und Weise; ***adverbs of manner*** ▶
■ **wo** und/oder **wann** etwas geschieht	▶ Ort und Zeit; ***adverbs of place and time*** ▶
■ **wie oft** etwas geschieht	▶ Häufigkeit; ***adverbs of frequency*** ▶
■ **ob** etwas **stärker oder schwächer** geschieht	▶ Grad, Ausmaß; ***adverbs of degree*** ▶
■ **wie** ein **ganzer Satz** gemeint ist	▶ Satzadverb; ***sentence adverbials*** ▶

A BILDUNG DES ADVERBS

Die ***adverbs of manner*** werden in den meisten Fällen nach dem folgenden Muster gebildet:

adjective + ly

Rechtschreibung:

„Normalfälle"			
adjective ▶	*adverb*	*adjective* ▶	*adverb*
slow	*slow**ly***	*basic*	*basic**ally***
awful	*awful**ly***	*fantastic*	*fantastic**ally***
		Ausnahme!	
		public	*public**ly***
„Sonderfälle"			
*luck**y***	*luck**ily***	*terri**ble***	*terri**bly***
*heav**y***	*heav**ily***	*simp**le***	*simp**ly***
Ausnahmen!			
shy	*shy**ly***	*dry*	*dry**ly***

manner	*slowly, awfully, fantastically, nicely, easily …* *They **walked slowly** into the garden.*	▶ ***how?***
place and time	*here, there, everywhere …; today, yesterday …* *We **saw** them **here yesterday**.*	▶ ***where? when?***
frequency	*always, often, frequently, hardly (ever), never, usually, sometimes, occasionally …* *Joe **always does** his homework.*	▶ ***how often?***
degree	*fairly, rather, very, really, quite* (ziemlich, eher, sehr, wirklich, recht) *James plays the piano **rather well**.*	▶ ***how (well)?***
sentence	*actually, fortunately, luckily, frankly, unfortunately* (eigentlich, glücklicherweise, ehrlich, leider) ***Unfortunately,** I fell and broke my leg.*	

A 9 **Bilde nach dem bekannten Muster die passenden *adverbs of manner*. Beachte dabei die Rechtschreibregeln!**

1. dangerous – weak – careless – bitter – narrow
2. strong – nervous – laughing – sad – polite
3. truthful – important – physical – busy – noisy
4. cold – angry – quick – beautiful – nice
5. spiritual – noble – hot – simple – stupid
6. clever – vertical – open – horrible – strange
7. mechanical – honest – smiling – harmless – dry
8. jealous – powerful – brilliant – useful – sudden

B VERSCHIEDENE BEDEUTUNG VON ADJEKTIV UND ADVERB

Einige *adverbs* sehen so aus, als wären sie „ganz normal" durch das Anhängen von *-ly* aus einem *adjective* entstanden. Doch hier trügt der Schein! In einigen Fällen haben **Adverb und Adjektiv verschiedene Bedeutung**.

adjectives		*adverbs*		*examples*
deep	tief	*deeply*	zutiefst	*You were in deep thoughts.* *We were deeply disappointed.*
direct	direkt	*directly*	gleich, sofort	*I want a direct answer!* *Send him to me directly, please!*
free	frei, gratis	*freely*	freimütig, ohne Scheu	*Free words in a free press!* *They walked around freely.*
hard	hart, schwer	*hardly*	kaum	*I worked hard all day.* *I hardly worked all day.*
high	hoch	*highly*	höchst, sehr	*It was high time to leave.* *TNT is highly explosive.*
late	spät	*lately*	vor kurzem, unlängst	*The bus leaves late at night.* *Have you seen Joe lately?*
most	am meisten	*mostly*	hauptsächlich	*What I hate most is milk!* *They played mostly Hip Hop.*
near	nahe	*nearly*	beinahe, fast	*Dad parked near the church.* *I nearly forgot to phone you.*

B 10 ***Adjective or adverb?* Welche Form passt? Überlege und streiche das falsche Wort durch.**

1. I think the post office is *near/nearly* the train station. Let's ask somebody!
2. Mum is *deep/deeply* worried because I had a "D" in my English test.
3. What tourist like *most/mostly* about Austria is the beautiful countryside in the mountains, but *hard/hardly* anybody knows the "Weinviertel".
4. Trudy is a vegetarian. She eats *most/mostly* salads and vegetable dishes.
5. William has been very busy *late/lately*. On some days he works until *late/lately* at night.
6. Peter says he can get us *free/freely* tickets to the Champions League matches! – Really? That's *hard/hardly* to believe, but let's hope it's true.
7. Uncle Sam drives only American cars, *most/mostly* Cadillacs or Lincolns.
8. How's the new physics teacher, Colin? – I *hard/hardly* know him, but they say he is *high/highly* respected by everyone.
9. If you ask me a *direct/directly* question, I will answer it *direct/directly*.

C „AUSNAHMEN"

- **Einige Adverbien** werden **nicht durch das Anhängen von *-ly*** gebildet. Entweder sie gleichen den Adjektiven oder sie sind „Sonderformen".

adject.	*adverbs*	Bedeutung	*examples*
good	*well*	gut	*This is a very good text.* *You've done it very well.*
fast	*fast*	schnell, rasch	*My dad always has fast cars.* *He likes to drive fast.*
hard	*hard*	hart, schwer	*This was a hard day for me.* *I had to work hard all day.*
high	*high*	hoch	*George loves high mountains.* *He has a house high on the mountain.*
early	*early*	früh, zeitig	*My mum is an "early riser".* *She gets up very early in the morning.*
late	*late*	spät	*Nick usually takes the late bus home.* *But he is never late for school.*

- Manche Adjektive auf *-ly* bilden keine Adverbien. Man verwendet in diesen Fällen die Wendung ***"in a (adjective) way"***.
  Zu dieser Gruppen zählen zB ***friendly, lonely, lovely*** und ***silly***.
  ▶ *Maggie is a **friendly** girl. She always smiles and laughs **in a friendly way.***

C 11 **Finde die passenden *adjectives and adverbs* und setze sie an die richtige Stelle.**

early – early – good – hard – hard – high – high –
high – late – late – late – lovely – silly – well

1. Mr. Franklin is never ... for a lesson. I think he waits outside the classroom.
2. My parents and the Bakers are ... friends, so I know Rosie Baker very ... .
3. Do you ever watch the ... night show on TV? – Yes, every Friday, because I don't have to get up ... on Saturday.
4. For many of my friends, school is ... work. They often study until ... at night.
5. Have you ever climbed a really ... mountain, Julie? – Well, I've been at the foot of the Matterhorn. Is that ... enough?
6. I think you work too ..., Mum. Why don't you go to bed now? You have to get up ... tomorrow morning.
7. That was a very ... question, Sammy! You should be ashamed of yourself!
8. Last summer we stayed at a ... little castle on a rock ... above a river.

Additional exercise Seite 153

D VERBEN, AUF DIE KEIN ADVERB FOLGT

Auf bestimmte Verben folgt das Adjektiv und nicht das Adverb. Diese Verben beschreiben **keine Handlungen, sondern Zustände** (siehe auch 1. Kapitel, A 2, Seite 8).

- Alle Formen von ***to be***:
  The boys ***are tired*** *after a match.*
  I'm sure the next test ***will be easy***.
  This week ***has been awful*** *so far.*

- Die Verben ***feel, look, smell, seem, sound*** und ***taste***, wenn sie einen **Zustand** beschreiben:
  I always ***feel good*** *when I see you.*
  Why do you ***look*** *so* ***sad*** *today, Linda?*
  Mmmmh, this soup ***smells wonderful****!*
  The children ***seem excited****; what's the matter?*
  You ***sound horrible****! What's wrong with you?*
  Grandma's goulash always ***tastes great***.

  ABER ▶ Adverb, wenn das Verb eine **Handlung** beschreibt
  Mary ***felt nervously*** *for my hand during the film.* ▶ Handlung
  Justin ***looked*** *at me* ***sadly****, but I had no idea why.* ▶ Handlung
  Our dog always ***smells carefully*** *at everything.* ▶ Handlung
  The shopkeeper ***sounded*** *the alarm* ***quickly*** *after the robbery.* ▶ Handlung

- Die Verben ***get, go, grow*** und ***become***, wenn sie „werden" bedeuten:
  In autumn, the nights ***get cold*** *very fast.*
  Mum will ***go mad*** *if you don't tidy your room now.*
  Look at Mr. Myers! He ***has grown old*** *this year, hasn't he?*
  Joe ***will become*** *very* ***successful****, I am sure.*

E STEIGERUNG – *COMPARISON OF THE ADVERB*

So wie das Adjektiv lässt sich auch das Adverb steigern:

Wie?	Was?	zum Beispiel:
more und ***most***	alle Adverbien, die sich durch das Anhängen von ***-ly*** aus einem Adjektiv ableiten lassen	***loudly – more loudly – most loudly*** ***carefully – more carefully – most carefully***
-(e)r und ***-(e)st***	alle Adverbien, die sich nicht durch Anhängen von ***-ly*** aus einem Adjektiv ableiten lassen	***fast – faster – fastest*** ***late – later – latest*** ***near – nearer – nearest***
unregelmäßig	*well* *badly* *little* (wenig)	***well – better – best*** ***badly – worse – worst*** ***little – less – least***

BCD 12 ***Adjective or adverb?* Wähle die richtige Wortart. Es gelten die Regeln von Seite 12, 13, 18, 19 und 20.**

1. Do you like Ms. Lennox? – The physics teacher? Yes, I do. I think she's an (*excellent*) teacher. Her lessons are (*interesting*) and she can explain things (*good*). I can follow her (*easy*). How about you? – Well, I don't know. She seems (*nice*), but I find some of her lessons (*boring*). And she (*hard*) ever makes any jokes.
2. What's this (*awful*) smell? Has somebody dropped a stink bomb? – No, it comes from the chemistry room. They are experimenting with butyric acid *(Buttersäure)*. It smells (*horrible*), doesn't it? That's why they (*real*) use it in stink bombs, you know? – No, I didn't know. Well, they should stop this experiment (*quick*) and let in some (*fresh*) air.
3. Gina, have you seen Mike (*late*)? – No, I haven't. I think it's (*high*) time that he calls or sends us an email. I think he's the (*lazy*) person I know.
4. My sister-in-law is a (*wonderful*) cook. Yesterday she made roast beef, and I've never eaten anything so (*good*). She says roast beef is (*typical*) English, and she always makes it in the (*typical*) way, with lots of gravy and green peas.
5. Why are you looking at me so (*angry*), Mum? What have I done? – Well, I (*real*) am (*angry*)! I told you (*very friendly*) to tidy up your room, but you haven't done it! Instead, you sit around (*quiet*), listening to this (*terrible*) music! Now get up and do as I said, and do it (*quick*)!
6. Charlie is the (*perfect*) boyfriend! He is (*handsome*) and (*athletic*), he behaves (*good*), he is (*good*) at sports, he has a (*beautiful*) voice and he dances (*fantastic*). And he is (*nice*) to my parents.
7. Drive (*careful*), Dad! The roads are (*icy*) and there is a (*strong*) wind blowing. – I know. I promise I won't drive (*fast*) today. So don't worry if I come home (*late*) than usual tonight.
8. My brother Anthony is four years (*old*) than I, but he is not the (*oldest*) child in the family. He is two years (*young*) than Reggie, who is our (*old*) brother.
9. Ireland is one of the (*expensive*) countries in Europa at the moment. Almost everything costs (*much*) than in Austria. In the past, it was the other way round: Ireland was a lot (*cheap*). So it's not (*easy*) to spend a long holiday there as it was before.

Additional exercise Seite 153

E 13 **Wandle die folgenden Adjektive in *adverbs* um und bilde die Mehr- und die Meiststufe *(comparative and superlative)*.**

examples: *slow* ▶ *slowly – more slowly – most slowly*
hard ▶ *hard – harder – hardest*

1. happy	4. beautiful	7. near	10. bad
2. stupid	5. heavy	8. honest	11. serious
3. wide	6. fast	9. early	12. high

Auch für das **Adverb** gelten die **Regeln der *word order***! (Siehe dazu Kapitel 26, Seite 148.)

F ORTS- UND ZEITANGABEN

Adverbs of place und ***adverbs of time*** stehen entweder **am Beginn oder am Ende des Satzes**. Am Satzende gilt außerdem „Ort vor Zeit" oder *"place before time"*.

> ***Yesterday*** *my dad bought me some blank CDs.*
> *My dad bought me some blank CDs* ***yesterday****.*
> ***Upstairs*** *it is much warmer.*
> *It is much warmer* ***upstairs****.*
> *Let's meet again* ***here tonight****!*

G HÄUFIGKEITSADVERBIEN

Die Häufigkeitsadverbien ***(adverbs of frequency)*** können an drei Stellen im Satz auftreten:

- **zwischen Subjekt und Prädikat**; das ist der „Normalfall":
  My brother never watches *love stories.*
  S adv P

- **nach der Form von *to be*:**
  My grandparents ***were always*** *the first to go to bed.*
  to be adv

- **nach dem ersten Prädikatsteil:**
  I ***will often think*** *of you.*
  P1 adv P2

H REIHENFOLGE BEI MEHREREN ADVERBIEN AM SATZENDE

Das Adverb der Art und Weise (Modaladverb, ***adverb of manner***) – im Wesentlichen also das Adverb, das mit ***-ly*** gebildet wird – steht **in den allermeisten Fällen am Satzende** (die Ausnahmefälle interessieren uns hier und jetzt nicht).
Soll auch noch eine Orts- und/oder Zeitangabe gemacht werden, dann gilt die alphabetische Reihenfolge: ***manner*** – ***place*** – ***time*** oder **Art** – **Ort** – **Zeit**:

manner (Art)	***place*** (Ort)	***time*** (Zeit)
how?	***where?***	***when?***

Sandra paints and draws ***beautifully****.*	▶	***how?***
The children played ***quietly indoors****.*	▶	***how? where?***
Jenny cried ***silently in her bed last night****.*	▶	***how? where? when?***
Fred walked home ***slowly today****.*	▶	***how? when?***

F 14 **Setze die angegebenen Adverbien an die richtige Stelle im Satz. Denke daran, dass es auch mehr als eine richtige Lösung geben kann.**

1. Somebody saw us. (*yesterday, here*)
2. They will tell us more about it. (*tomorrow*)
3. I could not find my English things. (*anywhere, yesterday*)
4. You shouldn't stay. (*today, indoors*)
5. Tom works at a café. I met him. (*yesterday, there*)
6. People study English. (*everywhere, today*)
7. You wanted to speak with me. Well, I am (*now, here*).
8. We'd really like to help you, but we haven't got the time. (*now*)
9. We could not play badminton. (*yesterday, outdoors*)
10. Let's go! (*inside, now*)

G 15 **Setze die *adverbs of frequency* an die passende Stelle.**

1. We could find our way out of the wood. (*hardly*)
2. Uncle Walter is at home at this time of the day. (*usually*)
3. They will tell us the whole story. (*never*)
4. We have thought of selling our house. (*sometimes*)
5. I copy my homework from a friend. (*hardly ever*)
6. Paula promised that she would write to me. (*frequently*)
7. Jill has asked herself why she is so unhappy. (*often*)
8. You must ask Henry about his girlfriends. (*never*)
9. Camembert is made from cows' milk. (*usually*)
10. My little brother wants pizza for lunch. (*always*)

H 16 **Alles gemischt! Setze die Adverbien wieder an die passende Stelle.**

1. My dad speaks English and French. (*very bad*)
2. The baby smiled at his mother. (*happily, today*)
3. The dogs ran around. (*outdoors, wildly*)
4. Has it rained? (*today, here*)
5. Everything will work out. (*tomorrow, well*)
6. Before the exam, I was walking around. (*nervously*)
7. This is Mr. Walker. He has been waiting for you. (*upstairs, patiently*)
8. It snowed. (*heavily, yesterday*)
9. They left the house. (*very quietly*)
10. We will have to work. (*fast, today*)

Additional exercise Seite 154

3. KAPITEL *THE ARTICLE* – DER ARTIKEL

Im Englischen gibt es – so wie im Deutschen – zwei Artikel:

- den **unbestimmten Artikel**
  the indefinite article ▶ ***a*** oder ***an***
- den **bestimmten Artikel**
  the definite article ▶ ***the***

Der unbestimmte Artikel ***a/an*** wird im Wesentlichen so verwendet wie im Deutschen. Allerdings gibt es auch ein paar **„Besonderheiten“**, die es zu beachten gilt!

A AUSSPRACHE: *"A"* ODER *"AN"*?

Ob der unbestimmte Artikel *"a" oder "an"* heißt, richtet sich nach der **Aussprache des danach folgenden Wortes:**

Der unbestimmte Artikel heißt ***an***, wenn das folgende Wort **mit einem Vokal** (Selbstlaut) **beginnt.**

an accident
an open window
an hour [auə]

Der unbestimmte Artikel heißt ***a***, wenn das folgende Wort **mit einem Konsonant** (Mitlaut) **beginnt.**

a picture
a window
a uniform [ju:nifɔ:m]

B BESTIMMTE ANGABEN ÜBER EINE PERSON

Angaben über Beruf, Herkunft oder Religion verlangen den unbestimmten Artikel.

*Uncle Edward is **a doctor**.* – Onkel Edward ist Arzt.
*This year's exchange student is **an Australian**.* – ... ist Australier.
*The new boy in my class is **a Buddhist**.* – ... ist (ein) Buddhist.

C AN NACHGEORDNETER STELLE NACH BESTIMMTEN WÖRTERN

Dabei musst du dir die „verkehrte“ Wortstellung merken:

half a, quite a, rather a, such a, what a, once/twice a, too (adjective) a

*Danny's dad won **half a million** dollars in the lottery.* – eine halbe Million
*The axolotl is **quite an ugly** animal.* – ein ziemlich hässliches Tier
*That's **rather a stupid** idea.* – eine ziemlich blöde Idee
*You have **such a nice** voice.* – so eine schöne Stimme
***What a sad** story!* – Was für eine traurige Geschichte!
*I visit my grandparents **once/twice a week**.* – einmal/zweimal pro Woche
*This is **too serious a** matter to laugh about!* – eine zu ernste Sache

A 17 *"a"* oder *"an"*? Die Aussprache des Folgewortes entscheidet!

1. The thief got into the house through ... open window.
2. You can have ... pink blouse or ... orange one.
3. I know that ... penguin is ... bird that can't fly, but what is ... emu? – It's ... Australian bird that doesn't fly.
4. Which has bigger ears, ... African elephant or ... Indian elephant? – I haven't got ... idea! Let's look it up in ... biology book.
5. Do you have to wear ... uniform at your school? – Yes, ... green jacket and black trousers or ... black skirt.
6. Many people want ... united Europe because they think ... united Europe is ... strong Europe.
7. I have ... absolutely crazy idea – let's all dress up as vampires tomorrow!
8. Philip always takes ... apple or ... banana to school with him.
9. Yesterday I spent ... afternoon with my grandparents. We went to ... excellent restaurant first, and then they invited me to ... tour of the city in ... doubledecker bus.

B 18 Finde heraus, welchen Beruf die folgenden Personen haben, woher sie sind oder welcher Religion sie angehören, und bilde entsprechende Sätze.

example: *Dennis repairs cars.* ▶ *Dennis is a mechanic.*

1. Herbert is from Berlin.
2. Malcolm comes from California.
3. Ali prays at a mosque every Friday.
4. My mother takes care of sick people at a hospital.
5. Bono sings and plays with "U2".
6. Betty goes to Holy Mass every Sunday morning.
7. My dad works at a school.
8. Mr. Simmons plans and builds engines.
9. Giovanni was born in Rome.

C 19 Wandle die folgenden Sätze so um, dass ein unbestimmter Artikel an nachgeordneter Stelle steht.

1. I've waited six months for this computer game. (→ *ein halbes Jahr*)
2. The show will begin in 30 minutes. (→ *in einer halben Stunde*)
3. The new Hobbit film is quite good. (→ *ein recht guter Film*)
4. The party at Tom's house was rather boring. (→ *eine recht fade Party*)
5. This room is so beautiful! I love it! (→ *so ein schönes Zimmer*)
6. The night was so cold that we couldn't sleep. (→ *so eine kalte Nacht*)
7. This is a nice surprise! (→ *Was für eine nette Überraschung!*)
8. That's a wonderful idea! (→ *Was für ...*)
9. Every Monday, Jack gets a letter from Canada. (→ *einmal pro Woche*)
10. We go on holiday in May and in September. (→ *zweimal im Jahr*)
11. This question is too difficult for me. (→ *eine zu schwierige Frage*)
12. Yesterday it was too cold for skiing. (→ *ein zu kalter Tag zum ...*)

D WENDUNGEN *(PHRASES)* MIT UNBESTIMMTEM ARTIKEL

- Die wichtigsten Wendungen, welche den unbestimmten Artikel verlangen, sind:

What a pity! It's a pity that …	Wie schade! Es ist schade, dass …
to have ***a headache***	Kopfweh haben
to be ***in a hurry***	es eilig haben, in Eile sein
in a minute	gleich, sofort
in a *(loud, low, shrill …)* ***voice***	mit (lauter, leiser, schriller …) Stimme

- **Der bestimmte Artikel** wird meist **für bestimmte Dinge** verwendet. Er kommt im Englischen seltener vor als im Deutschen, also Vorsicht im Umgang mit ***"the"***.

allgemeiner Fall ▶ ohne *"the"* **besonderer Fall ▶ mit *"the"***

E HERAUSHEBEN VON PERSONEN ODER DINGEN AUS DER ALLGEMEINEN MENGE

Boys *like football.*
(Buben im Allgemeinen, alle Buben)

We gave ***the boys*** *a new football.*
(ganz bestimmte Buben)

Life *can be very hard.*
(das Leben an sich, ganz allgemein)

*"****The Life*** *of Brian" is a great film.*
(das Leben eines bestimmten Mannes)

Water *freezes at 0° centigrade.*
(Wasser im Allgemeinen)

The water *is boiling. Let's make tea.*
(das Wasser auf dem Herd)

F TAGE, MONATE, JAHRESZEITEN

Summer *is my favourite season.*
(deutsch: Der Sommer ist …)

Do you remember ***the summer*** *of 2010?*
(ein ganz bestimmter Sommer)

This year, ***Friday*** *is the hardest day.*
(jeder Freitag; dt: der Freitag)

Bob leaves on ***the Friday*** *after Easter.*
(an dem Freitag …; bestimmter Tag)

February *is the shortest month.*
(das ist jedes Jahr so)

The February *of 2016 will have 29 days.*
(nicht jeder Februar, aber dieser schon)

D 20 Setze die passenden *phrases* mit dem unbestimmten Artikel ein.

1. I can't stop to speak with you. I'm ... (*es eilig haben*).
2. (*Wie schade*) ... that you didn't "fly" the London Eye on your last visit.
3. Mum has gone to bed because she ... (*Kopfweh haben*).
4. Please come in and sit down. Mr. Brown will be here ... (*sofort*).
5. (*es ist schade*) ... that we missed the beginning of the play.
6. The bride said ... (*mit lauter Stimme*), "I will!".
7. Joe was ... (*es eilig haben*) because he wanted to catch his train.
8. Please turn off the radio; I've got ... (*starkes Kopfweh haben*).
9. Waiter to new guests: "I'll be with you ... (*gleich*)!"
10. Our maths teacher always speaks ... (*mit leiser Stimme*) so we can't hear what she is saying.
11. Jane looks terrible. She says she's got ... (*schreckliches Kopfweh*).
12. "Help! Help!" somebody shouted ... (*mit schriller Stimme*).

E 21 Mit oder ohne *"the"*? Denke daran: Nur bestimmte Fälle verlangen den bestimmten Artikel! Streiche die falsche Lösung weg.

1. *Cheese/The cheese* you brought back from Italy tastes interesting.
2. A good teacher should like *children/the children*.
3. I like *music/the music* of "Captain America" better than the film!
4. Luke usually drinks *coffee/the coffee* after lunch.
5. *People/The people* in this shop all want to buy *CDs/the CDs*.
6. *Life/The life* would be very complicated without *computers/the computers*.
7. *Children/The children* are often noisy, but that's *life/the life*.
8. My brother hates *cheese/the cheese*, but I love it.
9. My dad can talk about *music/the music* for hours.
10. Did you take *coffee/the coffee* from *shelf/the shelf*? – Yes, why? – It's old.
11. We must all work together to protect *nature/the nature*.
12. *People/The people* say that Lionel Messi is the best living footballer.

F 22 Auch hier geht es um den bestimmten Artikel: einsetzen oder weglassen?

1. The longest night of the year is in ... December.
2. This week, there will be no school on ... Thursday.
3. For many old people, ... winter is the worst time of the year.
4. "Martin Luther King Day" is on ... third Monday in ... January.
5. ... winter of 2013 was unusually warm.
6. The last Olympic Games in Austria were in ... winter of 1976.
7. I love ... autumn, because all the leaves turn red or golden.
8. Both ... July and ... August have 31 days.
9. ... Saturday is my favourite day because there is no school.
10. In the USA, school starts after Labor Day. That's always ... first Monday in ... September.
11. Terry will always remember ... spring of 2001; that's when he met Sue.
12. I hate ... Monday because I have to go to school again.

G VORSICHT BEIM UMGANG MIT DIESEN WÖRTERN!

school – university/college – hospital – church – prison – bed – work

*In England, **school** starts at 9 o'clock.*
(der Unterricht, das Lernen)
*Tim is at **university** now.*
(er studiert)
*Oliver was in **hospital** last week.*
(zur Behandlung; er war krank)
*Do you often go to **church**?*
(zum Beten, in den Gottesdienst)
*Have you ever been to **prison**?*
(als Sträfling)
*You should stay **in bed** for a week.*
(weil du krank bist)
*Dad drives to **work** every morning.*
(die Arbeitsstätte, der Ort)

The school is near the train station.
(das Gebäude, der Ort)
*Let's meet behind **the university**!*
(das Gebäude, der Ort)
*We went to **the hospital** to visit him.*
(das Gebäude; der Ort; zu Besuch)
*We go to **the church** in State Street.*
(das Gebäude, der Ort)
*Where's **the prison**, please?*
(das Gebäude, der Ort)
*We slept **in the bed** of the King.*
(ein bestimmtes Bett; ein „Ort")
*He likes **the work** he is doing.*
(eine bestimmte Tätigkeit)

H VORSICHT AUCH BEI MAHLZEITEN, MATERIALIEN UND VERKEHRSMITTELN!

*This room is open only **for breakfast**.*
*My desk is **made of** expensive **wood**.*
*Mum goes to work **by bus**.*

***The breakfast** at our hotel was okay.*
*What happened to **the wood** I bought?*
*Joe was **on the bus** from Miami.*

I BESTIMMTER ARTIKEL – JA UND NEIN?

Kein bestimmter Artikel bei	Bestimmter Artikel bei
Namen von Personen (Einzahl)	Namen von Personen (Mehrzahl)
Ländernamen (Einzahl)	Ländernamen (Mehrzahl)
Bergen (Normalfall)	Gebirgen
Seen	Flüssen und Meeren
Straßen und Plätzen (Normalfall)	Straßen und Plätzen (Einzelfälle)
der Wendung *"most + noun"*	—
*I sit between **Joe** and **Maria** this year.*	*Our new neighbours are **the Millers**.*
*Pierre is from **Canada**, and …*	*… Mia is from **the United States**.*
***Mt. Logan** is Canada's highest mountain.*	*Skiing in **the Alps** can be expensive.*
***Lake Victoria** is one of the places where …*	*… **the Nile** comes from.*
*Shopping in **Oxford Street** is great!*	*There's a nice pub in **the High Street**.*
*In New York, you must see **Times Square**!*	***The Red Square** in Moscow is huge.*
***Most girls** play with dolls.*	—

G 23 Bestimmter Artikel oder nicht? Vorsicht – der Artikel ändert die Aussage des Satzes!

1. When ... school is over, my friends and I often walk home together.
2. If your fever doesn't go down, you'll have to go to ... hospital.
3. ... church in our town was designed by a famous architect.
4. Have you heard? Jenny's brother is in ... prison again!
5. Sorry I can't come with you. I've ... work to do today!
6. Can I speak with Tina, please? – I'm sorry, she's in ... bed with a cold.
7. When I'm older, I want to go to ... university and study economics.
8. How do you like ... bed in your room? – It's too soft for me. I like hard beds.
9. Is this ... hospital? – Oh no! ... hospital is next to ... school.
10. Many young people look for ... work in the summer months.
11. My mum and my dad went to ... school where I am now.
12. I'm dead tired. I think I'll go to ... bed now.
13. When will you finish ... work for your physics project, Frank?
14. Richard, there's a letter for you from ... university!
15. Uncle Eric works at ... prison in our town. He likes ... work of a guard.
16. Grandma goes to ... church every Sunday morning.

Additional exercise Seite 154

H 24 Besonderer Fall oder allgemeiner Fall? Artikel oder kein Artikel?

1. How did you like dinner/the dinner last night? – It was superb!
2. What did you do with salt/the salt I bought last week, Mum?
3. Hurry up, Joe! Train/The train leaves in five minutes!
4. We all need air/the air to survive.
5. In the US, lunch/the lunch consists of soup or a salad or a sandwich.
6. How many times do you change water/the water in your swimming pool?
7. I didn't know that you need salt/the salt for baking a cake.
8. Air/The air in this room is terrible!
9. Dinner/The dinner at the "Savoy" is always excellent, but very expensive.
10. How will you travel to Paris, Jasmine? – I think I'll go by train/the train.

I 25 Einzahl oder Mehrzahl? Kein Artikel oder doch einer?

1. ... Belgium and ... Netherlands are founding members of the EU.
2. In the past, ... most people could not read or write.
3. ... Broadway and ... Wall Street are famous streets in New York City.
4. Did ... Clintons go mountain climbing in ... Alps again? – No, they went to South America this year. They tried to climb ... Aconcagua, the highest mountain in ... Andes.
5. ... most young people like HipHop and ... most old people think it's rubbish.
6. ... Danube River flows through Vienna and Budapest. Later, it empties into ... Black Sea.
7. The Victoria Falls are on ... Zambezi River in Africa.
8. Which is larger, ... Atlantic or ... Pacific? – ... Pacific, of course.
9. The highest peak in ... Rocky Mountains is ... Mt. McKinley in ... Alaska.
10. In ... USA, ... most people speak English inside and outside their homes.

4. KAPITEL *CONDITIONS* – BEDINGUNGSSÄTZE

Du kennst die Bedingungssätze – auf Englisch ***conditional clauses*** – auch als **„*if*-Sätze"**, weil sie für gewöhnlich mit dem Wort ***if*** (wenn, falls) eingeleitet werden.

Die folgenden Punkte sind bei den Bedingungssätzen zu beachten:

- Eine Bedingung setzt sich immer aus **zwei Teilen** zusammen: dem **„wenn-Teil"** (der eigentlichen Bedingung; im Englischen der ***if*-Teil**; Gliedsatz) und dem **„dann"-Teil** (der Folge; sie tritt ein, wenn die Bedingung erfüllt wird; Hauptsatz).

Bedingung	►	**Folge**
If we run,		*we will catch the bus.*
If I had more time,		*I would play with you.*
If they had not left,		*they would have met you.*

- Die **Reihenfolge** von Gliedsatz (*if*-Satz, Bedingung) und Hauptsatz (Folge) lässt sich **umkehren**, ohne dass sich der Sinn der Aussage verändert. (In diesem Fall entfällt das Komma.)

We will catch the bus		*if we run.*
I would play with you		*if I had more time.*
They would have met you		*if they had not left.*
Folge	◄	**Bedingung**

- Es gibt **drei Stufen von Bedingungen**: die wirklichen, die möglichen und die unmöglichen. Sie verlangen ein ganz **bestimmtes Zusammenwirken der Zeitstufen.**

A „FALL DER WIRKLICHKEIT"

Wenn die **Bedingung (wirklich)** erfüllt wird, dann tritt die **Folge (wirklich)** ein.

Diese Art der Bedingung verlangt die folgenden Zeitstufen:

Bedingung *if*-Satz		Folge Hauptsatz	Folge Hauptsatz		Bedingung *if*-Satz
*If it **rains** today,*		*we **won't go** out.*	*We **won't go** out*		*if it **rains**.*
▼		▼	▼		▼
present tense	+	***future tense***	***future tense***	+	***present tense***

A 26 Hier findest du Bedingungen (*if*-Sätze) vor, zu denen du die passenden Folgen finden sollst.

I'll never speak with Monica again – his dad will buy him a laptop – we will win the championship – we will go for a walk – they will begin without us – he will say no – I will go – you will ruin your eyes

1. If I ask my dad for some money, ...
2. ... if it doesn't rain.
3. If Melissa invites me to her party, ...
4. ... if we win the last two games.
5. If we don't hurry, ...
6. ... if you read in the dark.
7. If Gary gets an "A" in his maths test, ...
8. ... if she doesn't say sorry.

A 27 Jetzt musst du zu den Folgen (Hauptsätze) die passenden Bedingungen finden.

if you don't tell them – if you ask him in a friendly way – if you don't shut the window – if I can find them – if I can get tickets – if you don't install a firewall – if you call before 5 p.m. – if he gets home early tonight

1. I'm sure Frank will lend you his bike ...
2. ... we will go and see "The Hunger Games" tonight.
3. Nobody will know about it ...
4. ... it will get very cold in the room.
5. Dad says he will help me with my model plane ...
6. ... your computer will be open to attacks.
7. I'll show you the pictures ...
8. ... nobody will be at home.

Additional exercise Seite 155

A 28 Setze nun die angegebenen Verben in die richtige Zeitstufe *(present tense* für die Bedingung, *future tense* für die Folge).

1. If Max (*lose*) his USB stick, he (*be*) in trouble.
2. If somebody (*see*) us here, they (*tell*) our parents.
3. If you (*like*) the bike, we (*buy*) it.
4. If our neighbours (*move*) away, we (*be*) very sorry.
5. If an asteroid (*hit*) the earth, many people and animals (*die*).
6. If you (*not show*) me how to play this game, I (*not play*) with you.
7. You (*not get*) any emails if you (*not write*) any.
8. Nothing (*happen*) if nobody (*tell*) our parents.
9. The river (*flood*) the streets if the rain (*not stop*) soon.
10. Andy (*win*) the tournament if he (*not make*) a mistake now.
11. Who (*water*) the flowers if you (*go*) away for a week?
12. Timothy (*not help*) us if we (*not ask*) him.

Additional exercise Seite 155

B „FALL DER MÖGLICHKEIT"

Wenn die **Bedingung erfüllt** wird, dann tritt die **Folge vielleicht** ein.

Diese Art der Bedingung verlangt die folgenden Zeitstufen:

Bedingung *if*-Satz	Folge Hauptsatz	Folge Hauptsatz	Bedingung *if*-Satz
*If you **asked** me,*	*I **would come**.*	*I **would come***	*if you **asked** me.*
▼ past tense	+ ▼ *conditional present*	▼ *conditional present*	+ ▼ past tense

conditional present/first conditional = would + infinitive (1st form)

Bitte beachten:

- Bei ***"to be"*** gilt im gehobenen Englisch für **alle Personen** ***"were"***, also auch bei *I, he, she* und *it*. Im Alltagsenglisch setzt sich allerdings immer mehr ***"was"*** durch. Man hört und liest also immer öfter beide Formen.

gehobenes Englisch	Alltagsenglisch
*If Joe **were** at home, ...*	*If Joe **was** at home, ...*
*If I **were** in your place, ...*	*If I **was** in your place, ...*
*If it **weren't** so hot, ...*	*If it **wasn't** so hot, ...*

- Immer stärker wird im Alltagsenglisch ***past tense*** **von** ***"would"*** **verdrängt**. Das hat sich aber noch nicht überall herumgesprochen, also Vorsicht!
  *If Mike **came** to the party, ...* *If Mike **would come** to the party, ...*

C „FALL DER UNMÖGLICHKEIT"

Die **Bedingung** kann nicht mehr erfüllt werden, es ist **unmöglich** geworden. Deshalb kann oder hat sich auch die Folge nicht ergeben.

Diese Art der Bedingung verlangt die folgenden Zeitstufen:

Bedingung *if*-Satz	Folge Hauptsatz
*If Mr. Smith **had been** at home,*	*he **would have answered** the phone.*
▼ *past perfect tense* +	▼ *conditional perfect*

conditional perfect = would have + past participle (3rd form)

B 29 **Bilde den „Fall der Möglichkeit" mit den folgenden Sätzen. Nicht vergessen: Bedingung = *past tense*, Folge = *conditional present (would + infinitive)*!**

1. If you (*do*) what I told you to do, you (*get*) better results in your exams.
2. If everybody (*be*) here, we (*begin*) with the film.
3. If we (*run*) a little faster, we (*catch*) the bus.
4. If Jackie (*take*) off her ear phones, she (*hear*) what I am saying.
5. If I (*not need*) your advice, I (*not ask*) you.
6. If I (*be*) you, I (*not believe*) all those stories.
7. The plants (*grow*) faster if you (*not forget*) to water them every day.
8. Your car (*start*) without problems if you (*buy*) a new battery.
9. We (*not be*) so afraid if you (*drive*) more carefully.
10. I'm sure Jenny (*feel*) very sad if you (*not ask*) her to dance with you.
11. You (*see*) the mountains from here if there (*not be*) such a fog.
12. Carl (*not come*) if he (*know*) that Cindy was there, too.
13. If Harry (*have*) a car, he (*drive*) me to the shopping centre.
14. Olivia (*stop*) crying if you (*kiss*) her.
15. If Ian (*not be*) my friend, I (*tell*) him what you said about him.
16. I (*look*) up the word in a dictionary if I (*not know*) its meaning.

Additional exercise Seite 155

C 30 **Bilde den „Fall der Unmöglichkeit" mit den folgenden Sätzen. Verwende *past perfect tense* für die Bedingung und *conditional perfect* für die Folge.**

1. If you (*help*) me to look for my bus ticket, I (*find*) it sooner.
2. If Dad (*tell*) us to wash his car, we (*do*) it.
3. If Mary (*not leave*) the door open, I (*climb*) in through the window.
4. If Sam (*do*) his part of the project, we (*not get*) such a bad mark.
5. If Nelly (*not leave*) her car keys at home, she (*not call*) a taxi.
6. If everything (*work*) out alright for Bill, he (*become*) a doctor or a lawyer.
7. Herman (*win*) the match if he (*not make*) some bad mistakes.
8. We (*go*) to the concert yesterday if Kevin (*not lose*) the tickets.
9. The bus driver (*not wait*) for us if he (*be*) in a hurry.
10. I'm sure Mike (*use*) my mobile phone if I (*leave*) it on my desk.
11. Ron (*drown*) if Harry (*not save*) him.
12. If you (*read*) the book, you (*understand*) the film better.
13. You (*not find*) the text so difficult if you (*learn*) the words in time.
14. If the dog (*not start*) to bark, we (*not notice*) the fire in the neigbours' house.
15. I (*oversleep*) this morning if you (*not phone*) me.
16. I (*return*) the book to the library if my dog (*not tear*) it to pieces.

Additional exercise Seite 156

5. KAPITEL *THE FUTURE* – DIE ZUKUNFT

A DIE ZUKUNFT MIT *"WILL"*

BILDUNG

1 In allen Personen mit *will (not) + base form (1st form)*

	will (not)	+ base form	
I	***will (not)***	***do***	*this any more.*
You	***will (not)***	***hear***	*from us again.*
He/She/It	***will (not)***	***be***	*late.*
We	***will (not)***	***buy***	*a new car soon.*
They	***will (not)***	***forget***	*what has happened.*

- **Die Kurzformen** verwendest du beim Sprechen, beim Schreiben von persönlichen Briefen und in Dialogen (denn da soll man ja schreiben, „wie man spricht"). Vorsicht: Einige Kurzformen sehen anderen Wörtern zum Verwechseln ähnlich!

  I'll = *I will* ≠ *ill* (krank)
  won't = will not ≠ *want* (wollen)
  he'll = *he will* ≠ *hell* (Hölle)
  she'll = *she will* ≠ *shell* (Muschel)
  we'll = *we will* ≠ *well* (gut)

2 Frage und Verneinung

Werden „direkt" gebildet, also **ohne *do/does***.

Will you *write to me? – I* ***will not/won't*** *write to you again.*

VERWENDUNG

3 Bei Annahmen (Erwartungen, Befürchtungen, Hoffnungen), Versprechungen und Vorhersagen

Das sind Ereignisse, über die der Sprecher keine wirkliche Kontrolle hat und über die er nicht wirklich bestimmen kann. Wörter, die oft auf die *future with will* hinweisen, sind:

maybe, perhaps, probably; expect, hope, think; (I'm) sure

I'm ***afraid*** *nobody* ***will like*** *my new dress.* (Annahme, Befürchtung)
I ***expect*** *they'****ll call*** *the police.* (Annahme, Erwartung)
Let's ***hope*** *everyone* ***will be*** *there.* (Hoffnung)
I ***promise*** *I'****ll do*** *it right now.* (Versprechen)
Believe *me, Joe* ***will pass*** *the exam.* (Vorhersage)

4 Bei plötzlichen Entscheidungen

Das sind Situationen, in denen man nicht genug Zeit zum Planen, Nachdenken oder Überlegen hat. Häufige Einleitung: *"I (don't) think" …*

*There's nothing on TV tonight. I think I'****ll go*** *to bed.*

A1 31 **Zunächst die einfachste aller Übungen. Setze die folgenden Sätze in die Zukunft. Verwende dabei die vorgegebenen Zeitangaben (wo sie vorhanden sind) und bilde auch die Kurzform.**

example: *Chris spoke with Claudia last week. (→ again, next week)* ▶
He will speak with her again next week./He'll speak ...

1. We saw Katy Perry in concert last summer. (→ *next spring*)
2. Cindy called this morning. (→ *again, tomorrow morning*)
3. It was very hot last week. (→ *this week, too*)
4. They went to Africa in 2005. (→ *again, in 2008*)
5. You liked "Man of Steel". (→ *"Iron Man", too*)
6. Yesterday and today the bus was late. (→ *tomorrow, again*)
7. George often dreams of Julia. (→ *in future*)
8. I had a date with Tony last weekend. (→ *many dates, this year*)

A2 32 **Bilde mit den folgenden Sätzen alle Fragen (Entscheidungsfrage sowie die Fragen nach den Satzteilen) und die Verneinung.**

1. Our neighbours will sell the house next spring.
2. Miriam will be here again at 7 o'clock.
3. The boys will like the hot dogs because they are hungry.

A3 33 **In dieser Übung geht es um Annahmen, Versprechen, Vorhersagen usw. Finde ein passendes Verb und setze es in der richtigen Form ein.**

land – like – get – not play – own – come – probably be – do

1. Twenty years from now everybody ... a personal robot.
2. I sent you the money yesterday. I hope you ... it tomorrow.
3. Dad has bought earrings for Mum. I think she ... them.
4. I've told lots of people about the party, and I'm sure many ... .
5. They haven't repaired our car yet, but they've promised they ... it this afternoon.
6. Doris wasn't on the 3 o'clock train, so she ... on the next one.
7. The Chinese say they ... a man on the moon in the next fifty years.
8. Adrian has had a shock. I expect he ... with fireworks again soon.

A4 34 **Jetzt sind rasche Entscheidungen gefragt! Finde wieder ein passendes Verb.**

never eat – have – miss – watch – talk – go

1. There's a good film on TV tonight. I think I ... it.
2. Don't forget, tomorrow is Eva's birthday. – What? I ... to get her a present!
3. I'm in a hurry right now, but I ... to you later.
4. I feel really sick after all this cake! I ... sweets again!
5. There's someone at the door! – I ... and see who it is.
6. We are very sorry that you have to leave so soon. We ... you very much!

B DIE ZUKUNFT MIT *"GOING TO"*

BILDUNG

1 ***am/is/are (not) + base form (1st form)***
(Ausnahme: Punkt 5 auf dieser Seite):

	to be +	*going to* +	*base form*	
I	***am (not)***	***going to***	***study***	*for tomorrow.*
You	***are (not)***	***going to***	***hear***	*a great story.*
He/She/It	***is (not)***	***going to***	***be***	*very surprised.*
We	***are (not)***	***going to***	***buy***	*a new car soon.*
They	***are (not)***	***going to***	***repair***	*my bike today.*

VERWENDUNG

2 **Bei festen Absichten oder Vorhaben**

Das sind Ereignisse, über die der Sprecher eine gewisse Kontrolle hat.

*I'm **going to show** you a film about turtles today.* (feste Absicht ...)
*My parents **are going to sell** the car.* (Vorhaben ...)

3 **Bei zukünftige Handlungen, die schon fest geplant sind**

Im modernen Alltagsenglisch zieht man hier eher ***present progressive*** vor.
Siehe dazu auch Abschnitt C auf Seite 38.

*Jill **is going to have** a party on Friday.* ► *Jill **is having** a party on Friday.*
(Die Gäste sind verständigt, die Getränke gekauft, die Eltern gehen aus ...)

*When **are** you **going to fly** to London?* ► *When **are** you **flying** to London?*
(So fragt man, wenn man annimmt, dass schon alle Termine feststehen.)

4 **Für die nahe Zukunft (*near future*)**

Man wendet sie dann an, wenn man glaubt oder weiß, dass etwas schon **sehr bald** – also in der „nahen Zukunft" – passieren wird. Meist gibt es **deutliche Hinweise** auf dieses Ereignis.

Take an umbrella with you. *It's **going to rain** today.*
(Dunkle Wolken stehen am Himmel, die ersten Tropfen fallen ...)

*Look at James! He **is going to repair** the roof of his garden shed.*
(Er hat die Werkzeugkiste bei sich und die Leiter in der Hand ...)

5 **Für Handlungen, die für die Vergangenheit geplant waren, aber nicht zustande kamen** ► ***was/were + going to***

Das entspricht den deutschen „Ich wollte ..., aber dann ..."-Sätzen.

*I **was going to phone** you last night, but then I forgot.*
*Joe **was going to come** today, but he remembered basketball practice.*

B1 35 **Zunächst eine einfachere Übung. Setze die folgenden Sätze in die *"going to"*-Zukunft.**

1. I (*paint*) my room one of these days.
2. Josie (*surprise*) her parents at Christmas this year.
3. The boys (*build*) an igloo in the garden.
4. Who (*prepare*) breakfast tomorrow morning?
5. My uncle (*buy*) a house in the Lake District.
6. We (*read*) "Romeo and Juliet" next.
7. I (*not forget*) what you said about me.
8. (*you, invite*) Nora to your party on Saturday?

B2/3 36 **Diese Übung handelt von festen Absichten, Vorhaben und Plänen. Finde das passende Verb und setze es ein. Verwende dabei *"future with going to"*.**

try out – win – leave – show – be – wash – visit – give up – start

1. They ... all parts of "Twilight" this Saturday. Can you come?
2. Who ... the dishes tonight? – I am. But tomorrow you'll have to do them.
3. I ... the next match. I know I can do it.
4. Dad says he ... smoking. I hope he is strong enough to do it!
5. My grandma ... a new recipe for roast turkey. It ... wonderful, I' sure.
6. We ... very early tomorrow morning because it's a long drive to Hamburg.
7. Jacob ... university in autumn. He wants to study geology.
8. We are ... the zoo next weekend. Who wants to come with us?

B4 37 **In den nächsten Beispielen deutet alles darauf hin, dass sehr bald etwas geschehen wird. Suche also passende Verben und bilde die „nahe Zukunft".**

start – fall asleep – be – not win – collapse – end – get – jump

1. The boys are playing very badly today. They ... .
2. I hope you can sleep long tomorrow, because this ... a long night.
3. Don't worry, Gina. Everything ... well.
4. I can hardly keep my eyes open! I ... very soon.
5. Quick, call the police and the ambulance! These men ... from the bridge!
6. You don't need a coat today, Charlie. They say it ... hot in the afternoon.
7. Look, they have switched off the lights. The play ... .
8. These houses are so old and neglected they ... very soon.

B5 38 **Was war geplant, was hat nicht geklappt? Bilde Sätze mit *was/were going to*.**

1. Mum (*drive*) me to school this morning, but then her car didn't start.
2. I (*wait*) for you, but then it started to rain and so I got on the next bus.
3. (*you, tell*) the police what you saw? – We were, but nobody asked us.
4. Wilma (*lock*) the doors when the phone rang. So she forgot about it.
5. Lawrence says he (*write*) to me, but I don't believe him.
6. (*Peter, not sell*) his mountain bike? – He was, but nobody wanted to buy it.

C *PRESENT PROGRESSIVE* ALS ZUKUNFT

Für **fix geplante zukünftige Handlungen oder Ereignisse** verwendet man meist *present progressive*. Dabei sollte der Zeitpunkt des Geschehens bereits feststehen.
(Auch *"future with going to"* ist möglich, wird aber in diesem Zusammenhang seltener angewendet; siehe auch Abschnitt B dieses Kapitels, Seite 36.)

*Mum **is meeting** her friends at a café on Saturday.*
(Die Tische sind reserviert, die Freundinnen haben zugesagt ...)

*When **are** your parents **coming** back from Sweden?*
(Dass sie demnächst kommen, steht fest; die Frage ist nur wann!)

Zur Erinnerung: ***present progressive = am/is/are + ing-form***

D *PRESENT SIMPLE* ALS ZUKUNFT

Im Zusammenhang mit **Zeitplänen, Stundenplänen, Fahrplänen, Tagesordnungen** und dergleichen weist *present simple* auch auf Zukünftiges hin.

*Hurry up! The bus **leaves** in ten minutes!*
*Tomorrow we **have** English and geography, my two favourite subjects.*
*The conference **ends** at 6 p.m., and dinner **is** served from 8.30 to 10.*

E *FUTURE PROGRESSIVE*

Future progressive ist eine „typisch englische" Form der Zukunft. Mit ihrer Hilfe lässt sich beschreiben, **was zu einem zukünftigen Zeitpunkt gerade passieren wird**. Diese Form der Zukunft kommt im Alltagsenglisch ziemlich selten vor.
Future progressive bildest du in allen Personen der Ein- und Mehrzahl gleich:

will be + ing-form

This time tomorrow afternoon — *I **will be riding** the bus home from school, Dad **will be working** in the office and my little sister **will be watching** TV.*

F *FUTURE PERFECT TENSE* (VORZUKUNFT PLUSQUAMPERFEKT)

Damit lässt sich sagen, **was zu einem zukünftigen Zeitpunkt schon geschehen sein wird.** Auch auf diese Form der Zukunft stößt man im Alltagsenglisch nicht oft.
Future perfect tense bildest du in allen Personen der Ein- und Mehrzahl gleich:

will have + 3rd form

This time tomorrow afternoon — *I **will have talked** to my guitar teacher, my little sister **will have had** lunch, but Dad **will not have finished** working yet.*

C 39 **Hier findest du Ausschnitte aus verschiedenen Zeitplänen. Bilde Sätze mit *present progressive* in zukünftiger Bedeutung.**

example: *Sunday – Matthew – go to zoo – parents* ▶
On Sunday, Matthew is going to the zoo with his parents.

1. Joe's brother – come back – from the USA – next Monday
2. Sylvia – celebrate – her birthday – at the weekend
3. H&M – open – a new shop – in our town – on Saturday
4. they – close down – the tyre factory – next month
5. the UN inspectors – leave – the country – this week
6. I – not go – to Norman's party – tonight
7. who – look after your dog – next week – ?
8. my parents – fly – to Spain – tomorrow

D 40 **„Offizieller Zeitplan" oder „persönliche Planung"? *Present simple* oder *present progressive*? Setze die richtige Form ein.**

1. Alex (*play*) two songs at the school concert on Thursday. The concert (*begin*) at 3 p.m.
2. Mum (*make*) my favourite cake for my birthday party next week.
3. I (*go*) to town with Mike and Daniel tonight, Mum. The bus (*leave*) at 7.
4. Have you heard? We (*leave*) for Canada tomorrow morning. – How (*you, travel*)? By plane or by ship? – By plane, of course. It (*leave*) at 9.30 and (*arrive*) at Toronto ten hours later.
5. (*you, come*) to the cinema with us tonight, Karen? – What time (*the film, start*)? – At 8. – I'm sorry, I can't. We (*write*) a paper tomorrow.
6. Dad (*attend*) a conference at the weekend. It (*open*) on Saturday morning and (*end*) on Sunday afternoon.
7. What (*you, do*) next Friday, Patrick? – Let me see ... Oh, yes! In the afternoon I (*play*) singles in the tennis club, and in the evening I (*go*) to the disco with my girlfriend.
8. When (*Grandpa's train, arrive*), Dad? – Tomorrow morning at 6.30. I (*drive*) to the station to pick him up. Do you want to come along?
9. Harry (*take*) the "Orient Express" to Venice this weekend. It (*leave*) from London on Friday and (*get*) to Venice on Saturday.

E F 41 ***Future progressive* (Was wird gerade passieren?) oder *future perfect* (Was wird schon passiert sein?)? Setze die passenden Formen ein.**

1. Dad (*grow*) melons in our garden next year.
2. Next Monday at this time of day Steve's ship (*arrive*).
3. Mr. Peterson won't be in his office at 10 o'clock tomorrow morning. He (*attend*) an important meeting.
4. When (*you, read*) my essay, sir? – By next Monday, Joe. I can't do it sooner.
5. A year from now, everybody (*hear*) of my rock band, believe me!
6. While you (*sleep*) tonight, I (*sit*) over my books, studying for an exam.

Additional exercise Seite 156

6. KAPITEL *THE GERUND*

Das **Gerund ist ein Verb, das wie ein Nomen verwendet wird.** Überall dort, wo ein Gerund vorkommt, kann auch ein „normales" Nomen stehen.
In der deutschen Sprache kommt das „hauptwörtliche gebrauchte Zeitwort" dem Gerund am nächsten, doch eine genaue Entsprechung gibt es nicht.

Das **Gerund ist eine *"ing-form"*.** Die *"ing-form"* bildest du aus ***base form*** *(1st form)* durch Anhängen der Silbe ***"-ing"***. (Siehe auch Kapitel 17, ab Seite 94.)

walk + ing ▶ ***walking*** ***cry + ing*** ▶ ***crying***

A RECHTSCHREIBUNG

- **Wegfall des „stummen e"** am Ende der *base form*:
  wake + ing ▶ *waking* *hide + ing* ▶ *hiding*
- **Verdoppelung des Enkonsonanten** bei kurzer *base form*:
  hit + ing ▶ *hitting* *run + ing* ▶ *running*
- ***ie*** ▶ ***y*** bei diesen drei Verben:
  lie ▶ *lying* (liegen, lügen) *die* ▶ *dying* (sterben) *tie* ▶ *tying* (binden, knüpfen)

B GERUND ALS SUBJEKT ODER ALS OBJEKT

Wie jedes „normale" Nomen kann das Gerund als **Subjekt** (Satzgegenstand) und als **Objekt** (Ergänzung) auftreten. Dabei kann ein Artikel das Gerund begleiten, aber das muss nicht sein. (Alles Wesentliche über den Artikel erfährst du in Kapitel 3, ab Seite 24.)

S: ***Dancing*** *can be great fun.* (Tanzen kann sehr lustig sein.)
The crashing *of the waves got louder.* (Das Krachen der Wellen ...)

O: *We were woken by* ***the barking*** *of the dog.* (... vom Bellen des Hundes.)
Can you hear ***the chirping*** *of the birds?* (... das Zwitschern der Vögel.)

C GERUND NACH VERBEN, DIE VORLIEBE ODER ABNEIGUNG AUSDRÜCKEN

Zu dieser Gruppe der Verben zählen unter anderem:

like – love – enjoy – dislike – hate

Do you ***like*** *or* ***dislike walking*** *in the rain, Julia? – I love it!*
I always ***enjoy getting*** *a letter from you, Grandma.*
My dad ***loves cooking****, but he really* ***hates washing*** *up afterwards.*
When Willy was young, he ***loved playing*** *with his toy trains.*
Where ist Polly? She knows I ***hate waiting****.*

A 42 **Bilde die *"ing-forms"* der folgenden Verben und beachte dabei besonders die Rechtschreibregeln.**

answer – attack – bite – buy – catch – come – do – drink – end – enter – fight – forget – give – grin – have – hurt – install – invite – joke – jump – keep – kick – let – lie – map[1] – meet – negate[2] – nod[3] – open – order – pet[4] – put – question[5] – quit – ride – ring – say – speak – take – tie – understand – use – vary[6] – vibrate – waste – yell[7]

[1]kartieren, [2]verneinen, [3]nicken, [4] streicheln, [5] befragen, [6] abwechseln, [7] schreien

B C 43 **Versuche, die folgenden Sätze in „gutes" Deutsch zu übersetzen. Wo bleibt das englische Gerund im deutschen Satz ein Nomen? Wo musst du dir eine andere Lösung einfallen lassen (zB einen Gliedsatz)?**

Da das Gerund so „typisch Englisch" ist, gibt es nicht immer ein deutsches Gegenstück dazu. Manchmal sehen die deutschen Sätze sehr ähnlich aus, oft aber unterscheiden sie sich deutlich. Du erkennst diese Ähnlichkeiten und Unterschiede am besten, wenn du englische Sätze ins Deutsche und deutsche Sätze ins Englische übersetzt.

1. Diving is better than snorkelling.
2. My dad enjoys riding his motorbike.
3. Herbert's favourite hobby is making model planes.
4. Willy loves playing with his toy trains.
5. Feeding the animals is not allowed.
6. Listen to the whispering of the leaves in the wind!
7. Do you enjoy doing crossword puzzles, too?
8. With the ringing of the church bells the ceremony began.
9. Swimming under the bridge is dangerous.
10. My mum dislikes talking about her school days.
11. A huge comet caused the dying out of the dinosaurs.
12. I really like skiing, but I must say snowboarding is even better.
13. George hates loading and unloading the dishwasher.
14. Wearing a helmet is a must.
15. Asking me for the way is no good – I'm not from here.
16. Smoking can kill!

C GERUND NACH FÜGUNGEN MIT *"TO BE"*

Nach bestimmten **Fügungen mit *"to be"*** ist das **Gerund** zwingend.

to be afraid of	(sich vor etwas fürchten, Angst haben)	*Alfred **is afraid of losing** his mobile phone.*
to be (in)capable of	(un)fähig sein zu/für etwas, in der Lage sein	*I **was capable of answering** every question.*
to be far from	weit davon entfernt sein (etwas zu tun)	***We're far from finishing** the job.*
to be fond of	etwas gerne tun/gerne haben	*Tony **is fond of going** out at the weekend.*
to be good at	bei/in etwas gut sein	*Who **is** really **good at doing** crosswords?*
to be interested in	an etwas interessiert sein, sich für etwas interessieren	***I'm interested in finding** out who she is.*
to be proud of	auf etwas stolz sein	*You can **be proud of attending** this school.*
to be responsible for	für etwas verantwortlich sein, schuld sein an etwas	*Who **is responsible for tidying** up the room?*
to be surprised at	von/über etwas überrascht sein	***Were** you **surprised at seeing** me again?*
to be tired of	etwas satt haben	***Are** you never **tired of playing** this game?*
to be tired from	von etwas müde sein	***I'm** often **tired from doing** homework.*
to be used to	an etwas gewöhnt sein	***I'm** not **used to staying** up so late.*

D GERUND NACH BESTIMMTEN VERBEN

Bestimmte Verben verlangen zwingend* das **Gerund.** Die wichtigsten davon sind:

admit	(zugeben, gestehen)	*I will never **admit taking** the money.*
avoid	(vermeiden)	*Why do you **avoid looking** at me?*
consider	(denken an, überlegen)	*Sam **considers buying** a car.*
finish	(beenden, fertig werden)	***Finish reading** and **start writing**.*
imagine	(sich etwas vorstellen)	*Can you **imagine going out** with me?*
mention	(erwähnen)	*John **mentioned seeing** you in town.*
mind	(etwas dagegen haben)	*Do you **mind waiting** outside, please?*
miss	(vermissen)	*I really **miss talking** to Giovanni.*
practise	(üben)	*I must **practise singing** every day.*
risk	(riskieren)	*You'll **risk breaking** a leg if you fall.*
suggest	(vorschlagen)	*Who **suggested buying** this machine?*

* Auf eine andere Gruppe von Verben kann ein Gerund folgen, auf eine weitere Gruppe darf keines folgen. Siehe dazu Kapitel 10, Seite 64.

C 44 **Zur Gewöhnung an das Gerund eine leichtere Übung: Setze die passenden Wörter aus der *box* als Gerund an die richtige Stelle. Verwende jedes Wort nur einmal.**

tell – read – go – be – hear – get – dance –
clean – listen – find – finish – wake

1. You look tired, Jane. – Well, I'm not used to ... up so early in the morning.
2. I'm tired from ... all night. I think I'll go home now.
3. I was very surprised at ... about Mike! Did he really win the first prize?
4. This room is a mess! – Well, I'm not responsible for ... up the place!
5. I really like you, Frank. I'm proud of ... your friend.
6. No more excuses, please! We're tired of ... to your lies!
7. I don't want to go to the disco alone, but Joe is not interested in ... .
8. Ask Judy for help. She's really good at ... things on the internet.
9. Are you fond of ..., Terry? – Yes, but only good books.
10. I still have a lot of work to do. I'm far from ... the project.
11. Nobody believes that you are capable of ... a lie.
12. When Sue was little, she was afraid of ... up in a dark room at night.

C 45 **Etwas schwieriger: Übersetze die 12 Mustersätze aus der oberen Tabelle von Seite 42 in gutes Deutsch.**

D 46 **Finde wieder die passenden Wörter und setze sie als Gerund ein. Du darfst jedes Wort nur einmal verwenden.**

ask – buy – dance – hurt – live – play – ski –
speak – swim – take – talk – wait – work

1. It is snowing heavily, so I suggest ... the bus.
2. I don't do much sport because I don't want to risk ... myself.
3. We will practise ... for the ball all of next week, I promise.
4. In winter, I miss ... in the lake, and in summer I miss ... in the mountains.
5. Take your time, Mum. I really don't mind ... for you.
6. Did anybody mention ... pizza for dinner? – No, but it's a wonderful idea!
7. Paris is a great city! I could imagine ... there for a year or two.
8. Dad finished ... an hour earlier today, so we can watch TV together.
9. Have you ever considered ... your grandmother for some pocket money?
10. What's wrong with Vicky? She avoids ... with me when she sees me.
11. Come on, Bill! Why don't you admit ... to Danielle behind my back?

D 47 **Übersetze die 11 Mustersätze aus der unteren Tabelle von Seite 42 in gutes Deutsch.**

E GERUND NACH *"VERB + PREPOSITION"*

Das **Gerund** folgt zwingend auf bestimmte Kombinationen von „Verb und Präposition".
Diese Kombination nennt man auch ***"phrasal verb"***.
Die folgende Liste enthält einige wichtige *phrasal verbs*:

apologise for	sich entschuldigen	*I **apologise for being** late again.*
believe in	glauben an, für richtig halten	*We **believe in telling** the truth.*
care about	es ist wichtig für einen	*Joe **cares about helping** others.*
feel like	zumute sein nach	*I **feel like winning** today.*
give up	etwas aufgeben	*You should **give up calling** Tina.*
go on/keep on	weitermachen mit	***Go on talking. – Keep on going.***
insist on	bestehen auf	*I **insist on getting** an answer now.*
keep from ***prevent from***	abhalten von, hindern an	*They could not **keep/prevent** me **from leaving** the room.*
look forward to	sich freuen auf	*I'm **looking forward to seeing** you.*
put off	verschieben	*Don't **put off sending** the letter.*
succeed in	gelingen	*We **succeeded in doing** the puzzle.*
talk about	sprechen über	*Let's **talk about buying** a new PC.*
talk of	sprechen von	*Tim often **talks of leaving** town.*
thank for	danken für	*I **thanked** Ali **for calling** us.*
think of/about	denken an/über	*Ian **thinks of/about getting** married.*
worry about	sich Sorgen machen	*You **worry about losing** the match?*

F GERUND NACH EINIGEN *"PHRASES"*

Auch bestimmte Wendungen oder Fügungen verlangen zwingend das Gerund.

be busy	mit etwas beschäftigt sein, eifrig dabei sein	*Mum **was busy packing** our suitcases, so she did not hear the phone.*
cannot help	einfach etwas tun müssen, nicht anders können als	*I **can't help thinking** of Moira whenever I look at these photos.*
cannot stand	nicht ausstehen/ ertragen können	*Let's go, please! I **can't stand listening** to this nonsense any longer!*
it's little use ***it's no use*** ***it's no good***	es hat keinen/wenig Sinn; es bringt nichts	***It's little use asking** Ron about it.* ***It's no use crying** over spilt milk.* ***It's no good planting** tea in Austria.*
be worth	es wert sein	*"Gravity" **is worth seeing**.*

E 48 **Setze passende Gerunds ein. Du darfst jedes Wort nur einmal verwenden.**

save – look – talk – fight – be – find – lose – ask – spend – finish – become – see – pay – waste – run – kiss – do – forget

1. These days, many people worry about … their job and not … a new one.
2. Have you ever thought about … Dora for a date?
3. Ladies and gentlemen, let me thank you for … here tonight!
4. My friends sometimes talk of … a year at a high school in the USA.
5. Grandpa often talks about … in the war.
6. Tamara succeeded in … the race in under 10 minutes. She is very good.
7. I really didn't want to put off … to you, but I was so busy last week.
8. We are looking forward to … you again. Let's hope it will be soon.
9. Why do you always insist on … for me? Why don't you let me invite you?
10. Don't stop now, Bill! Keep on …! You can still be first!
11. After a week, the police gave up … for our car. We never saw it again.
12. You look happy, Sally! – I am! I feel like … everyone I see today!
13. Patrick is a good boy. He really cares about … the right thing.
14. Money is important to me. I believe in … it, not in … it!
15. Sir, I apologise for … to do my homework for today. I'll bring it tomorrow.
16. I sometimes think of … a doctor or a dentist when I'm older.

E 49 **Übertrage die Mustersätze aus der oberen Tabelle von Seite 44 in gutes Deutsch.**

F 50 **Finde das passende Wort und setze es als Gerund an der richtigen Stelle ein. Jedes Wort nur einmal verwenden!**

listen – wait – try – talk – visit – prepare – fall – ask – cry – think

1. We can't go to the pool because we are busy … for the camping trip.
2. Have you ever been to New York? No? Let me tell you, it's worth …!
3. Whenever Joshua tells a story, I can't help … asleep.
4. It's no good … Nick for help. He never helps anyone!
5. I can't stand … about Nina and her stupid problems. Let's talk about something else.
6. Stop it, Dad! It's no use … to start the car when the battery is dead.
7. When the film was over, Karla couldn't help … because it was so sad.
8. It's little use … any longer. They're not going to come today.
9. Forget William, Alice! He's not worth … about!
10. Haven't you got any heavy metal CDs? I can't stand … to so much techno.

F 51 **Übertrage die 10 Sätze aus Übung 50 in einwandfreies Deutsch.**

G GERUND NACH *"INSTEAD OF"* UND *"WITHOUT"*

Grundsätzlich kann nach jeder Präposition (Vorwort) ein Gerund folgen. Normalerweise treten die Präpositionen aber gemeinsam mit einem Verb auf – siehe Abschnitt E, Seite 44, über *"phrasal verbs"*.

Die Präpositionen ***"instead of"*** (statt, anstatt) und ***"without"*** (ohne zu) treten aber ohne engere Bindung an ein Verb auf.

> *Marty played with the dog **instead of tidying** his room.*
> (... statt sein Zimmer aufzuräumen.)
>
> ***Instead of waiting** for her dad, Kathy took the bus home.*
> (Anstatt auf ihren Vater zu warten ... .)
>
> *Dad threw away the letter **without reading** it.*
> (... ohne ihn zu lesen.)
>
> ***Without thinking** about the consequences, I started Dad's car.*
> (Ohne über die Folgen nachzudenken ... .)

H GERUND ANSTELLE VON TEMPORALSÄTZEN (ZEITSÄTZEN)

Die **Verkürzung von Gliedsätzen** mit Hilfe des Gerunds ist eine „typisch englische" Sache. Das ist sehr eleganter, „gehobener" Stil und kommt daher eher in der geschriebenen Sprache vor.

Diese Satzverkürzung ist nur möglich, **wenn Hauptsatz und Gliedsatz dasselbe Subjekt aufweisen**. Dabei ist es unwichtig, welcher Teil des Satzgefüges an erster Stelle steht.

> ***When Fred opened** the door, **he** saw that his car was snowed in.*
> ***On opening** the door, Fred saw that his car ... .*
>
> ***Before Nina told** me the story, **she** made sure nobody could hear us.*
> ***Before telling** me the story, Nina made sure ... .*
>
> ***Claudia** went to bed **after she had finished** the book.*
> *Claudia went to bed **after finishing** the book.*

! **Beachte:** ***when*** ► ***on*** ***before*** ► ***before*** ***after*** ► ***after***

I *"BY + GERUND"* ANSTELLE EINES „INDEM-SATZES"

„Indem-Sätze" sind Modalsätze. Sie sagen uns, auf welche Art und Weise etwas geschieht oder geschah.

> *They got into the house **by breaking** through a wall.*
> (... indem sie eine Wand durchbrachen.)
>
> ***By passing** the ball back to Joe, I surprised the players of the other team.*
> (Indem ich den Ball zurück zu Joe spielte, überraschte ich ... .)

G 52 **Was macht mehr Sinn, *"instead of"* oder *"without"*? Setze das Wort ein, von dem du glaubst, dass es besser passt.**

1. Never jump into water ... checking the temperature first.
2. ... staring out of the window, you could read a book or play with your sister.
3. Gilbert turned round and left ... answering my questions.
4. ... saying that she was sorry, Lydia got into the car and drove off.
5. You should call Andy and talk to him ... sitting at home crying.
6. The old man opened the door ... asking who was there.
7. ... calling us, you could send us an email.
8. Let's paint the rooms ourselves ... hiring a painter.

G 53 **Verbinde die folgenden Sätze mit *"instead of" oder "without"* plus Gerund.**

1. Dad left the house this morning. He did not take an umbrella with him.
2. You should do your homework. You shouldn't watch TV.
3. The burglars left the house. They didn't find the jewels.
4. We shouldn't complain about the food. We should enjoy the beaches.
5. Leo was so tired that he went to bed. He did not brush his teeth.
6. I've told you before: You can't just use my pen! You have to ask me first!
7. Let's try to do it ourselves! Let's not ask somebody else for help.
8. Why don't you tell me what you want? Why are you wasting my time?

Additional exercise Seite 157

H 54 **Verkürze die folgenden Temporalsätze mit Hilfe des Gerunds. Vorsicht – nur die Gliedsätze dürfen verändert werden, nicht die Hauptsätze.**

1. Before Mum goes to bed, she turns off all the lights in the house.
2. Nicky gave many interviews after she had received the gold medal.
3. When Maurice saw what he had done, he was very satisfied with himself.
4. After the passengers had got off the train, they waited for the tour buses.
5. Max always brushes his teeth before he leaves the house.
6. When the "Eagle" landed on the moon surface, it raised a cloud of dust.
7. After Eric had told Suzie he loved her, he asked her to marry him.
8. Eric told Suzie he loved her before he asked her to marry him.

Additional exercise Seite 158

I 55 **Verbinde oder verkürze die folgenden Sätze mit *"by + gerund"*.**

1. The President opened the new motorway. He cut a red ribbon in two.
2. If you look through the telescope, you can see the climbers.
3. Joe always makes friends quickly. He invites them to a round of drinks.
4. Emily qualified for the quiz show. She answered nine out of ten questions.
5. If you put A and B together, you will get a picture of the whole machine.
6. You can open the secret door if you touch a certain stone in the wall.
7. Mr. Zacharias really impressed his class. He did a backflip from the stand.
8. The male cricket tries to attract the female. It rubs its legs against its body.

Additional exercise Seite 158

J GERUND MIT UND OHNE *"PERSONAL"* ODER *"POSSESSIVE PRONOUN"*

Vergleiche die folgenden zwei Sätze und versuche ihre unterschiedliche Bedeutung zu erkennen!

(a) *I **hate looking** at these pictures!*

(b) *I **hate his/him looking** at these pictures!*

Der Unterschied ergibt sich aus dem Wort ***his*** oder ***him*** in Satz (b). In der deutschen Übersetzung ist das leicht zu erkennen:

(a) Ich hasse es, diese Bilder anzuschauen.
(Das heißt, **ich** mag sie mir nicht anschauen.)

(b) Ich hasse es, wenn **er** sich diese Bilder anschaut.
(Das heißt, ich mag nicht, dass sie sich **jemand anderer** anschaut.)

Die Möglichlichkeit, mit Hilfe eines Fürworts *(pronoun)* den Sinn des Satzes zu verändern, besteht bei vielen Gerund-Sätzen. Das eingeschobene *me/my, you/your, him/his* ... gibt dem Satz eine ganz andere Bedeutung.

Dazu einige Beispiele von vielen möglichen:

*Julia **dislikes being** late.* (**Sie** kommt nicht gern zu spät.)	*Julia **dislikes me being** late.* (Sie mag es nicht, wenn **ich** mich verspäte.)
*We don't **mind waiting** here.* (Es macht **uns** nichts aus, zu warten.)	*We don't **mind your waiting** here.* (Es stört uns nicht, wenn **ihr** wartet.)
*I **can't stand talking** to you.* (**Ich** halte es nicht aus, mit dir zu reden.)	*I **can't stand him talking** to you.* (Ich ertrage es nicht, wenn **er** mit dir spricht.)
*Everything **depends on arriving** in time.* (Alles hängt davon ab, dass **wir** rechtzeitig ankommen.)	*Everything **depends on their arriving** in time.* (Alles hängt davon ab, dass **sie** rechtzeitig ankommen.)
*I'm not **used to ironing** my shirts.* (**Ich** bin es nicht gewöhnt, meine Hemden zu bügeln.)	*I'm not **used to her ironing** my shirts.* (Ich bin es nicht gewöhnt, dass **sie** meine Hemden bügelt.)
*I **don't like laughing** at others.* (**Ich** lache nicht gern über andere.)	*I **don't like you laughing** at others.* (Ich mag es nicht, wenn **du** über andere lachst.)
*Tom **insists on paying** for everyone.* (**Tom** besteht darauf, für alle zu bezahlen.)	*Tom **insists on us paying** for everyone.* (Tom besteht darauf, dass **wir** für alle bezahlen.)

J 56 **Bilde jeweils zwei Gerund-Sätze, einen mit Fürwort *(personal or possessive pronoun)*, einen ohne. Das Beispiel zeigt dir, wie das geht.**

example: *Dad – proud – win the finals – (I)*
Vater war stolz darauf, das Finale zu gewinnen.
Vater was stolz darauf, dass ich das Finale gewonnen habe. ▶
Dad was proud of winning the finals.
Dad was proud of me/my winning the finals.

1. *Mum – doesn't like – work – till late at night – (we)*
   Mutter arbeitet nicht gern bis spät in die Nacht.
   Mutter mag es nicht, wenn wir bis spät in die Nacht arbeiten.
2. *my dad – tired of – play – the piano – every day – (I)*
   Vater hat das tägliche Klavierspielen satt.
   Vater hat es satt, dass ich jeden Tag Klavier spiele.
3. *we – look forward to – meet – Jacob's girlfriend – (you)*
   Wir freuen uns schon darauf, Jacobs Freundin kennen zu lernen.
   Wir freuen uns schon darauf, wenn ihr Jacobs Freundin kennen lernt.
4. *Robert – apologised – be – late – (we)*
   Robert entschuldigte sich für sein Zuspätkommen.
   Robert entschuldigte sich für unser Zuspätkommen.
5. *I – break a glass – without – notice – (she)*
   Ich zerbrach ein Glas, ohne es zu bemerken.
   Ich zerbrach ein Glas, ohne dass sie es bemerkte.
6. *I – not mind – watch – the movie – (you)*
   Ich habe nichts dagegen, mir den Film anzusehen.
   Ich habe nichts dagegen, dass du dir den Film ansiehst.
7. *were you surprised – find – right key – (I)*
   Warst du überrascht, den richtigen Schlüssel zu finden?
   Warst du überrascht, dass ich den richtigen Schlüssel fand?
8. *do you mind – help Grandpa – with the puzzle – (we)*
   Macht es dir etwas aus, Großvater bei dem Puzzle zu helfen?
   Macht es dir etwas aus, wenn wir Großvater bei dem Puzzle helfen?
9. *I – often worry – get – into trouble – (she)*
   Ich mache mir oft Sorgen, dass ich in Schwierigkeiten gerate.
   Ich mache mir oft Sorgen, dass sie in Schwierigkeiten gerät.
10. *I – not interested – see – this photo – (he)*
    Ich habe kein Interesse daran, das Foto zu sehen.
    Ich habe kein Interesse daran, dass er das Foto sieht.

Additional exercise Seite 158

7. KAPITEL *THE IMPERATIVE* – DIE BEFEHLSFORM

Die **Befehlsform *(the imperative)* sieht genauso aus wie die Nennform *(the infinitive, 1st form, base form)***, wird aber **ohne *"to"*** verwendet. Zwischen der Ein- und Mehrzahl gibt es keine Unterschiede.

infinitive	*imperative*
to come, to show	*Boys, **come** here and **show** me your exercise.*
to call, to tell	*Mum, please **don't call** Grandma and **tell** her to come.*
to go, to watch	*Come on, let's **go** and **watch** a video.*

A BEFEHLSFORM IN BITTEN, BEFEHLEN UND VERBOTEN

- Eine **Bitte** ist immer freundlicher und höflicher als ein Befehl oder ein Verbot. Das „Kennwort" einer Bitte ist normalerweise ***"please"***. Etwas bestimmter im Ton ist die **Aufforderung mit *"will you?"***.

  ***Please tell** Michelle to call me.* — Bitte sag Michelle, sie soll mich anrufen.
  ***Tell** Michelle to call me, please.*

  Tell** Michelle to call me, **will you? — Sag Michelle doch, sie soll mich anrufen.

- Ein **Befehl** ist viel bestimmter im Ton und kommt in der Regel ohne *"please"* oder *"will you?"* aus.

  *Boys, **leave** the girls alone!*
  (... lasst die Mädchen in Ruhe!)

  *Frederick, **stop** talking and **start** working!*
  (Hör auf zu reden und fang an zu arbeiten!)

- Ein **Verbot** bedeutet, dass man etwas nicht tun soll oder darf. Es lässt sich sehr direkt mit ***Don't ...!*** oder als Bitte mit ***Please don't ...!*** ausdrücken.

  ***Don't touch** the red button, Joe!*
  (Nicht den roten Knopf berühren!)

  ***Please don't talk** to me like that!*
  (Bitte sprich nicht so mit mir!)

B BEFEHLSFORM MIT *"LET'S ...!"* ALS VORSCHLAG ODER AUFFORDERUNG

***Let's watch** the match on TV!* — Schauen wir uns das Spiel im Fernsehen an!
***Let's not tell** her about the fight.* — Sagen wir ihr nichts von dem Streit!

A 57 **Die folgenden Situationen verlangen eine Bitte, eine Aufforderung, einen Befehl oder ein Verbot. Setze das passende Verb in der richtigen Form ein.**

example: *Max, please … to your room but … a noise! [go – not make]* ►
Max, please go to your room but don't make a noise!

not drink – get – ask – not look – look – help – hold – give – not switch – not shoot – call – run – eat – not tell – take – not invite – shut – go – put – do – not forget

1. I must get in touch with Fiona at once. Please … me her phone number!
2. This ladder doesn't look very stable. … it for me while I climb up, will you?
3. Hey, … off the lights! I'm reading!
4. Mum, please … me with this exercise. I can't do it!
5. … at me so angrily! I didn't do anything wrong!
6. Julia, please … Dad at the office and … him when he will be home tonight.
7. If you want to stay healthy, … lots of fruit and vegetables, but … alcohol.
8. Lenny, … these letters to the post office, will you? I can't do it myself.
9. When you talk to Joe next time, … him that we've met.
10. Norah, please … Kevin to your party! I can't stand him!
11. …, boys, or you'll be late again!
12. When you are in London, … to the Tower and … at the crown jewels!
13. Walter, please … to water the flowers while I'm away.
14. Police: "… out of the car and … your hands on the roof! Now!"
    Man: "… me, please! I didn't do anything! You've got the wrong person!"
    Police: "… up and … what I say and nothing will happen to you!"

B 58 **Übersetze diese Aufforderungen mit Hilfe von *"let's" oder "let's not".***

1. Hören wir uns das Neujahrskonzert an!
2. Gehen wir heute abend doch ins Kino!
3. Streiten wir doch nicht! *(streiten = to fight, to argue)*
4. Warten wir nicht länger; gehen wir!
5. Fragen wir Frank! Er weiß alles.
6. Fangen wir an! Es gibt viel zu tun.
7. Bestellen wir heute keine Pizza, sondern *(but)* Spaghetti.
8. Kaufen wir uns etwas zum Trinken!
9. Hören wir auf mit der Arbeit! Ich bin müde.
10. Drehen wir den Fernseher ab und gehen wir schlafen!

8. KAPITEL *THE INDIRECT OR REPORTED SPEECH* – DIE INDIREKTE REDE

Wenn man jemand mitteilen möchte, was jemand anderer gesagt hat, verwendet man die „indirekte Rede". Sie umfasst Aussagen, Fragen, Bitten, Befehle und Verbote.

Für die richtige Bildung der indirekten Rede sind die **einleitenden Verben** ***(reporting verbs)*** von besonderer Bedeutung. Dazu zählen:

answer – ask – complain – explain – inform – know – mention – wonder – remember – report – say – tell – think – want to know – write

A DER INDIREKTE BEFEHL – *THE INDIRECT COMMAND*

- Der indirekte Befehl umfasst von seiner sprachlichen Form her **Befehle, Aufforderungen, Bitten und Verbote.**

  Die häufigsten ***reporting verbs*** sind:

  tell (bei Befehlen, Aufforderungen und Verboten)
  ask (bei Bitten)

- Für die Bildung des indirekten Befehls braucht man nur den **Infinitiv** ***(base form, 1st form)***.
  (Bei einer anderen – komplizierteren – Art des indirekten Befehls wird aus dem direkten Befehl ein indirekter Aussagesatz mit ***should/should not***.)

  - *Grandma said (to us), "**Come** again soon!"* ▶ **Aufforderung**
    *Grandma **told** us **to come** again soon!"*
    *(Grandma said/told us **that we should come** again soon.)*
  - *Mr. Klein said, "**Open** your test books and **start** writing!"* ▶ **Befehl**
    *Mr. Klein **told** us **to open** our test books and **(to) start** writing.*
    *(Mr. Klein said **we should open** our test books and start writing.)*
  - *Sally said, "Please **put** the things in the fridge!"* ▶ **Bitte**
    *Sally **asked** me **to put** the things in the fridge.*
    *(Sally said **that I should put** the things in the fridge.)*
  - *Mum said, "**Don't speak** with Marcus!"* ▶ **Verbot**
    *Mum **told** me **not to speak** with Marcus.*
    *(Mum said **that I shouldn't speak** with Marcus.)*

A 59 **Verwandle die folgenden Befehle, Aufforderungen, Bitten und Verbote in die indirekte Rede. Verwende *told me* und *asked me* als Einleitung.**

1. Dad: "Feed the dog!"
2. Benjamin: "Close your eyes and count to ten!"
3. Samantha: "Put the books on the shelves!"
4. Policeman: "Switch off the engine and show me the first aid box!"
5. Vera: "Bring me something to read from the library, please!"
6. Mrs. Stone: "Take your feet off the desk and sit up straight!"
7. Alice: "Please load the dishwasher!"
8. Harry: "Push the green button and pull the door open!"
9. the stranger: "Give me a dollar, please!"
10. Gloria: "Don't touch the picture!"
11. our neighbour: "Don't make such a noise, please!"
12. Martina: "Don't call and don't send any emails!"
13. Maria: "Please don't wait outside!"
14. Mum: "Don't open the presents before Christmas!"
15. Dad: "Don't cross the street without looking!"
16. Grandma: "Don't mess up the living room, please!"
17. everybody: "Don't believe the newspapers!"
18. Richard: "Don't forget Mum's birthday!"
19. Kathy: "Please don't use so much water!"
20. Mum: "Hold the door open, please!"
21. Dad: "Don't drop the bottles!"
22. the postman: "Sign at the bottom of the page, please!"
23. Mr. Marks: "Read pages 12 to 15!"
24. Grandpa: "Lock the doors and switch off the lights!"
25. Allison: "Please don't show the photos to anyone!"
26. the old man: "Don't play in front of the house!"
27. Claire: "Watch the 10 o'clock news!"
28. the shop assistant: "Please pay at the cash desk!"
29. the gardener: "Don't step into the flower beds!"
30. the gym teacher: "Run to the ropes and climb up!"

B VERSCHIEBUNG DER ZEITSTUFEN – *CHANGE OF TENSES*

Wenn das ***reporting verb in past tense*** steht – zum Beispiel: *I asked, Joe said, We wanted to know, They thought* –, dann kommt es zu einer Verschiebung der Zeiten; das heißt, in der indirekten Rede werden andere Zeitstufen verwendet als in der direkten Rede. Dabei folgt man einem ziemlich strengen Schema:

direct speech	▶	*indirect speech*
present tense	▶	***past tense***
present perfect tense	▶	***past perfect tense***
past tense	▶	***past perfect tense***
future with will	▶	***conditional present ("would")***
*Samantha **said**,*	▶	*Samantha said (that) ...*
*"I **like** the new school."*	▶	*... she **liked** the new school.*
*"They **have done** a good job."*	▶	*... they **had done** a good job.*
*"It **took** two years to build it."*	▶	*... it **had taken** two years to build it.*
*"My friends **will like** it, too."*	▶	*... her friends **would like** it, too.*

C VERÄNDERUNGEN BEI DEN FÜRWÖRTERN – *CHANGE OF PRONOUNS*

Die Veränderungen bei den persönlichen und besitzanzeigenden Fürwörtern *(personal and possessive pronouns)* ergeben sich aus der jeweiligen Situation:
Wer spricht mit wem über wen?

*The boys said to Mary, "**We** know that **you** are not **our** friend."* ▶
*The boys informed Mary (that) **they** knew (that) **she** wasn't **their** friend.*

*Bianca said to me, "**I** like **my** room better than **yours**.* ▶
*Bianca told me (that) **she** liked **her** room better than **mine**.*

D VERÄNDERUNGEN BEI ORTS- UND ZEITANGABEN – *CHANGE OF ADVERBIALS*

Die Orts- und Zeitangaben verändern sich sinngemäß, weil sich der Standpunkt des „Weitererzählers" von dem des (direkten) Sprechers unterscheiden kann: „Hier" bleibt nicht „hier", wenn man seinen Standort verändert, und „heute" ist nicht mehr „heute", wenn man etwas einen oder zwei Tage später weitererzählt.
Hier findest du die wichtigsten Veränderungen:

direct speech	► *indirect speech*	*direct speech*	► *indirect speech*
this	► ***that***	*(a week) ago*	► ***(the week) before***
these	► ***those***	*last (month)*	► ***(the month) before***
yesterday	► ***the day before***	*next (year)*	► ***the following (year), (the year) after***
today	► ***that day***		
tomorrow	► ***the day after, the next/following day***	*here*	► ***there***

B C 60 **Bilde die indirekte Rede aus den folgenden Sätzen. Leite sie mit einem Verb in *past tense* ein *(said, explained, mentioned, remembered, thought, told ...)* und achte besonders auf die Verschiebungen bei den Zeitstufen und die Veränderungen bei den persönlichen und besitzanzeigenden Fürwörtern. Gehe davon aus, dass die jeweiligen Personen mit dir/euch gesprochen haben; Abweichungen sind leicht erkennbar (zB Satz 3, 5 ...)**

1. Emily: "My cousins and I have always wanted to visit Disney World."
2. Mr. and Mrs. Sadler: "Our son likes his new job very much."
3. I told Sarah, "I'm not speaking about your boyfriend."
4. The boys: "We are going to meet our friends in town."
5. Agatha: "You will all like my new book."
6. Edgar to Jennifer: "You haven't returned my books yet."
7. Leo: "Marcia and her sister will be at my party, too."
8. Theresa: "I've sent you three emails since Friday."

D 61 **Wie bei Übung 60: Bilde die indirekte Rede! Jetzt musst du aber zusätzlich auf die Veränderung der Orts- und Zeitangaben achten!**

1. Grandma: "I will call you again next week."
2. the new teacher: "We are going to write an essay today."
3. shopkeeper: "I sold over 50 games this morning."
4. Mum: "I've been waiting for this letter since last week."
5. man: "I bought this car last month and I've got problems with it already."
6. woman: "My husband was the mayor of this town until last year."
7. Aunt Lucy: "We are looking forward to your visit next month."
8. the officer to the soldier: "You have to get a haircut before tomorrow."
9. Florence: "Ernest got back from his trip yesterday."

E "REPORTING VERB" IN PRESENT (PERFECT) TENSE

Wichtige Abweichung vom „Gesetz der Zeitenverschiebung": Wenn das *reporting verb* in *present tense* oder *present perfect tense* steht *(Charlie says ...; They have told us ...)*, dann findet **keine Verschiebung der Zeitstufen** statt.
Auch die **Orts- und Zeitangaben bleiben unverändert**; nur die Fürwörter *(personal and possessive pronouns)* ändern sich sinngemäß.

direct speech	▶	*indirect speech*
*Samantha **says/has said,***	▶	*Samantha **says/has said** that ...*
*"I **like** the new school."*	▶	*... she **likes** the new school.*
*"They **have done** a good job."*	▶	*... they **have done** a good job.*
*"It **took** two years to build it."*	▶	*... it **took** two years to build it.*
*"My friends **will like** it, too."*	▶	*... her friends **will like** it, too.*

F FRAGEN IN DER INDIREKTEN REDE – *INDIRECT QUESTIONS*

- Die Bildung der indirekten Frage hängt von der Art der Frage ab:
Entscheidungsfrage oder Ergänzungsfrage?

direkte Entscheidungsfragen Antwort: JA oder NEIN	**direkte Ergänzungsfragen** Antwort: ein Satzglied (Ort, Zeit ...)
"Can we go now?"	*"Why can't we go now?"*
"Is Gwendolyn at home?"	*"Where is Gwendolyn?"*
"Do you like my new dress?"	*"How do you like my new dress?"*
"Have you dyed your hair?"	*"What have you done with your hair?"*

indirekte Entscheidungsfragen werden mit ***if/whether*** eingeleitet; beide Wörter bedeuten **„ob"**	**indirekte Ergänzungsfragen** werden mit dem **gleichen Fragewort** eingeleitet wie die direkte Frage
Helena wanted to know ...	*Helena wanted to know ...*
*... **if** they **could** go now.*	*... **why** they **couldn't** go now.*
*... **if** Gwendolyn **was** at home.*	*... **where** Gwendolyn **was**.*
*... **whether** I **liked** her new dress.*	*... **how** I **liked** her new dress.*
*... **whether** I **had dyed** my hair.*	*... **what** I **had done** with my hair.*

- Was man bei der Umwandlung einer direkten Frage in eine indirekte noch beachten muss: Die **indirekte Frage** ist keine Frage, sondern eine Aussage, daher schließt der Satz mit **Punkt statt** mit **Fragezeichen.**

E 62 **Bilde die indirekte Rede, wobei das einleitende Verb in *present tense* oder *present perfect tense* stehen muss *(says, has told us ...)*.**

1. The reporter says, "Three people were hurt in a fire yesterday."
2. Eric complains, "My new maths teacher doesn't like me."
3. Jill has said, "These cucumbers grew in my garden."
4. Victor remembers, "My family used to live in a two-room flat."
5. The text on a pack of cigarettes says, "Smoking can kill you."
6. Uncle Alfred writes, "We will try to visit you on our way to Italy tomorrow."
7. The coach complains, "My team played well last night, but they lost again."
8. In the play, Hamlet thinks, "I must find out who has killed my father."
9. Mum has said, "I'm going to visit a friend of mine this afternoon."
10. The newspaper informs us, "The bridge will be closed for a week."

F 63 **Bilde die indirekte Frage aus diesen direkten Entscheidungsfragen. Achte darauf, ob das *reporting verb* in *present (perfect) tense* oder in *past tense* steht.**

1. Jim wants to know, "Did you see a good film last weekend?"
2. Polly asked me, "Will you go to the dance with Wilma tonight?"
3. Thomas wondered, "Have I done the right thing?"
4. Joe often asks himself, "Am I crazy?"
5. Gordon wanted to know, "Can we park our car here?"
6. Nobody asked us, "Do you like this kind of music?"
7. Lucy wonders, "Does Linus still love me?"
8. Mum often asks me, "Have you called Grandma lately?"
9. Sandra wanted to know, "Did you talk to my brother yesterday?"
10. Ian asked me, "Will you send me your picture?"

F 64 **Bilde nun indirekte Fragen aus diesen Ergänzungsfragen. Achte wieder darauf, in welcher Zeitstufe die *reporting verbs* stehen.**

1. Ali asked me, "What are you doing this afternoon?"
2. Bill wants to know, "When can I have my football back?"
3. I've often asked myself, "How does a fax machine work?"
4. Mrs. Eisner wanted to know, "Why aren't you in my class this year?"
5. Monica wondered, "Where have I put my keys?"
6. Angela asked her dad, "Why do you want to meet my new friends?"
7. Graham wanted to know, "Who has seen my trainers?"
8. Herbert wondered, "Who told you about my accident yesterday?"
9. Dan wants to know, "Why doesn't Sonja like me?"
10. Quentin asked me, "How much did you pay for your new iPhone?"
11. Silvia wondered, "What did I do to make Mum so angry?"
12. Tristan wanted to know, "When will I hear from you again?"

Additional exercise Seite 159

9. KAPITEL *THE INFINITIVE* – DIE NENNFORM

Die Nennform kennt man auch als Infinitiv, 1. Stammform des Verbs oder – auf Englisch – ***base form*** oder ***1st form***.
Der Infinitiv tritt **mit und ohne *"to"*** auf. Weil er aber meistens mit *"to"* vorkommt, nennt man ihn auch die ***"to-form"***.

A INFINITIV NACH BESTIMMTEN VERBEN MIT *"TO"*

Nach bestimmten Verben ist der Infinitiv mit *"to"* zwingend vorgeschrieben.
Die folgende Liste enthält die wichtigsten dieser Verben:

afford	leisten	*We can't **afford to lose** the next two matches.*
agree	zustimmen	*They **agreed to show** us the secret room.*
ask	bitten	*I've **asked** Dan **to go** to the supermarket for me.*
attempt	versuchen	*You have never **attempted to find** out the truth.*
decide	beschließen	*We **decided to forget** the fight and make peace.*
expect	erwarten	*Sue **expects to get** an answer soon.*
forget	vergessen	*Don't **forget to send** Grandma some flowers.*
happen	„zufällig geschehen"	*I **happened to be** there ...* Ich war zufällig dort.
hesitate	zögern	*... but I **hesitate to tell** you what happened.*
hope	hoffen	*Everybody **hopes to find** a good job after school.*
learn	lernen	*A child must **learn to tell** right from wrong.*
manage	es schaffen	*I'm sure you have **managed to learn** this.*
offer	anbieten	*They have **offered to buy** our old car.*
pretend	so tun als ob	*Dad **pretends to like** my cake, but he doesn't.*
promise	versprechen	*I **promised** Dad not **to bake** another cake soon.*
plan	planen	*Andy is **planning to spend** a week with us.*
refuse	ablehnen, sich weigern	*I **refuse to listen** to this nonsense.*
seem	scheinen	*Wilson **seems to know** everything.*
want	wollen	*Do you really **want to leave** the party so soon?*

B INFINITIV NACH BESTIMMTEN VERBEN OHNE *"TO"*

Dieser kommt **seltener** vor. Er tritt uns in den folgenden Fällen entgegen:

- mit den ***modal verbs*** ▶ *can, may, must, will ...*
  *I know you **can do** it! – We really **must stop** now. – You **may go**!*
- mit *"let"* und *"make"* in der Bedeutung von „lassen"/„veranlassen"
  *Please, let me **say** something! – They made us **leave** the room.*
- mit ***had better not*** und ***had rather not***
  *We'**d better start** soon!* ▶ Wir sollten lieber bald anfangen!
  *I **had rather not play** today.* ▶ Ich würde heute lieber nicht spielen!
- nach ***see, hear, watch*** und ***feel*** bei schon abgeschlossener Handlung
  *We **watched** them **drive** away.* Siehe Seite 64 und 96, Kapitel 17 D.

A 65 **Welches Verb aus der Tabelle von Seite 58 passt am besten zu den einzelnen Sätzen? Bilde gute englische Sätze und versuche sie anschließend in ebenso gutes Deutsch zu übersetzen.**

1. Rudy ... to become an important scientist when he gets older.
2. We will need the electric torch when it gets dark. We can't ... to lose it!
3. Look, Andrea ... to know the answer! Let's go and ask her!
4. Many people would ... to work for less money if they only had a job.
5. This is nonsense! I absolutely ... to believe it!
6. One day I will ... Dad to let me drive the car.
7. What will you do with this old car? – I'm ... to repair it and drive it.
8. The burglars ... to get away through the garden, but they were caught.

B 66 **Setze das passende englische Wort als *"infinitive without to"* ein.**

1. George, you must (*antworten*) ... each of these questions.
2. Sometimes Dad lets me (*verwenden*) ... his laptop.
3. Nobody will make me (*tun*) ... something I don't want to do.
4. Martha, I think you had better (*zuhören*) ... to your mother!
5. Coke or orange juice, Carl? – I'd rather (*haben*) ... a glass of water, please.
6. I often see you (*verlassen*) ... the house at night.
7. Marianne never lets me (*anschauen*) ... at her photos.
8. Boys, you'd better (*gehen*) ... home now. It's past 9 o'clock.

B 67 **Übersetze die folgenden Sätze mit Hilfe des Infinitivs ohne *"to"*.**

1. Wir würden morgen lieber zu Hause bleiben.
2. Hast du jemand in das Haus gehen gesehen?
3. Mrs. Hoffman ließ uns nach der Schule die Klasse aufräumen.
4. Ich glaube, du solltest mir alles erzählen.
5. Wir hören dich oft am Nachmittag Klavier spielen.
6. Ihr müsst den Aufsatz heute fertig schreiben.
7. Du solltest lieber nicht hier parken.
8. Lass deinen Hund nicht ohne Leine (= *leash*) herumlaufen.

C INFINITIV NACH EINEM ADJEKTIV

Der Infinitiv tritt häufig in Verbindung mit einem Adjektiv auf, oft als Ergebnis einer „typisch englischen" Satzverkürzung. Das sieht dann zum Beispiel so aus:

*We were **happy to hear** that you were alright.*
Anstelle von ▶ *We were happy when we heard that you were alright.*

*Linda is **sorry to miss** the first day of school, but she is ill.*
*Is it **important to know** all these words?*

D INFINITIV NACH EINEM FRAGEWORT

Wieder ein „typisch englisches" Sprachgebilde! Mit seiner Hilfe lassen sich holprig klingende Sätze vermeiden und elegant klingende Sätze bilden.

I don't remember where I should put the photo albums. ▶
*I don't remember **where to put** the photo albums.*

Mum can't decide what she should wear tonight. ▶
*Mum can't decide **what to wear** tonight.*

Do you know when you must be there? ▶
*Do you know **when to be** there?*

E INFINITIV NACH BESTIMMTEN NOMEN

Eine Reihe von Hauptwörtern (Nomen) verlangen den Infinitiv mit *"to"*. Dazu zählen die folgenden Wörter (Auswahl der wichtigsten):

ability	Fähigkeit	*Animals don't have the **ability to think**.*
chance	Gelegenheit	*This is our only **chance to get** out of here.*
opportunity	Möglichkeit	*We had the **opportunity to see** the Queen.*
command	Befehl	*Who gave the **command to attack**?*
order	Befehl	*My **orders** are **to let** nobody in.*
courage	Mut	*Nobody had the **courage to say** anything.*
decision	Entscheidung	*It's your **decision to stay** or **to go**.*
freedom	Freiheit	*I need the **freedom to do** what I want.*
permission	Erlaubnis	*Do we need your **permission to stay** here?*
possibility	Möglichkeit	*There was no **possibility to find** decent work.*
reason	Grund	*I have **reason to believe** that Joe is coming.*
right	Recht	*They say everyone has the **right to live** free!*
time	Zeit	*It's **time to say** good-bye.*
way	Art, Weise	*There must be a **way to stop** the fight.*
wish	Wunsch	*It was Tina's **wish to speak** with us.*

F INFINITIV NACH *"TOO + ADJECTIVE"* UND *"ENOUGH + NOUN"*

*I'm **too tired to work**.* (statt: *I'm so tired that I can't work.)*
*There's not **enough time to finish** the project.* (*... so little time that ...*)

C 68 Suche zu jedem Satz ein passendes Adjektiv aus der „Box" und setze es ein.

sorry – hard – silly – possible – dangerous – ready – nice – good

1. I wasn't ... to say which was better, the chocolate cake or the apple pie.
2. Our coach says it will be very ... to win the championship.
3. Where are you, Martin? We are ... to go!
4. Nobody was ... to hear that Chris had got an "F" in maths.
5. It's very ... to spend a week or so at the seaside every year.
6. Be careful! It can be ... to swim here.
7. It's ... to have a friend like you, John!
8. I think it's ... to dress up like a clown.

D 69 Wandle die folgenden Sätze mit Hilfe von *"question word + infinitive"* um.

1. The plan in the book told us how we could find the treasure.
2. Children, you know who you can ask if you have a question.
3. Please tell me when I should begin.
4. Dad was not sure where he should hide Mum's birthday present.
5. I never know what I should order at an expensive restaurant.
6. Can somebody show me how I can open this stupid box?
7. Tom has no idea what he should do in his spare time.
8. We would like to know where we should go now! Left or right?

Additional exercise Seite 160

E 70 Suche zu jedem Satz das passende Verb, so dass sich sinnvolle Sätze mit *"noun + infinitive"* ergeben.

buy – do – lose – see – shout – stay – tell – visit

1. Joe did not have the courage to ... his parents the truth.
2. This is no reason to ... at me!
3. It was Uncle Stanley's greatest wish to ... the Tadj Mahal by moonlight.
4. We had the opportunity to ... four CDs for the price of three.
5. The doctor did not give us permission to ... Grandpa after the operation.
6. I think it was the right decision to ... at this hotel; it's very nice here.
7. My dad has the ability to ... several things at the same time.
8. Lying is the best way to ... a friend.

F 71 Verkürze die folgenden Sätze mit Hilfe von *"too"* oder *"enough"*.

1. The river was so deep that we could not cross it.
2. It's so cloudy that we won't see the stars tonight.
3. After Christmas I had so much money that I could buy a game station.
4. There's so little snow that we can't ski today.

G VERB + OBJEKT + INFINITIV

Die Fügung *"verb + object + infinitive"* kommt im Englischen häufiger und in anderen Zusammenhängen vor als im Deutschen.

	verb +	*object*	*+ infinitive*	
■ **wie auf Deutsch**				
Grandma Oma	***asked*** bat	***me*** mich	***to come.*** zu kommen.	▶ mit *"to"*
Mum Mutter	***lets*** lässt	***us*** uns	***try*** *on her shoes.* ihre Schuhe probieren.	▶ ohne *"to"*
■ **anstelle eines „dass-Satzes"**				
Grandpa *Norah*	***expects*** ***wants***	***you*** ***me***	***to feed*** *the dog.* ***to go out*** *with her.*	
Opa Norah	erwartet, möchte,	dass du den Hund fütterst. dass ich mit ihr ausgehe.		

Die folgenden Verben eignen sich besonders für diese Fügung:

advise	(be)raten, einen Rat geben	*Let me **advise you to get** a new bike.*
allow	gestatten, erlauben	*Dad doesn't **allow me to use** his laptop.*
ask	bitten, ersuchen	*Joe **asked us to visit** him again.*
expect	erwarten	*I **expect Fred to say** he's sorry.*
help	helfen	*Can you **help me to open** this door?*
invite	einladen, auffordern	*They **invited me to play** in their band.*
know	wissen, kennen (als)	*You **know me to be** a good friend.*
order	befehlen	*They **ordered us to leave** the building.*
remind	(jemand) erinnern	*Please **remind me to return** the books.*
teach	lehren, beibringen	*Let's **teach them** (how) **to behave.***
tell	sagen, befehlen	*Who **told you to do** this exercise?*
want	wollen, mögen	*Mum **wants us to go** shopping today.*
wish	wünschen, wollen	*I **wish you to leave** me in peace.*
would like	mögen, wollen	*I'd **like you to meet** my boyfriend.*

H INFINITIV NACH EINEM „EXTREMWORT"

Zu den „Extremwörtern" zählt man:

- **Ordnungszahlwörter**
  first, second ...
- **Superlative**
  best, last ...
- ***"the only"***
  (der einzige)

The easiest *thing* ***to do*** *would be to give up.*
As usual, I was ***the only*** *one* ***to know*** *the answer.*

G 72 **Übersetze mit Hilfe von *"verb + object + infinitive"* in gutes Englisch.**

1. Walter bat mich, seinen Vater zu informieren.
2. Charlie erlaubte mir, sein neues iPad auszuprobieren. (*try out*)
3. Ich rate dir, nicht mit Gerry zu sprechen.
4. Mein Bruder half mir, das Bild fertigzustellen. (*finish*)
5. Claudia lud mich ein, eine Woche auf dem Boot ihrer Eltern zu verbringen.
6. Der Polizist befahl dem Fahrer, aus dem Auto zu steigen.
7. Ich erinnerte meine Schwester, ein Geschenk für Vater zu kaufen.
8. Kannst du mir beibringen, das auf Spanisch zu sagen?
9. Niemand erwartet, dass du alles weißt.
10. Möchtest du, dass ich gehe oder bleibe?
11. Sag mir nicht, dass ich diesen Unsinn glauben soll!
12. Lori hätte gern, dass du mit ihr tanzt.
13. Wir wollten nicht, dass ihr das wisst.
14. Ich möchte dich bitten, für mich einkaufen zu gehen.
15. Wir wissen, dass du ein hervorragender (*outstanding*) Schwimmer bist.
16. Soll ich dir eine lustige Geschiche erzählen? (= Möchtest du, dass ich dir eine lustige Geschichte erzähle?)
17. Ich werde es nicht erlauben, dass ihr so früh geht (*leave*).
18. Niemand hat mich erinnert, dass ich den Müll hinaustrage.
19. Opa wünscht sich, dass ich eines Tages seine Uhr (*watch*) bekomme.
20. Sie sagten, wir sollten nächste Woche anrufen.

Additional exercise Seite 160

H 73 **Verkürze die folgenden Sätze mit Hilfe von *"extreme word + infinitive"*.**

example: *It would be best if you told your parents everything.* ►
It would be best to tell your parents everything.

1. Peter was the only person who tried to stop the fight.
2. I was the last person that heard about the party.
3. The worst thing that happened in 2004 was the tsunami.
4. The fifth person that comes into the room gets a prize.
5. Jimmy is the only boy that reads love stories.
6. The captain should be the last person that leaves the ship.
6. It would be best if we stopped here for the night.
7. The Russians were the first that sent a man into space.
8. Dad is the first that comes in the morning and the last that leaves at night.
9. Michael Schumacher is the only driver that won seven championships.
10. Frank, you are the second person that finished the race. How does it feel?
11. The best wine that goes with fish is white wine.
12. The kiwi is the most unusual bird that you can see in New Zealand.
13. Reinhold Messner was the first that climbed Mt. Everest without oxygen.
14. English is one of the easiest languages that you can learn.
15. For a few years, the "Concorde" was the fastest plane that flew from Europe to North America.

10. KAPITEL *INFINITIVE* ODER *"ING-FORM"*?

Oft stellt sich die Frage, ob nach einem Verb ein Infinitiv oder eine *"ing-form"* (Gerund oder *present participle*) folgt.
In den entsprechenden Kapiteln (**Gerund** ab Seite 40; ***present participle*** ab Seite 94) erfährst du, in welchen Fällen diese Fügungen zwingend sind.
Es gibt aber auch einige Verben, die **sowohl mit dem Infinitiv als auch mit einer *"ing-form"*** auftreten. Dabei muss man drei Möglichkeiten unterscheiden:

verb + infinitive und ***verb + "ing-form"***		
1. mit gleicher Bedeutung	**2. mit geringem Unterschied in der Bedeutung**	**3. mit großem Unterschied in der Bedeutung**
begin – start – continue *He began to sing.* *= He began singing.* ***like – love – prefer – hate*** *We prefer to walk.* *= We prefer walking.*	***verb + infinitive*** eher allgemein gehalten; keine einzelne Handlung *We often hear you sing.* ***verb + "ing-form"*** eher bei bestimmten, beobachtbaren Handlungen *We can hear you singing.*	Bei einigen Zeitwörtern ändert sich die Bedeutung der Aussage, je nachdem, ob man sie mit dem Infinitiv oder mit der *"ing-form"* verwendet.

Zu dieser 3. Gruppe von Verben, deren Bedeutung davon abhängt, ob ein Infinitiv oder eine *ing-form* folgt, zählen die folgenden:

verb + infinitive	***verb + "ing-form"***
*Louisa **forgot to feed** her hamster.* ▶ notwendige Handlung (hätte sie tun sollen, hat sie aber vergessen)	*You won't **forget riding** this horse.* ▶ Erinnerung an schon Geschehenes (wird man nie vergessen ...)
*I **need to know** what you think.* ▶ Notwendigkeit, Zwang (aktiv) (das muss geschehen, das muss sein)	*Jill **needs talking** to, I think.* ▶ Notwendigkeit, Zwang (passiv) (das müsste mit ihr geschehen, sie braucht das)
***Remember to call** me tomorrow.* ▶ notwendige Handlung (darf man nicht vergessen)	*I **remember talking** to Joe on Friday.* ▶ Erinnerung an Vergangenes, schon Geschehenes (ich erinnere mich daran)
*We **stopped to ask** for the way.* ▶ eine Tätigkeit unterbrechen, um etwas anderes zu tun; „um zu"	***Stop asking** those people. Let's drive on!* ▶ eine Tätigkeit beenden, einstellen
*Joe **tried to find** his keys, but he had lost them.* ▶ Versuch, etwas zu tun (er hat es versucht)	*We can **try selling** the books. Perhaps somebody wants them.* ▶ Vorschlag (zur Lösung des Problems) (wir könnten es ja versuchen)

74 Infinitiv (mit oder ohne *"to"*) oder *"ing-form"*? Finde die richtige Verbform. Streiche die falsche Verbform durch, so dass sich ein richtiger Satz ergibt.

1. We *tried to phone/tried phoning* them the other day, but nobody answered.
2. I think I *remember to see/remember seeing* these people at Joe's party.
3. While he was working in the garden, Dad *stopped to smoke/stopped smoking* a cigarette.
4. Brian, you *need to be/need being* more careful when you ride your bike.
5. How awful! You *forgot to call/forgot calling* Grandma on her birthday? She will never forgive you.
6. *Remember to send/Remember sending* Max an email. He's waiting for it.
7. *Try to ask/Try asking* Richard for help. I'm sure he will do it.
8. Dad doesn't like Oliver. He says I must *stop to see/stop seeing* him.
9. Charles *forgot to tell/forgot telling* us the joke, so he told it again.
10. Look at you car, Mum! It *needs to wash/needs washing* badly.

75 Setze die richtige Verbform ein: Infinitiv oder *"ing-form"*.

1. My parents have always told me (*say*) … thank you when somebody gives me something, and I never forget (*do*) … it.
2. Lukas is so cute! The girls can't help (*talk*) … about him all the time.
3. I don't want you (*use*) … my pen again without (*ask*) … me first, okay?
4. My German teacher made me (*feel*) … very proud by (*read*) … my essay in class in front of everybody, but since that day, George refuses (*speak*) … with me. I think he is jealous.
5. Go on (*write*) …, Sally, and don't forget (*read*) … your essay again before (*hand*) … it in.
6. Grandpa forgot (*feed*) … the dog, so he was surprised (*see*) … that the dog didn't want to eat.
7. Please stop (*talk*) …, Mike! I'm trying (*concentrate*) … on my work.
8. Harry came (*run*) … downstairs, (*shout*) … wildly. He had just seen himself on TV for the first time.
9. Your shoes need (*clean*) …, Dad. I can (*do*) … it for you if you let me (*use*) … your laptop this afternoon.
10. After (*listen*) … to Gloria for a while, I began (*understand*) … why everybody thinks she is crazy.
11. If we continue (*walk*) … in this direction, we will never get there. Let's (*stop*) … (*ask*) … somebody for the way.
12. The guests are coming! I hear them (*talk*) … and (*laugh*) … in the street.
13. Dad, have you finished (*take*) … pictures? We'd like (*continue*) … the tour.
14. One of my favourite sports is (*jog*) …, but I can't stand (*do*) … it alone.
15. Ron looked so funny in that suit! We couldn't help (*laugh*) … when we saw him. That made him angry, of course, so we apologised for (*be*) … so silly.
16. At first, I enjoyed (*take*) … the dog for a walk, but now I hate (*go*) … out in all kinds of weather. Sometimes I'd rather (*stay*) … indoors (*watch*) … TV.
17. We'd better (*wait*) … for Mike. It's too late now (*leave*) … without him.

Additional exercise Seite 161

11. KAPITEL | *MODAL VERBS* – HILFSVERBEN DER AUSSAGEWEISE

Die Hilfszeitwörter der Aussageweise (Modalverben) geben genauere Auskunft über die **Art und Weise**, wie eine Handlung abläuft. Sie sagen uns zum Beispiel, ob etwas **geschehen kann, darf, muss** oder **soll**.
Die wichtigsten ***modal verbs*** der englischen Sprache sind ***can***, ***may*** und ***must***. Außerdem interessiert uns, wie man **„sollen“** und **„lassen“** auf Englisch ausdrücken kann.

A *CAN – COULD – TO BE ABLE*

- **"Can"** bedeutet **können** oder **dürfen**.
- Es gibt eine Form für ***present tense*** ▶ ***can***
  und eine für ***past tense*** ▶ ***could***.
- In allen Zeitstufen gibt es eine **Ersatzform**.
  Diese heißt ▶ ***to be able to*** + ***base form***. (*"able"* heißt „fähig“, „in der Lage“)

  *We **are able to help** you.*
  *The boys **were able to build** the tree house.*
  *I **haven't been able to get** in touch with Mary.*
  *Nobody **will be able to solve** this riddle.*

- *"can"* und *"could"* drücken **sowohl Fähigkeit als auch Erlaubnis** aus.
  Die **Ersatzform** ***"to be able to + base form"*** steht aber **nur bei Fähigkeit**.

Erlaubnis	Fähigkeit
*You **can read this letter.*** (Du darfst = kannst ihn lesen.)	*This letter is in French, but Bill **can read** it.* (Er ist in der Lage, ihn zu lesen, obwohl ...) ▶ *..., but Bill **is able to read** it.*
*Joe **could invite** ten friends.* (er durfte = er konnte)	*I couldn't invite you because I was ill.* (ich war dazu nicht in der Lage) ▶ *I **wasn't able to invite** you because ...*

- Für ***if*-Satz** und **höfliche Frage** gilt: ***could*** = **könnte**
  ***Could** you give us your phone number, please?*
  *Michael would call us tonight if he **could**.*
- Die **Verneinung** (***negation***) sieht so aus:

can ▶ *cannot/can't*	*could* ▶ *could not/couldn't*
am able ▶ ***am not able***	*was able* ▶ ***was not able***
is able ▶ ***is not able***	*were able* ▶ ***were not able***
will be able ▶ ***will not be able***	*had been able* ▶ ***had not been able***
have been able ▶ ***have not been able***	*has been able* ▶ ***has not been able***

Diese Punkte gelten für alle *modal verbs*:

- ***Modal verbs*** treten nicht allein, sondern immer **gemeinsam mit einem Hauptzeitwort** (Vollverb) auf. Dies gilt nicht bei Kurzantworten und in *tag questions*. Das Hauptzeitwort erscheint dabei immer im **Infinitiv** *(base form)*, aber immer **ohne *"to"***.
- Den ***modal verbs*** **fehlen bestimmte Formen und Zeitstufen.** Nicht vorhanden sind:
  - **Infinitiv** *(base form, 1st form)*
  - ***past form*** (2. Stammform), außer ***"could"***
  - ***past participle*** (3. Stammform, Mittelwort der Vergangenheit)
- ***Modal verbs*** bilden **Frage und Verneinung ohne *"do – does – did"***.
- ***Modal verbs*** sehen **in allen Personen gleich** aus. Es gibt keine unterschiedlichen Endungen, wie zum Beispiel *3rd person -s*.
- ***Modal verbs*** haben **Ersatzformen** für die fehlenden Formen. Man braucht sie, um alle Zeitstufen bilden zu können.

A 76 **Ersetze *can* und *could* durch eine passende Form von *"to be able to + base form"*.**

1. Nobody and nothing can stop a tsunami.
2. We cannot give you this information.
3. I can say what's good and what's bad.
4. Who can explain what I have just said?
5. Can everybody hear what the speakers are saying?
6. We could not take a good look at the room.
7. Sandra could catch the vase before it fell to the floor.
8. Could Alex finish the test?
9. Who could translate the last two sentences?
10. We couldn't get tickets for the show.

A 77 **Forme die folgenden Sätze so um, dass in jedem Satz „können" in irgendeiner Weise vorkommt (*can, could, are able, was able ...*).**

1. Dad bought some glue for the model planes.
2. We hear you, but we don't see you. Where are you?
3. I hope Judy will tell us more when we see her again.
4. Frank hasn't used the internet since Friday.
5. Did Herbert repair your computer?
6. After falling from the ladder, Ruth did not get up again.
7. I think man will never fly to Mars.
8. The girls finished their dresses in time.
9. I have spoken with the headmaster several times.
10. Ben is sorry, but he won't come tonight.
11. The questions were easy, but we did not answer them.
12. Darren has skied since he was three years old.

B *MAY – MIGHT – TO BE ALLOWED*

- *"May"* bedeutet **dürfen** oder **„vielleicht"**.
- Es gibt eine Form für ***present tense*** ▶ ***may***
  und eine, die aussieht, als wäre sie ***past tense*** ▶ ***might***.
- In allen Zeitstufen gibt es eine **Ersatzform.**
  Diese heißt ▶ ***(to) be allowed to*** + ***base form***. (*"allowed"* heißt „erlaubt")

  *We **are allowed to stay** up late.*
  *The boys **were allowed to leave** the room.*
  *I **haven't been allowed to get** in touch with Mary.*
  *Nobody **will be allowed to cheat** during the test.*

- *"May"* drückt **sowohl Erlaubnis als auch Möglichkeit** aus.
  Die Ersatzform ***"to be allowed to + base form"*** steht aber **nur bei Erlaubnis.**

Erlaubnis	Möglichkeit
*You **may read** this letter.* (du darfst; ich erlaube es) *You **are allowed to read** it.*	*Gina **may read** this letter or she **may not**.* (**vielleicht** liest sie ihn, **vielleicht nicht**)
*Joe **was allowed to** invite friends.* (er durfte; man erlaubte es ihm)	*I **couldn't invite** you because I was ill.* (ich hatte nicht die Möglichkeit dazu)

- ***may*** ▶ **„vielleicht", „mag sein"**; kann durch *"perhaps"* oder *"maybe"* ersetzt werden
- ***might*** ▶ bedeutet ebenso **„vielleicht"**, ist aber unsicherer als *may*

- Beim Punkt **„Erlaubnis"** lässt sich eine Abstufung von „normal" über „höflich" bis „sehr höflich" erkennen:

normal (üblich)	höflich (häufig)	sehr höflich (seltener)
can I?	***could I?***	***may I?***
***Can I go** now?*	***Could we go** now?*	***May I go** now, please?*

- Die **Verneinung (*negation*)** hängt von der Bedeutung ab:

Erlaubnis/Verbot		Möglichkeit
sanftes Verbot (selten)	**strenges Verbot (häufiger)**	***may not*** ***might not***
*No, you **may not** keep it.*	*No, you **must not** keep it.*	*This **may not** be true.* *This **might not** be true.*
Nein, du **darfst** es **nicht** behalten. (Der Tonfall ist entscheidend!)		Wer weiß, das ist vielleicht alles nicht wahr!

B 78 **In den folgenden Sätzen kommt *"may"* nicht vor. Forme sie so um, dass in jedem Satz „dürfen" in irgendeiner Form vorkommt (*may, may not, must not, is not allowed, was not allowed, will not be allowed ...*). Achte also auf die Zeitstufe der Vorlage!**

example: *We have not spoken with Joe for two weeks.* ▶
We have not been allowed to speak with Joe for two weeks.

1. You will see Miriam again when she leaves hospital.
2. I do not play Dad's CDs.
3. My brother has often driven the family car since he got his driver's licence.
4. We took part in the opening of the new theatre in town.
5. Lucy usually stays at Julia's place on Saturday.
6. Nobody under the age of 18 rides a motorbike.
7. Can I say a few words, too?
8. Why don't you talk to me, Sally?
9. We would sell the house if it belonged to us.

B 79 **Verwende abwechselnd *may* und *might* anstelle von *"perhaps"* oder *"maybe"*.**

example: *Take your photos with you, Ron. Perhaps we want to see them. (~/≈)* ▶
Take your photos with you, Ron. We may/might want to see them.

1. Dad collects stamps. Maybe they will be worth a lot of money one day.
2. Mr. Hopkins wasn't at the office today. Perhaps he'll come in tomorrow.
3. Perhaps we won't recognise you! What do you look like?
4. You should go to the concert, Jenny. Maybe you'll like the music.
5. I hope my dad doesn't come home early. Maybe he won't like to see you here.
6. You should be nice to Vanessa. It is perhaps her last week here.
7. Where's the pink dress from the shop window? – Perhaps they've sold it.
8. I can't find my notes anywhere. Perhaps I've thrown them away.
9. There's a lot of traffic today. Perhaps we'll be late for the film.

B 80 **Erlaubt oder verboten? Bilde Sätze nach dem folgenden Muster:**

example: *We took pictures of the monkeys, but we did not feed them.* ▶
We could/were allowed to take pictures of the monkeys, but we weren't allowed to feed them.
Look at the pictures, but don't touch them. ▶
You can look at the pictures, but you mustn't touch them.

1. They went to the disco, but they did not stay out all night.
2. Have a glass of wine, but don't drink the whole bottle.
3. We looked at the books, but we did not take them home.
4. I sat in Werner's Ferrari, but I did not drive it.
5. We caught some fish, but we did not eat them.
6. Have a picnic on the beach, but don't camp overnight.

C *MUST – TO HAVE*

- *"Must"* bedeutet **müssen**.
- Es gibt nur die Form für ***present tense*** ▶ ***must***
- In allen Zeitstufen gibt es eine **Ersatzform**.
  Diese heißt ▶ ***(to) have to + base form.***

  *We **have to help** the poor people.*
  *The boys **had to build** the tree house again.*
  *I **have had to write** letters to Mary for many years.*
  *Nobody **will have to answer** this question.*

- *"must"* und *"have to"* haben weitgehend die **gleiche Bedeutung** und sind daher in den meisten Fällen austauschbar.

must	*have to*
Der **Sprecher selbst** findet eine Sache zwingend und unvermeidbar.	Der Sprecher will vor allen Dingen **eine Anordnung** weitergeben.
*We **must go** soon.* (ich finde, wir müssen)	*Mum says we **have to go** soon.* (Mutter sagt, wir müssen)

- Die **Verneinung *(negation)*** sieht so aus:

must	▶	***need not/do not have to/does not have to***
have to/has to	▶	***need not/do not have to/does not have to***
had to	▶	***did not have to***
will have to	▶	***will not/won't have to***
have had to	▶	***haven't had to***
has had to	▶	***hasn't had to***

*You **must be** back soon, but you **need not hurry/don't have to hurry**.*
*Jesse **has to get up** early today, but he **need not go/doesn't have to go** to work.*
*We **had to wear** nice clothes, but luckily we **didn't have to dance**.*
*They **will have to use** a laptop, but they **won't have to buy** it.*
*I've **had to work** hard all my life, but I **haven't had to go** to hospital.*
*Jack **has had to move** many times, but he **hasn't had to leave** town.*

C 81

In den folgenden Sätzen kommt *must* nicht vor. Verändere sie so, dass in jedem Satz „müssen" in der richtigen Form und Zeitstufe aufscheint *(must, need not, have to, has to, had to, do/does/did not have to ...)*.

example: *I'm sad because I said good bye to Thomas.* ▶
I'm sad because I had to say good bye to Thomas.

1. Where I live, we don't go to school on Saturday.
2. If you make a mess, you will clean it up again.
3. Is Allison here? – No, she went to the dentist.
4. Have you still got those videos? – No, I have taken them back already.
5. During the week, my parents get up at 5.30 every morning.
6. If you drop these glasses, you will buy new ones.
8. When Grandpa was a young man, he worked in a coal mine for some time.
9. We were there at 8 o'clock, but we didn't do any work for another hour.
10. The CD player costs more than I thought, so I have borrowed some money from my grandparents.
11. If I could not afford my hobbies, I would give them up.
12. After Hurricane Katrina hit New Orleans, many people left the city.
13. Harry won't do it if he is too tired.
14. Linda's fever has got worse, so we've called the doctor.

C 82

Was ist erforderlich, was nicht? Bilde Sätze nach dem folgenden Muster. Verwende abwechselnd *must* und *have to* beziehungsweise *need not* und *do/does/did not have to*.

example: *Wipe off your shoes before you go in, but don't take them off.* ▶
You must/have to wipe off your shoes ..., but you need not/don't have to take them off.

1. Eat something, but don't order the most expensive dish on the menu.
2. Take Jenny to a nice disco, but don't pay for everything.
3. Buy Mum a nice present, but don't spend all your money.
4. Come here quickly, but don't rush.
5. Speak with your parents, but don't tell them everything.
6. Don't read the whole book, but study the first two chapters.
7. Don't mow the lawn, but water the flowers.
8. Don't throw away your old CD player, but get a new one.
9. Don't tidy up the whole house, but pick up the things in the living room.
10. Don't visit all the sights of London, but go to the London Dungeon.

Additional exercise Seite 162

D „SOLLEN“

- ***"shall"*** kommt im modernen Alltagsenglisch ausschließlich **in Fragen** vor:
  Shall *we* ***dance****?* – Sollen wir tanzen?
- Es gibt eine Form für ***present*** ▶ ***shall***
  und eine, die aussieht, als wäre sie ***past tense*** ▶ ***should***.
- ***"should"*** oder ***"ought to"*** verwendest du, wenn du jemand einen **Rat** gibst oder um Rat fragst.
  You ***should/ought to ask*** *somebody for help.* – Du solltest um Hilfe bitten.
- ***"to be supposed to + base form"*** teilt mit: A will, dass B etwas tut.
  *You****'re supposed to call*** *your parents as soon as you get here.*
  Du sollst deine Eltern anrufen, sobald du hier bist.
  We ***were not supposed to be*** *in this room.*
  Wir hätten nicht in diesem Zimmer sein sollen.
- ***"had better + infinitive without to"*** heißt **„sollte lieber“**. (9B, Seite 59)
  *Joe, you****'d better do*** *what I say or there will be trouble.*

E „LASSEN“

- ***"let"*** und ***"allow to"*** ▶ lassen, zulassen, erlauben, gestatten
  Dad is very nice. He often ***lets*** *me* ***use/allows*** *me* ***to use*** *his laptop.*
- ***"keep", "make"*** und ***"force to"*** ▶ lassen, veranlassen, zwingen
  Please don't ***keep*** *me* ***waiting****!*
  Mr. Wilcox ***made*** *us* ***write*** *the whole text. = …* ***forced*** *us* ***to write*** *…*
- ***have + (something) + 3rd form*** ▶ (sich etwas) machen lassen
  Diese „typisch englische“ Fügung ist ganz anders aufgebaut als ihr deutsches Gegenstück und verdient daher besondere Beachtung:

Mum	***has***	***her dresses***	***made***	*by a friend.*
I	***had***	***the films***	***developed***	*in Italy.*
We	***will have***	***the goods***	***sent***	*home.*
Joe	***has had***	***his hair***	***cut***	*again!*
	▼	▼	▼	
	"have"	***(something) = object***	***3rd form***	

Mum … ▶ Mum **lässt** sich ihre Kleider von einer Freundin **machen**.
I … ▶ Ich **ließ** die Filme in Italien **entwickeln**.
We … ▶ Wir **werden** uns die Waren nach Hause **schicken lassen**.
Joe … ▶ Joe **hat** sich die Haare schon wieder **schneiden lassen**.

Vorsicht – Falle! Nicht mit ***present perfect tense*** verwechseln!

We ***have mowed*** *the lawn.*	≠	*We* ***have*** *the lawn* ***mowed****.*
Wir haben den Rasen gemäht.		Wir lassen ihn mähen.

D 83 **Setze passende Formen von „sollen“ ein; Mehrfachlösungen möglich!**

1. Mum says we (*be home*) … by eight o'clock.
2. Hey, where (*we, put*) … these things?
3. I think you (*see*) … a doctor if the fever doesn't go down.
4. You (*not use*) … dirty words in public.
5. Ben, you (*go*) … now or you'll be in trouble.
6. When a teacher tells you to do something, you (*not talk*) … back!
7. I (*tell*) … Cindy that I like her before she goes out with someone else.
8. We (*ask*) … somebody who lives here or we'll never get there.
9. (*I, give*) … you some good advice? I think you (*not wear*) … this awful dress!
10. Charlie, you (*show*) … more interest or you won't pass this semester.

Additional exercise Seite 162

E 84 **„Erlauben“ (zulassen, gestatten) oder „zwingen“ (veranlassen, dazu bewegen)? Entscheide dich für *"let/allow to"* oder *"make/force to"* und setze ein.**

1. What's the matter? Why are you so angry? – Well, Mum ... me hoover the floor in every room of the house! It took me two hours to do it!
2. Please ... me explain the situation! I'm sure you'll understand.
3. The soldiers ... the prisoners to march all day and all night.
4. Tina wanted to speak with her boss, but his secretary did not ... her in!
5. I think Mr. Roberts is crazy! He ... us run 20 laps around the park today!
6. Did they ... you to watch the whole programme?
7. Our neighbours are really nice! Sometimes they even ... us use their pool.
8. I hate family parties! Mum always ... me wear this awful pink dress!
9. They won't ... us into the house if we don't clean our boots first.
10. The strong wind ... the boats to sail back to the harbour.

E 85 **In den folgenden Sätzen hat sich jemand etwas machen lassen. Drücke das mit der „Formel“ *have + (something) + 3rd form* aus. Achte dabei vor allem auf die richtige Zeitstufe!**

1. My school (*new brochures – print*) every year.
2. This morning, Dad (*our car – take*) to the mechanic because it did not start.
3. Don't worry, madam, I (*the dress – send*) to your address this week.
4. I need 500 copies of this poster. Can I (*them – do*) here?
5. Dad did not build the garage himself. He (*it – plan and build*) by experts.
6. That's a nice jacket, Uncle Ed! – Thanks! I (*it – make*) in Hong Kong last week.
7. If you don't like the colour of the walls, we can (*them – paint*) again.
8. Is my car ready, Mr. Simms? – Not yet, but we (*it – repair*) by Friday.
9. When Tommy (*his hair – cut*) for the first time, he screamed a lot.
10. Sally (*her nose – pierce*) if her mum allowed it.

Additional exercise Seite 162

12. KAPITEL *THE PASSIVE VOICE* – DIE LEIDEFORM

A UNTERSCHIED ZWISCHEN AKTIV UND PASSIV

Das Aktiv (die Tätigkeitsform) und das Passiv (die Leideform) lassen uns erkennen, **wer etwas tut** oder **mit wem etwas geschieht**.

passive voice (Leideform)	*active voice* (Tätigkeitsform)
■ **Mit dem Subjekt** des Satzes **geschieht etwas**; das Subjekt „erleidet" etwas; es ist „passiv".	■ **Das Subjekt** des Satzes **tut etwas**; es ist „aktiv".
■ Das Passiv verwendet man eher dann, wenn der **„Täter" unwichtig oder unbekannt** ist; es ist nicht wichtig, „wer" etwas tut, sondern „was" getan wird.	■ Das Aktiv wird eher dann verwendet, wenn der **„Täter" bekannt** ist; man erfährt nicht nur, „was" geschah, sondern auch, „wer" es getan hat.
■ Wenn man den „Täter" doch nennt, verwendet man ***"by + object"***.	
Two skiers were buried by an avalanche. (Zwei Schifahrer wurden von einer Lawine verschüttet.)	***The soldiers saved** them.* (Die Soldaten retteten sie.)

B BILDUNG DES PASSIVS

Das Passiv bildet man nach dieser „Formel":

	"to be" + 3rd form (past participle)			
tense	***subject***	***"to be"***	***3rd form***	
infinitive (+ modal verb)	*The river*	***can be***	***seen***	*from here.*
present tense	*I*	***am***	***loved***	*by everyone.*
	Steel	***is***	***made***	*from iron.*
	Toyotas	***are***	***produced***	*in Japan.*
past tense	*Gold*	***was***	***found***	*in Alaska.*
	The children	***were***	***sent***	*home.*
future with will	*The hotel*	***will be***	***opened***	*next year.*
present perfect tense	*We*	***have been***	***invited***	*to the party.*
	Nobody	***has been***	***informed***	*!*
past perfect tense	*Dinner*	***had been***	***served***	*when we came.*
conditional present	*The bridge*	***would be***	***closed***	*if it were necessary.*

A 86 **Tut das Subjekt etwas oder geschieht etwas mit ihm? Lies dir die folgenden Sätze aufmerksam durch und teile sie zu: aktiv oder passiv?**

example: *Rugby is played outside Great Britain, too.* ▶
passiv; das Subjekt (Rugby) tut nichts, sondern es geschieht etwas mit ihm (es wird gespielt)
George plays in a Rugby team. ▶
aktiv; das Subjekt (George) tut etwas (er spielt)

1. The first computers came from the USA.
2. They were sold to big companies, not to private people.
3. Now many people own a PC or a laptop.
4. Computers are used almost everywhere.
5. My dad has worked with computers for more than twenty years.
6. I was given my first PC when I was ten years old.
7. It was also used by my brother.
8. We gave it away last week because it wasn't fast enough.

B 87 **Setze die angegebenen Verben in die „Formel" *"to be + 3rd form"* ein, so dass passive Sätze entstehen. Achte dabei besonders auf die richtige Zeitstufe.**

example: *The newspaper says that the stolen picture (find) in an empty flat.* ▶
The newspaper ... the stolen picture has been found *in an empty flat.*

1. The Empire State Building (*build*) in the 1930s.
2. The Cherokees (*drive*) from the land of their fathers by American soldiers.
3. Today, many Native American children (*sent*) to schools outside the reservations.
4. Oil from Alaska (*pump*) through a famous pipeline for more than thirty years.
5. More oil (*produce*) in Alaska in the next years.
6. The Statue of Liberty (*restore*), and now it looks better than ever.
7. The Grand Canyon (*visit*) by five million people every year.
8. The two towers of the World Trade Center (*destroy*) by terrorists in 2001.

Und jetzt ein kurzer zusammenhängender Text. Bilde wieder passive Sätze.

9. A short time before the Second World War, the atom (*split*) for the first time, and some years later the first atomic bomb (*build*) by American scientists. In 1945, two bombs (*drop*) on Japanese cities, and thousands of people (*kill*) or (*injure*). Since then, no more atomic bombs (*use*), but many countries use the power of the atom to produce energy.
After serious accidents, atomic power stations (*shut*) down in several countries. The only Austrian nuclear power plant at Zwentendorf (*never, open*). Experts believe that in future more atomic power stations (*build*) all over the world and that a lot of uranium (*need*). Today most of the uranium (*produce*) by Russia, China and the USA, and only very little can (*buy*) on the world market.

C PASSIVE PROGRESSIVE

Passive progressive gibt es nur in *present tense* und *past tense*. Sie drückt aus, was **jetzt gerade** oder zu einem **bestimmten Zeitpunkt** mit dem Subjekt geschieht oder geschah. Du bildest die Form wie folgt:

	"to be" + being + 3rd form
present tense:	*Help! I'm **being eaten** by those mosquitoes!* *Fred **is being questioned** about the accident.* *My favourite trousers **are being washed**.* ▶ das alles passiert **jetzt gerade**
past tense:	*Water **was being pumped** into the pool when we arrived.* *Joe called and said that our cars **were being towed** away.* ▶ das alles passierte **zu einem bestimmten vergangenen Zeitpunkt** (als wir hinkamen; als Joe anrief)

D PASSIVE INFINITIVE

Passive infinitive bildest du **immer mit einem *modal verb***:

	modal verb + be + 3rd form
can(not)	*What you did to Mary **can(not) be forgiven**.*
may (not)	*These bikes **may (not) be used** by everyone.*
must (not)	*The windows **must (not) be opened** at night.*
should (not)	*Children **should (not) be told** about these things.*
need not	*The carpets **need not be vacuumed** every day.*

E PASSIV FÜR NEUTRALE AUSSAGEN („MAN-SÄTZE")

Mit bestimmten Verben lassen sich neutrale Aussagen treffen, bei denen der Urheber der Handlung (wie in einem deutschen **„man-Satz"**) nicht genannt wird.

believe – expect – know – report – say – think

People believe that "13" is an unlucky number.
It's believed that "13" **is** an unlucky number.*
*"13" **is believed to be** an unlucky number.*

They expected that the conference would last a week.
***It was expected** that the conference **would last** a week.*
*The conference **was expected to last** a week.*

We know that some athletes take drugs to perform better.
***It is known** that some athletes **take** drugs to perform better.*
*Some athletes **are known to take** drugs to perform better.*

C 88 **Bilde passive Sätze mit *progressive form* – so wie im Beispiel.**

example: *I can't use my PC right now. It (check) for viruses.* ►
... right now. It's being checked for viruses.
(Er wird gerade auf Viren geprüft.)

1. Mum couldn't park in our street last night because the snow (*remove*).
2. I can't lend you my bike today because it (*repair*).
3. When we arrived at the concert hall, the doors (*close*).
4. We can't take Main Street today because the road (*pave*).
5. Grandpa is still in hospital. His heart (*still, test*).
6. Be careful when you cross the park today. The trees (*spray*).
7. Where are the girls? – In the dressing room. Their dresses (*prepare*) for the show tonight.
8. Where are the things I ordered last week? – Don't worry! They (*take*) to your house at this moment.
9. Why is the park closed today? – Don't you know? Some scenes of a TV show (*shoot*) there.

D 89 **Bilde passive Sätze mit *passive infinitive.***

1. These photos must not (*see*) by anybody, do you understand?
2. You should not tell Mr. Brown. He need not (*inform*) about everything.
3. What an offer! These three books can (*buy*) for the price of two.
4. In case of a fire, this number must (*call*) at once.
5. What you say is perhaps true, but it may not (*say*) in public.
6. When Mrs. Berger looks like this, she should not (*provoke*).
7. If my dad can't repair this radio, it cannot (*repair*) by anyone else.
8. The concert may (*repeat*) next month.
9. You know, these wheels should (*oil*) regularly.
10. All the questions on the test sheet must (*answer*).

Additional exercise Seite 163

E 90 **Gestalte die folgenden Sätze mit Hilfe der nebenstehenden Verben um, so dass sich neutrale Aussagen auf Englisch ergeben. Siehe Beispielsatz!**

example: *People believe that the price of petrol will rise.* ►
It is believed that the price ... . – The price ... is believed to rise.

1. People believe that Brazil will win the World Cup again.
2. They expect that the heat wave will end soon.
3. They have reported that fighting continues in Iraq.
4. People say that snowboarding is easier to learn than skiing.
5. They think that tornadoes will develop in the next hours.
6. They believe that nobody has survived the plane crash.
7. People expected that our team would win.
8. Today we know that the universe is more than 10 billion years old.
9. They say that my mum makes the best apple pies.
10. People believed that the earth was a disc.

F AKTIVE UND PASSIVE WIEDERGABE EINER HANDLUNG

Ob man ein Geschehen aktiv oder passiv wiedergibt, hängt davon ab, **wer oder was im Mittelpunkt der Aussage** steht:
„**Wer** hat etwas getan?“ oder „**Was** ist mit jemand geschehen?“

Aus diesem Grund sollte man wissen, wie man ein bestimmtes Ereignis sowohl aktiv als auch passiv ausdrückt. Man muss dazu Sätze **umformen** können: vom **Aktiv zum Passiv und umgekehrt**.

1 *active to passive*

Subjekt	Prädikat (Verb)	Objekt	Ergänzung
The Chinese	***invented***	***gunpowder***	*long before us.*
Gunpowder	***was invented***	***by the Chinese***	*long before us.*
They	***drink***	***lots of beer***	*in Ireland.*
Lots of beer	***is drunk***	–	*in Ireland.*

- Das **aktive Objekt** *(gunpowder, lots of beer)* **wird zum passiven Subjekt**; das heißt, es „wandert“ an die erste Stelle im Satz.
- Das **aktive Prädikat** *(invented, drink)* **wird zum passiven Prädikat**; das heißt, es teilt sich in eine Form von ***"to be"*** **und die *3rd form*** *(was invented,* is drunk).
- Das **aktive Subjekt** *(the Chinese, they)* **wird nur dann zum passiven Objekt**, wenn es dabei um jemand Bestimmten geht (zB *the Chinese,* nicht aber *they*). Es wird mit ***"by"*** an den Satz gebunden (*"by-object"*).
- Vorhandene Ergänzungen (Orts- oder Zeitangaben oder dergleichen) werden von diesen Vorgängen nicht betroffen.

F 1 91 **Verwandle die folgenden Sätze von aktiv auf passiv. Achte dabei darauf, ob das *"by-object"* sinnvoll ist und daher gebraucht wird oder nicht.**

1. Columbus reached America in 1492.
2. Brazil exports lots of coffee.
3. The mayor will open the new bridge on Saturday.
4. My friends have built these model ships.
5. The tourists can buy many nice souvenirs here.
6. They have found the stolen car.
7. They make many useful things from oil.
8. They will change the rules of the game.

2 *passive to active*

Subjekt	Prädikat (Verb)	Objekt	Ergänzung
These clothes	*were designed*	*by Armani*	*in 2005.*
Armani	*designed*	*these clothes*	*in 2005.*
The money	*will be sent*	----	*to Africa.*
They	*will send*	*the money*	*to Africa.*

- Wenn es im passiven Satz ein ***by-object*** gibt, dann **wird** es **zum aktiven Objekt** *(Armani)*.
  Wenn es **kein *by-object*** gibt, wählt man ein **neutrales aktives Subjekt** (meist *they*, aber auch *people, you, we*).
- Das **passive Prädikat** *(were designed, will be sent)* **wird zum aktiven Prädikat** *(designed, will send)*; das heißt, es **„verliert“** die Form von ***to be***, und das Verb wird an die entsprechende Zeitstufe angepasst (hier: *past tense* und *future with will*).
- Das **passive Subjekt** *(these clothes, the money)* **wird zum aktiven Objekt**.
- Vorhandene Ergänzungen (Orts- oder Zeitangaben oder dergleichen) werden von diesen Vorgängen nicht betroffen.

F 2 92 **Verwandle die folgenden Sätze von passiv auf aktiv. Suche nach Möglichkeit verschiedene „neutrale“ Subjekte für den aktiven Satz.**

1. St. Paul's Cathedral in London was hit by German bombs during the war.
2. Our lawn is mowed by the neighbours' son every weekend.
3. The New Year's concert will be seen by millions of people.
4. These numbers have been called by you several times since last Sunday.
5. This towel has already been used by someone!
6. The next conference will be organised in Portugal.
7. Your essays must be written on the computer.
8. Dinner would be served on the terrace if the weather were fine.
9. My bags have been stolen!
10. The documents were hidden behind a stone wall.
11. Tickets are sold only between 2 and 3 o'clock in the afternoon.
12. Our car has been repaired.
13. The stolen jewels could not be found.
14. I hope we will be shown many interesting sights.

Additional exercise Seite 163

G SÄTZE MIT ZWEI OBJEKTEN

- Manche englische Sätze haben zwei Objekte. Man nennt sie **„Personalobjekt“** und **„Sachobjekt“**. Anders als im Deutschen können beide zum Subjekt eines aktiven Satzes werden.

They sent	***us***	***an invitation.***
They gave	***Grandma***	***a present.***
I'll show	***you***	***all the photos.***
	▼	▼
	Personen	***Sachen***

- Im modernen Alltagsenglisch kommt das **Passiv mit dem Personalobjekt** häufig vor. Man nennt diese Form des Passivs ***personal passive***.
Im Deutschen ist das gar nicht möglich! Man bildet stattdessen meist „man-Sätze“.

    We were sent *an invitation.* ▶ **Man** schickte uns eine Einladung.
    Grandma was given *a present.* ▶ **Man** gab Oma ein Geschenk.
    You will be shown *all the photos.* ▶ **Man** wird euch alle Fotos zeigen.

- Das **Passiv mit dem Sachobjekt** ist auch möglich, aber in vielen Fällen nicht üblich. Es ist meist interessanter zu wissen, **wer** etwas erhält als **was**.

    An invitation was sent *us by them.* ▶ gar nicht gut!
    A present was given *to Grandma.* ▶ möglich!
    All the photos will be shown *to you by me.* ▶ eher nicht!

H PASSIV AUS *VERB + PREPOSITION (PHRASAL VERB)*

Aus der Verbindung *verb + preposition* ergibt sich eine eigene Form des Passivs; ***phrasal verbs*** darf man **nicht trennen!**

*We must **look into** the matter carefully.* ▶ *The matter must be **looked into** carefully.*
*We **switched off** the lights.* ▶ *The lights were **switched off**.*

Diese Liste enthält einige *phrasal verbs*, mit denen *passive voice* möglich ist.

break down	(Tür) aufbrechen	***put off***	verschieben
close down	(endgültig) schließen	***put out***	(Feuer) löschen
cross out	durchstreichen	***switch on/off***	auf-/abdrehen
fill in	(Formular) ausfüllen	***take off***	ausziehen, abheben
knock out	niederschlagen	***throw away***	wegwerfen
look after	sich kümmern um	***try on***	anprobieren
look at	betrachten	***turn down***	leiser drehen
look for	suchen	***turn up***	lauter drehen
look up	nachschlagen	***wait for***	warten auf
pick up	aufheben, mitnehmen	***wake up***	aufwachen, wecken

G 93 **Die folgenden Sätze enthalten zwei Objekte: ein Personalobjekt und ein Sachobjekt. Bilde das Passiv mit Hilfe des Personalobjekts, der weitaus häufigeren Variante.**

1. They sent me the wrong things again!
2. Karen showed us her new room.
3. They gave me a lot of work to do.
4. People have told me a funny story.
5. They will not tell us the end of the story before Saturday.
6. You must inform them of the accident at once.
7. George promised me a nice surprise.
8. They have paid Joe a lot of money for his records.
9. They served us sandwiches and coke.
10. The Academy has awarded Steven Spielberg two Oscars so far.
11. Herbert offered me 100 $ for my stamp collection.
12. They gave me a medal for reporting the burglary.
13. We have already told the police everything.
14. I'm sure they will ask me many silly questions.
15. They said they would report us to the headmaster if we did not pay them.
16. They made me the speaker of the group.

H 94 **Verwandle die folgenden Sätze jeweils in die „andere" Form, also von aktiv auf passiv und von passiv auf aktiv. Achte darauf, dass du ein *phrasal verb* nicht zerreißen darfst!**

active to passive

1. Policemen broke down the door of the apartment.
2. The government will close down the power plant next year.
3. You must not cross out these words.
4. Visitors should not take off their hats in a synagogue.
5. A branch that fell from the tree almost knocked me out.
6. You should fill in all the spaces on this form.
7. Look, they have put out the fire at last!
8. You must not switch off these lights!
9. We will pick you up in front of the station at 8.30.
10. You can try on all these clothes if you want to.

passive to active

11. We were woken up by a loud bang in the middle of the night.
12. It became warmer in the room after the heat was turned up.
13. Paper and glass must not be thrown away.
14. The man in this photo is being looked for everywhere.
15. The text has been deleted by mistake.
16. The meeting will be put off until next week.
17. After some time we were picked up by a taxi.
18. The alarm cannot be switched off easily.
19. New words can be looked up in a dictionary.
20. I promise, this factory will never be closed down completely.

13. KAPITEL	*THE PAST PERFECT TENSE* – DIE VORVERGANGENHEIT/ DAS PLUSQUAMPERFEKT

A BILDUNG

Past perfect tense ist für alle Personen gleich und sieht so aus:

I	***had***	***read***	*the book before I saw the film.*
They	***had not***	***heard***	*the story until it was in the papers.*
Joe	***had never***	***seen***	*anybody as pretty as Anne.*
	▼	▼	
	had	***+ 3rd form***	

B BEDEUTUNG

- ***Past perfect tense*** teilt mit, **welche von** (mindestens) **zwei vergangenen Handlungen <u>vor</u> der** (den) **anderen geschehen** ist. Die frühere (= erste) Handlung war schon beendet, als die spätere (= zweite) Handlung begann. Dabei ist die Reihenfolge im Satz egal.

  *After I **had read** the book, I **saw** the film.*
  *I **had read** the book before I **saw** the film.*

  ▼ frühere Handlung ***past perfect tense*** — ▼ spätere Handlung ***past tense***

  *When Dad **came** home from work last night, I **had gone** to bed already.*
  später — **früher**

- Wenn vergangene Handlungen **nacheinander** wiedergegeben werden – also in der zeitlich richtigen Reihenfolge –, wird ***past simple*** verwendet.

  *First I **read** the book and then I **saw** the film.*
  *We **went** to bed and then Dad **came** home from work.*

C *PAST PERFECT SIMPLE* ALS VERGANGENHEIT VON *PAST SIMPLE* UND *PRESENT PERFECT SIMPLE*

Past perfect simple ist die Vergangenheit von *past simple* und *present perfect simple.* Das zeigt sich auch in der **Veränderung der Zeitstufen** im Rahmen der **indirekten Rede**. (Siehe dazu auch Kapitel 8B, Seite 54.)

*Jill said, "I am hungry because I **haven't eaten** a lot."*
*Jill said that she **was** hungry because she **hadn't eaten** a lot.*

▼ **später** — ▼ **früher**

A 95 **Vervollständige die folgenden Sätze mit Hilfe der angegebenen Verben. Stelle dir vor, du hast vorige Woche – nach längerer Zeit wieder einmal – den Ort besucht, wo du deine Kindheit verbracht hast. Du musstest feststellen, dass es seit deinem letzten Besuch einige Veränderungen gegeben hat!**

1. We left the town seven years ago because my parents (*found*) better jobs.
2. After we (*move*) to our new house, we did not often go back.
3. This time the town looked very friendly because they (*paint*) many of the houses in different colours.
4. The train station was much bigger because they (*build*) a new wing.
5. I noticed that they (*cut*) down some of the big trees in the town park, but they (*plant*) lots of young trees, too.
6. I also walked through the street where we (*live*).
7. Our old house was still there, and it (*not change*) very much.
8. Instead of the small park where I (*play*) as a child there were now garages.

B 96 **Mit den folgenden Beispielen übst du das Erkennen der Zeitenfolge: Was geschah vorher, was nachher?**
***Past perfect* für die <u>frühere</u> Handlung, *past simple* für die <u>spätere</u>.**

1. Dad (*cannot*) drive to work this morning because he (*lose*) the car keys.
2. I (*meet*) all my friends at Joe's party because he (*invite*) so many people.
3. After Cathy (*read*) the email, she (*feel*) very worried.
4. We (*go*) skiing after it (*stop*) snowing.
5. I (*know*) nothing about the movie because nobody (*tell*) me about it.
6. The man (*jump*) from the train before it (*stop*).
7. After the bus (*come*) to a stop, four men and a woman (*get*) off.
8. The cat (*kill*) the mouse after she (*play*) with it for some time.
9. My bus (*arrive*) late today because there (*be*) an accident on the way.
10. The boys (*tell*) the policeman that they (*watch*) someone climbing into that house through an open window.

B 97 **Wie Übung 96; die Sätze mit * sollst du auch so anordnen, dass die Handlungen hintereinander passieren (und somit zweimal *past tense* aufscheint).**

1. Chuck (*leave*) the house before I (*call*).
2. Soon after we (*go*) to bed, we (*hear*) strange noises outside.
3. I (*stay*) at home last night because Dad (*promise*) to play chess with me. *
4. Sue (*feel*) much better after she (*tell*) her mother everything. *
5. We (*not know*) the boys because we (*never, see*) them before.
6. Tim (*never, go*) out with a girl, so he (*be*) very nervous before his first date.
7. Mike (*pass*) the driving test because he (*practise*) a lot for it. *
8. Fred (*get*) really mad this morning because someone (*break*) his pen.
9. My stomach (*make*) funny noises because I (*not have*) enough to eat for breakfast this morning.*

Additional exercise Seite 164

D BILDUNG VON *PAST PERFECT PROGRESSIVE*

We	***had***	***been***	***waiting***	*all night before Sandra arrived.*
The boys	***had***	***been***	***smoking***	*for some time when Mum found them.*
Joe	***had***	***been***	***working***	*for hours when he fell asleep.*
	▼	▼	▼	
	had +	***been +***	***ing-form***	

E VERWENDUNG VON *PAST PERFECT PROGRESSIVE* UND *PAST PROGRESSIVE*

- Wenn man ausdrücken will, **wie lange eine Handlung schon andauerte, bevor eine zweite Handlung geschah**, verwendet man ***past perfect progressive***.
  Dabei sollte auch immer die betroffene **Zeitspanne** angegeben werden.

  *We **had been waiting all night before Sandra arrived.***
  *They **had been smoking for some time when Mum found them.***
  *Joe **had been working for hours when he fell asleep.***

  ▼ **länger andauernde Handlung** — ▼ **Zeitspanne** — ▼ **zweite, dazu kommende Handlung**

- Wenn man ausdrücken will, dass zwei Handlungen **zum selben Zeitpunkt** geschahen – ohne Angabe, seit wann oder wie lange schon –, nimmt man für die längere Handlung ***past progressive***. (Siehe auch Kapitel 20, ab Seite 114.)

  *When Joe **came** into the room, everyone **was writing**.*

F *PAST PERFECT PROGRESSIVE* ALS VERGANGENHEIT VON *PRESENT PERFECT PROGRESSIVE*

Past perfect progressive ist die Vergangenheit von ***present perfect progressive***. Das zeigt sich auch in der **Veränderung der Zeitstufen** im Rahmen der **indirekten Rede**. (Siehe Seite 54.)

*Jill said, "I'll go to bed now. I **have been working** for hours."* ▶
*Jill said that she would go to bed because she **had been working** for hours.*

G VERBEN IN *SIMPLE FORM*

Einige Verben werden fast ausschließlich in *simple form* verwendet; die wichtigsten findest du in dieser Liste. Allerdings gibt es da auch Ausnahmen (*). Siehe Seite 88, 14D.

believe	***have****	***love***	***realise***	***see****
belong	***hear****	***mean***	***recognise***	***seem***
forget	***know***	***need***	***remember***	***want***
hate	***like***	***prefer***	***understand***	***wish***

E 98 **Forme die Sätze mit Hilfe von *past perfect progressive* (Wie lange dauerte das schon an, bevor .../als ...?) und *past simple* (Und was geschah dann?) um. Beachte das Beispiel.**

example: *Little Red Riding Hood was walking through the wood. After some time the big, bad wolf blocked her way and ...* ▶
Little Red Riding Hood *had been walking* through the wood *for some time when the big, bad wolf blocked* her way and ...

1. The boys were playing basketball. After only thirty seconds, Mario scored the first points for his team.
2. It was raining heavily. After four days the first dams broke along the river.
3. George was waiting for Gina outside her house. After an hour he saw her and Bob leaving together.
4. Brian was playing computer games. After some time he remembered to put out the garbage.
5. Serena was looking at one dress after another. After half an hour she finally found one that she liked.
6. My parents were thinking of selling our house. After some weeks they decided to put an ad in the newspaper.
7. Dad was driving home from work. After a few minutes a deer jumped in front of his car.
8. The children were playing on the beach. After some time somebody shouted, "There's a shark in the water!"

E 99 **Passierten die beschriebenen Handlungen gleichzeitig *(past progressive)* oder fand eine vor der anderen statt *(past perfect)*?**

1. When I came to the bus stop this morning, several people (*wait*) already.
2. I was very tired last night. I (*play*) tennis all day.
3. We saw you in town yesterday. You (*look*) at the shop windows.
4. Anne (*read*) all afternoon when she remembered her maths homework.
5. Anne (*read*) when her telephone rang.
6. People (*dance*) for some time before the show began.
7. I checked all the drawers in the bedroom. I (*look*) for my new bracelet.
8. Dad's hands were full of dirt and grease because he (*repair*) his car all day.

Additional exercise Seite 164

14. KAPITEL *THE PAST TENSE* – DIE MITVERGANGENHEIT/ DAS IMPERFEKT

A FORMEN VON *PAST TENSE*

Wie bei jeder Zeitstufe im Englischen gibt es auch bei ***past tense*** zwei Formen: ***simple form*** und ***progressive form***.

simple form		*progressive form*
regular verbs	***irregular verbs***	keine Unterscheidung zwischen *regular* und *irregular*
*borrow**ed*** *hop**ed*** *wait**ed***	***came*** ***kept*** ***took***	***was** borrow**ing**/**were** com**ing*** ***was** hop**ing**/**were** keep**ing*** ***was** wait**ing**/**were** tak**ing***
▼	▼	▼
base form + (e)d	***past form/2nd form***	***was/were + ing-form***

Rechtschreibung!
- **Konsonant + y:** ***y*** ▶ ***i,*** **zB:** *study + ed* ▶ *stud**ied***
- **Endkonsonant** (bei einsilbigen Verben): **Verdoppelung,** **zB:** *drop + ed* ▶ *drop**ped***

B FRAGE UND VERNEINUNG

Frage und Verneinung *(question and negation)* folgen den üblichen Regeln: Man braucht für jede Frage (mit Ausnahme der Frage nach dem Subjekt) und für jede Verneinung ein **Hilfs(zeit)wort.**

past simple	*past progressive*
***Joe** found **the gun in the park**.*	***They** were dancing **boogie in school**.*
***Did** Joe find the gun in the park?*	***Were** they dancing boogie in school?*
*Joe **did not** find the gun in the park.*	*They **were not** dancing boogie ... .*
***Who found** the gun in the park?*	***Who was** dancing boogie in school?*
***What did** Joe find in the park?*	***What were** they dancing in school?*
***Where did** Joe find the gun?*	***Where were** they dancing boogie?*

Die Frage nach dem Subjekt verlangt **immer *3rd person singular***!
Daher heißt die Frage in *past progressive* immer ***"Who was ...?"***

A 100 **Bilde *past simple* und *past progressive* mit den gegebenen Personen und Verben.**

example: *Marion – run away* ▶
Marion ran away – Marion was running away

1. we – buy drinks
2. I – cut wood
3. you – drink tea
4. Joe – eat a roll
5. Sheila – freeze
6. they – give money
7. you – hold on
8. we – keep up
9. you – make the bed
10. it – rise
11. she – sleep well
12. they – think of me
13. I – write a text
14. we – drive a car
15. he – put up a tent
16. he – brake
17. they – carry a bag
18. we – decorate the tree
19. it – end well
20. I – fill the bottle
21. you – glide
22. we – help them
23. she – jump up and down
24. he – kiss her
25. I – listen
26. she – mend socks
27. they – open the doors
28. we – pet the dog
29. they – question me
30. I – stay here

B 101 **Bilde die Entscheidungsfrage und die Verneinung und frage nach den unterstrichenen Satzteilen.**

1. Elizabeth put a new poster on the wall yesterday.
2. Ian was helping his grandfather in the garden.
3. The boys were watching a film at midnight.
4. Uncle Max sold his car because he needed money.
5. Peter's parents lived in England for ten months.
6. Aunt Julia was telling the children a good-night story.
7. They could put out the fire by throwing a blanket on it.
8. Jasper spoke French very well.

Additional exercise Seite 165

B 102 **Bilde Fragen mit *past simple*: Freunde waren im Urlaub in den USA, und du möchtest jetzt so allerlei wissen!**

1. how? – get to America
2. who? – with you
3. where? – go
4. visit – Disney World?
5. how much? – cost – holiday
6. what? – like best
7. what? – weather like
8. Americans friendly?
9. have any adventures?
10. how long? – stay

C ANWENDUNG VON *PAST SIMPLE* UND *PAST PROGRESSIVE*

past simple	*past progressive*
(a) zur Wiedergabe von **Ereignissen aus der** Vergangenheit, **die vorbei und abgeschlossen** sind;	**(c)** wenn **zu einem bestimmten, schon vergangenen Zeitpunkt eine Handlung gerade** im Ablaufen **war**;
	(d) wenn **zwei oder mehrere Handlungen gleichzeitig abliefen** (meist durch *"while"* miteinander verbunden);
(b) zum **Erzählen von Geschichten**; *past simple* ist die „ganz normale" englische Erzählzeit;	**(e)** wenn **eine Handlung noch nicht beendet** war, **als eine andere Handlung begann** („kurze Handlung" = *past simple* unterbricht „längere Handlung" = *past progressive*; meist durch *"when"* miteinander verbunden).

(a) *Last Monday my mum **bought** me a cool sweatshirt.*
(b) *I **liked** it when I first **saw** it. I **put** it on at once and **showed** it to my sister. She **said** she **did not like** it so much because it **had** too much green in it.*
(c) *Yesterday morning I **was wearing** my new sweatshirt to school.*
(d) *While I **was walking** to school, I **was thinking** what my friends were going to say about it.*
(e) *All of my friends **were looking** at me when I **came** into the classroom.*

D VERBEN, DIE NORMALERWEISE NUR IN *SIMPLE FORM* VORKOMMEN

Einige Verben werden fast ausschließlich in *simple form* verwendet; die wichtigsten findest du in dieser Liste. Allerdings gibt es da auch Ausnahmen (*).
Siehe dazu auch Seite 84, 13G.

believe	***have****	***love***	***realise***	***see****
belong	***hear****	***mean***	***recognise***	***seem***
forget	***know***	***need***	***remember***	***want***
hate	***like***	***prefer***	***understand***	***wish***

Große **Verwechslungsgefahr** besteht zwischen ***past tense*** und ***present perfect tense***, vor allem bei *simple form*.
Alles Wesentliche erfährst du dazu ab Seite 108, 18E.

CD 103 **Wähle aus: *past simple or past progressive?* Streiche die falsche Variante durch, so dass ein richtiger Satz übrig bleibt.**

1. You *slept/were sleeping* when I *came/was coming* home from the cinema.
2. When I *left/was leaving* the room, nobody *looked/was looking* at me.
3. Sally *read/was reading* while she *waited/was waiting* for Chris.
4. Most people *slept/were sleeping* when the fire *broke/was breaking* out.
5. While I *studied/was studying* for today's test, I *fell/was falling* asleep.
6. I *tried/was trying* to tell you the story, but you *did not listen/weren't listening*. Now you have no idea what's going on.
7. Fred *worked/was working* in Barcelona when he *met/was meeting* Isabel. He *fell/was falling* in love with her, and two months later he *asked/was asking* her to marry him.
8. Danny *sat/was sitting* in a café when he *noticed/was noticing* Lorie on the other side of the street. She *talked/was talking* to a stranger.
9. While Judy and Erin *put/were putting* on their costumes, their dad *got/was getting* the car ready.
10. Grandma *walked/was walking* down the stairs when she *stumbled/was stumbling* and *fell/was falling*. Unfortunately she *hurt/was hurting* her elbow, and so we *took/were taking* her to hospital for an X-ray.

CD 104 **Setze ein: *past simple or past progressive?***

1. When we (*get*) to the airport, they (*already, call*) our flight.
2. Jack and Jill (*watch*) TV when somebody (*knock*) at the door.
3. Gertrude (*sing*) loudly while she (*walk*) home through the park.
4. While the children (*do*) their homework, mother (*take*) a nap.
5. The wind (*get*) stronger and stronger while we (*try*) to put up the tent.
6. Tim and I (*walk*) through the park when it (*begin*) to rain.
7. The sun (*set*) behind the mountains when we (*come*) home from skiing.
8. Bob and Julia (*dance*) while Simon and I (*listen*) to my CDs.
9. The girls (*take*) a shower when a boy (*walk*) into the shower room.
10. As Dad (*drive*) home yesterday, he (*notice*) that he (*have*) a flat tyre.

CD 105 **„Zwei gleichzeitige Handlungen" oder „eine Handlung nach der anderen"? Entscheide dich und setze ein: *past simple or past progressive?***

1. At the beginning of the year, I (*not understand*) what the teachers (*say*) because I (*not speak*) the language, but I (*learn*) it fast.
2. Mum (*send*) me to the post office because she (*need*) some stamps.
3. When Jacqueline finally (*get*) here, we (*can*) start the film.
4. I (*look*) out of the window this morning and I (*see*) that it (*still, rain*).
5. Aaron (*not want*) to go out last night because he (*read*) a good book.
6. What (*you, do*) at 5 o'clock on Friday? – I (*sit*) on the bus home from work.
7. (*you, meet*) interesting people while you (*travel*) through India?
8. When Dad (*come*) back from China, Mum (*serve*) a delicious dinner.
9. When the UFO (*land*) in Mike's garden, he (*call*) the TV station at once.
10. Yesterday Gina (*ask*) me if I (*remember*) her! Of course I did!

Additional exercise Seite 165

15. KAPITEL | *THE POSSESSIVE CASE* – DER 2. (BESITZANZEIGENDE) FALL

Der zweite Fall (Genitiv, *genitive, possessive case*) zeigt die **Besitzverhältnisse** und/oder die **Zugehörigkeit** an. Er sagt uns, wem oder zu wem jemand oder etwas gehört.

A GENITIV MIT …*'S* ODER …*S'*

Diese Form des zweiten Falls nennt man auch den ***Saxon Genitive***, weil er ein Überbleibsel aus der Zeit der Angelsachsen ist. Du verwendest ihn fast nur bei **Personen**. Achte dabei immer darauf, wo der **Apostroph** („das Stricherl") stehen muss:

…*s'* ▶ Mehrzahlwörter **auf -s**	… *'s* ▶ Wörter, die **nicht auf -s** enden
the boys' room ▶ das Zimmer **der** Buben	*the boy's room* ▶ das Zimmer **des** Buben
the Coopers' car ▶ das Auto der Coopers	*Mr. Cooper's car* ▶ das Auto von Herrn Cooper

In **einigen Fällen** wird der *Saxon Genitive* auch bei Nicht-Personen verwendet oder weicht von der „s-Regel" ab, zum Beispiel bei:

- Eigennamen auf -s: *St. James**'s** Park* *the Jones**'s** house*
- (Haus-)Tieren: *the lion**'s** teeth* *"Fido**'s**" water bowl*
- Ländern und Städten: *Austria**'s** capital* *New York**'s** skyscrapers*
- Zeitangaben: *an hour**'s** walk* *yesterday**'s** news*

B GENITIV MIT *"THE … OF …"*

Dieser Genitiv kommt weitaus häufiger vor als *Saxon Genitive*. Du kannst ihn im Prinzip immer verwenden, doch bei Personen und Eigennamen klingt *Saxon Genitive* besser.

***the** size **of** my shoes* ▶ die Größe meiner Schuhe
***the** legs **of** the table* ▶ die Beine des Tisches, die Tischbeine
***the** wheels **of** the car* ▶ die Räder des Autos
***the** colour **of** your eyes* ▶ die Farbe deiner Augen

*"**The** Life **of** Brian"* ≈ *Brian**'s** life*
***the** castle **of** King Arthur* ≈ *King Arthur**'s** castle*
***the** job **of** my father* ≈ *my father**'s** job*

C BESITZANZEIGENDE FÜRWÖRTER – *POSSESSIVE PRONOUNS*

Alles, was du über *possessive pronouns* wissen musst, erfährst du in Abschnitt 21B ab Seite 118.

AB 106 **Bilde von allen Beispielen den zweiten Fall. Wo es möglich ist, wende *Saxon Genitive* an.**

1. Julia – new dress
2. street – name
3. my sister – boyfriend
4. Dad – boss
5. bird – feathers
6. tiger – eyes
7. hotel – rooms
8. Mozart – operas
9. Jack – camera
10. Uncle Bob – motorbike

11. Charles – parents
12. my parents – wedding picture
13. moon – light
14. London – Underground
15. my boyfriend – father
16. Alexander – address
17. river – length
18. our new dog – name
19. a baby – hair
20. France – provinces

21. Vienna – museums
22. tickets – price
23. week – days
24. my school – new headmaster
25. cake – colour
26. cheese – smell
27. the girls – books
28. Mr. Simmons – job
29. house – windows
30. Frank – trainers

Additional exercise Seite 166

16. KAPITEL *PREPOSITIONS* – VORWÖRTER/PRÄPOSITIONEN

Die wichtigste Aufgabe der Präpositionen ist es, **Beziehungen zwischen einem Verb und anderen Satzteilen herzustellen**. Der Sinn einer Aussage hängt entscheidend von den Präpositionen ab.

*In class, Laura sits **behind/in front of/next to/...** Mona this year.*
*Let's meet **at/after/before/around/...** six o'clock tomorrow.*

Beziehungen, die durch Präpositionen hergestellt werden		
wo? *prepositions of place*	wann? *prepositions of time*	Sonstiges *"other" prepositions*
at, beside, below, in, next to, on, under ...	*at, before, for, since, from ... to, till, after ...*	*about, against, for, from, with, without ...*

Es gibt keine „Regeln“ für die Verwendung von Präpositionen, und viele Präpositionen haben mehr als eine Bedeutung. Deshalb sollte man sich Vorwörter immer **im Zusammenhang mit einem Verb oder einem Nomen** merken, wie zum Beispiel:

*to look **after**, to insist **on**, **at** the corner, **in** the picture, **below** zero ...*

A ZEITANGABEN – *PREPOSITIONS OF TIME*

Das folgende „Zeitlineal“ enthält die wichtigsten Vorwörter der Zeit und erklärt ihre Anwendungen:

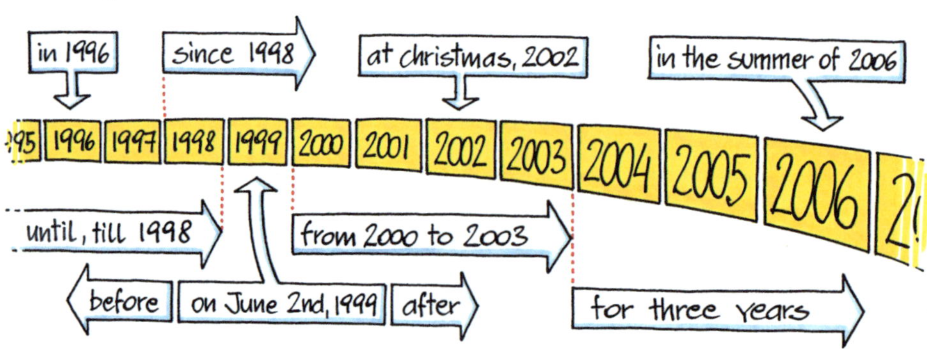

B ORTSANGABEN – *PREPOSITIONS OF PLACE*

Die „Szene aus dem Weltall" enthält alle wesentlichen Vorwörter des Ortes und illustriert ihre Anwendungen:

A 107 **Die folgenden Aufgaben lassen sich mit Hilfe des „Zeitlineals" lösen:**

1. My family moved to this town (*1996/im Jahr 1996*).
2. Dad has been working for "ABC" (*seit 1998*).
3. (*Bis 1998*) he used to work for "XYZ".
4. (*am 2. Juni 1999*) my sister Mary was born.
5. (*vor jenem Tag*) I was my parents' only child,
6. and (*nach jenem Tag*) there were two children.
7. But then my brother Andy was born (*zu Weihnachten 2002*).
8. (*von 2000 bis 2003*) I was at primary school,
9. and now I have been at my present school (*seit drei Jahren*).

B 108 **Bilde „Sätze aus dem Weltall" nach dem folgenden Muster:**

*"Big Eyes" is flying **between** two robots.*
*One UFO is coming **out of** the cleaning tube, the other one is flying **into** it.*
*"Big Mouth" is sitting **beside/next to** Max the Astronaut.*

17. KAPITEL *THE PRESENT PARTICIPLE* – DAS MITTELWORT DER GEGENWART

A BILDUNG

Present participle (Mittelwort der Gegenwart, 1. Mittelwort, Partizipium Präsens) ist eine ***"ing-form"***. Du bildest sie nach dieser Formel:

base form + ing

Rechtschreibung!
Beachte bei der Bildung von *present participle* diese **drei Rechtschreibregeln** (siehe auch Abschnitt 6, *The Gerund*, ab Seite 40):

- **Wegfall des „stummen e" am Wortende:** *hope* ▶ *hoping*
- **Verdoppelung des Endkonsonanten:** *win* ▶ *winning*
- **Umwandlung von *-ie* zu *-y* bei:** *lie* ▶ *lying; die* ▶ *dying; tie* ▶ *tying*

B *PRESENT PARTICIPLE* ALS TEIL DER *PROGRESSIVE FORM*

Progressive form bildest du so :

"to be" + present participle

Die Form von *"to be"* passt sich an Person und Zeitstufe an, während *present participle* seine Form nicht verändert. Dazu einige Beispiele:

	is	*playing*	*basketball at this moment.*
	was	*playing*	*basketball when I last saw him.*
Simon	***will be***	*playing*	*basketball at this time tomorrow.*
	has been	*playing*	*basketball since his ninth birthday.*
	had been	*playing*	*basketball for years before I met him.*

(Genaue Informationen über Bildung und Anwendung von *progressive form* erhältst du in den Kapiteln zu den einzelnen Zeitstufen sowie in Kapitel 20, ab Seite 114.)

C *PRESENT PARTICIPLE* ALS ADJEKTIV

Wie jedes andere Adjektiv dient auch ***present participle*** der näheren **Beschreibung eines Nomens** (Hauptwort, *noun*). Vergleiche dazu Kapitel 1, ab Seite 8.

*The **weeping willow** is a tree. In German it's called "Trauerweide".*
*I really like reading, but I read only **interesting books**.*
*The natives called this river the "**Whispering Water**".*
*People said Rasputin had **burning eyes**, like the devil.*

A 109 Bilde die *ing-form* mit den folgenden Verben:

ask – bring – cry – dry – empty[1] – freeze – grow – hide – injure[2] – judge[3] – knock – leave – make – nag[4] – organise – push – quit[5] – rise – shake – try – use – visit – wait – yearn[6]

[1] leeren; [2] verwunden, verletzen; [3] urteilen; [4] nörgeln; [5] aufgeben; [6] sich sehnen

B 110 Bilde mit den angegebenen Personen und Verben *progressive form* in der richtigen Zeitstufe. Achte auf die Rechtschreibung!

example: Joe dances ▶ Joe *is dancing* Dolly cried ▶ Dolly *was crying*

1. my tooth aches
2. Mum bakes a cake
3. they came up the hill
4. I will do it
5. Sam has eaten
6. the leaves fall
7. Alex grinned
8. we hiked
9. Dora will jump
10. I kneel on the floor
11. Jill lies in the sun
12. Dad made tea
13. she has opened letters
14. they will put up tents
15. we will read about it
16. Nick spoke with you
17. you have talked a long time
18. they use my pen
19. he yelled at me
20. Sue will write letters

C 111 Setze die *present participles* aus der *"box"* an der passenden Stelle als Adjektiv ein.

barking – drinking – dying – fascinating – fishing – freezing – reading – rising – running – sleeping – talking – visiting – winning

1. If you want to catch fish in this lake, you must get a ... licence.
2. I can't fall asleep! – Well, then you should take a ... pill in the evening.
3. In many fairy tales there are ... animals.
4. The ... numbers are 5, 17, 33, 38 and 41. – Really? I've got them!
5. What a ... story! I could go on reading it for ever!
6. An old saying goes, "... dogs don't bite", but I don't think it's true!
7. The room was very simple; there was no light, and there was no ... water.
8. You need a ... lamp or you will ruin your eyes!
9. It is ... cold today! It must be 30 degrees below zero!
10. One of Dad's favourite songs is "The House of the ... Sun". I like it, too.
11. ... hours at the hospital are from 2 to 5 in the afternoon.
12. Have you got an envelope and some ... paper, Jack? Tina is waiting for a letter from me.
13. "The ... Swan" is one of the most beautiful ballets.
14. If you travel through the Sahara, you must take a lot of ... water with you.

D *PRESENT PARTICIPLE* NACH VERBEN

- Auf **Verben der Sinneswahrnehmung** kann ***present participle*** oder ***infinitive*** folgen. Vergleiche dazu auch Kapitel 9, ab Seite 58.

see – watch – hear – feel – notice

Present participle folgt eher bei einzelnen, nicht wiederholten Handlungen, doch ist der Unterschied zu *verb + infinitive* nicht sehr groß (siehe auch Kapitel 10, ab Seite 64).

*We didn't **see** (hear, notice ...) you **coming** into the room just now.*
*(We never see/hear/notice you **come** into the room.)* ▶ *eher allgemein*

- ***Present participle*** folgt **zwingend** nach:

go – come – keep – catch

*We usually **go swimming** every Tuesday.*
*Don't **come crying** to me if you have a problem; I can't help you!*
*Why do you **keep looking** at me like that?*
*Mum **caught** me **opening** my presents before my birthday.*

E *PRESENT PARTICIPLE* ZUR VERKÜRZUNG ODER VERKNÜPFUNG VON SÄTZEN

Mit Hilfe von *present participle* lassen sich Handlungen miteinander verknüpfen, wenn folgende Bedingungen erfüllt werden:

- die Handlungen finden **gleichzeitig** oder knapp hintereinander statt;
- alle Handlungen haben das **gleiche Subjekt**.

Dabei bleibt die **„Haupthandlung"** unverändert, die **„Nebenhandlung"** wird durch ***present participle*** ausgedrückt.

*Tammy **was walking** home from school. She **was thinking** of Leo all the time.*

▶ *Tammy **was walking** home from school, **thinking** of Leo all the time.*
▼ **„Haupthandlung"** ▼ **„Nebenhandlung"**

▶ ***Walking** home from school, Tammy **was thinking** of Leo all the time.*
▼ **„Nebenhandlung"** ▼ **„Haupthandlung"**

- Bei knapp aufeinander folgenden Handlungen kann die **zuerst stattfindende Handlung** durch ***present participle*** ersetzt werden.

*Britney **took** her dancing shoes and **went** to the disco.*

▶ ***Taking** her dancing shoes, Britney **went** to the disco.*

D 112 **Übersetze die Verben ins Englische, setze sie als *present participle* ein und übertrage den gesamten Satz in gutes Deutsch.**

example: *The sailors watched the storm (werden) ... stronger and stronger.* ▶
The sailors watched the storm getting stronger and stronger.
Die Seeleute beobachteten, wie der Sturm immer stärker wurde.

1. Did you notice some strangers (*herumstehen*) ... yesterday?
2. The hunters came (*reiten*) ... across the fields.
3. Let's watch the kids (*spielen*) ... "Ludo". They seem to enjoy it.
4. Robert, they will catch you (*weggehen*) ... before the end of the lesson.
5. Please, don't keep us (*stehen*) ... in the cold! Let us in!
6. In winter, we go (*Schi fahren*) ... almost every weekend.
7. I watched you (*sprechen*) ... to a man I don't know. Who is he?
8. Where were you, Monica? Couldn't you hear me (*anklopfen*) ...?
9. I know you work hard, Joe, but you keep (*bekommen*) ... bad marks.
10. Julia could feel her toothache (*werden*) ... worse and worse.
11. Richard, the girls are here! I can hear them (*lachen*) ...!
12. After the earthquake, avalanches came (*donnern*) ... down the mountainside.
13. I've noticed you (*blicken*) ... at Marilyn. Do you like her?
14. After sunset, thousands of bats come (*fliegen*) ... out of the cave.
15. Doris feels bad; she keeps (*denken*) ... that she has made a silly mistake.

E 113 **Baue in die folgenden Sätze mindestens ein *present participle* ein. Bei gleichzeitig ablaufenden Handlungen sind auch zwei Mittelwort-Konstruktionen möglich (*).**

example: *Fred was sitting in the library. He was working for his history project.* * ▶
Fred was sitting in the library, working for his history project.
Sitting in the library, Fred was working for his history project.

1. Maria sat on the terrace of her house. She watched the birds and the bees. *
2. Dad took his briefcase and left for work.
3. Leslie opened the door to the kitchen. She noticed a strange smell.
4. Nelly prepared herself a cup of tea. She thought of her meeting with Tim. *
5. I looked across the street and saw a very pretty girl on the other side.
6. Mr. Smithers walked into the classroom today. He looked very worried.
7. Irene put on her shoes this morning. She decided to buy a new pair.
8. The boys were sitting on the railing. They were watching the girls. *
9. The President waved to the journalists and got on the plane.
10. Michael studied the picture carefully. He thought it was fantastic.
11. I was jogging along the river. I enjoyed the fresh air and the warm sun. *
12. Joe rode his bike down the hill. He was hit by a car.
13. Dad was lying on the couch. He was reading the newspaper.*
14. Tom stood on the top of the mountain. He felt very proud of himself.*
15. Martina came out of the shop. She looked very pleased.*

Additional exercise Seite 166

F *PRESENT PARTICIPLE* ANSTELLE EINES GLIEDSATZES MIT *AFTER, AS, BECAUSE, WHEN* ODER *WHILE*

Das ist wieder eine „typisch englische" Konstruktion! Sie ist sehr elegant und stilvoll und daher hört man sie im gesprochenen Englisch auch nicht sehr oft.

- **Gleiches Subjekt** in Hauptsatz und Gliedsatz ▶ nur zwingend bei Sätzen, die **mit *"while"* eingeleitet** werden:

  ***While** **Max** was waiting for Laura, **he** had a wonderful idea.*
  ***Waiting** for Laura, **Max** had a wonderful idea.*

  *After **Mrs. Hamilton** had returned from China, **she** had a lot to tell.*
  ***Having returned** from China, **Mrs. Hamilton** had a lot to tell.*

  *As **we** had not enough money left, **we** decided to stay at home.*
  ***Not having** enough money left, **we** decided to stay at home.*

- **Verschiedene Subjekte** in Hauptsatz und Gliedsatz ▶ bei allen Einleitungen außer *"while"* möglich; *present participle* muss am Anfang des Satzes stehen:

  S1 **S2**
  *When **the guests** had left, **my parents** could go to bed.*
  ***The guests having left**, **my parents** could go to bed.*

  *As **taxis** were too expensive, **we** decided to walk.*
  ***Taxis being** too expensive, **we** decided to walk.*

  *After **the fire** had gone out, **the room** became quite cold.*
  ***The fire having gone** out, **the room** became quite cold.*

G *PRESENT PARTICIPLE* ANSTELLE EINES RELATIVSATZES

Nur einschränkende Relativsätze können durch *present participles* ersetzt werden. Siehe dazu auch Kapitel 23, ab Seite 138.

*People **who live on the coast** are often fishermen.*
*People **living** on the coast are often fishermen.*

H MEHRERE *PRESENT PARTICIPLES* IN EINEM SATZ

Auch längere Satzgefüge können durch *present participles* „vereinfacht" werden:

*When Joe opened the door, he **noticed** a strange smell that was coming from the kitchen.*
▶ ***Opening** the door, Joe **noticed** a strange smell **coming** from the kitchen.*
▼
unveränderte Haupthandlung

F 114 **Ersetze die Gliedsätze durch *present participles.* Achte dabei besonders auf das Subjekt des Gliedsatzes – ist es gleich oder anders als das des Hauptsatzes?**

1. When Dad goes to work, he usually meets his colleagues on the bus.
2. As Gilbert wants to travel to China in summer, he saves all his money.
3. When Edna was walking home through the park, she heard strange noises.
4. As I have no school today, I stayed up late last night.
5. While Simon was waiting for his friends, he decided what they would do.
6. When Ben left the sweets shop, he saw that his bike was gone.
7. As Gerry is a very good goalkeeper, many teams want him to play for them.
8. As winter was so cold, Gina bought herself a warmer coat.
9. When the sun had gone down, the vampires came out of the caves.
10. As the doors are always open, everybody can come and go as they like.

G 115 **Ersetze den Relativsatz *(who ..., that ...)* durch ein *present participle.***

1. In Africa, we saw many people who were collecting firewood for cooking.
2. Everyone who left the room was carefully checked.
3. They cut down all the trees that stood in the way of the new road.
4. People who speak several languages are called "polyglot".
5. Did you see all those pictures that hung on the walls?
6. Is this my DVD that is lying on the floor?
7. The police arrested four men who were selling drugs in the park.
8. At the dance, Mum noticed a woman who was wearing the same dress.
9. My parents are very good friends with the people who live next door.
10. Is there anybody who wishes they were not here?

H 116 **In den folgenden Sätzen ist Platz für mehr als ein *present participle.***

1. As I was walking through the town, I noticed many people who were trying to find a parking space for their cars.
2. When Fred left the shop, he saw a blind man who was crossing the street.
3. When Max opened the window, he heard the ambulance that was coming round the corner.
4. As we looked down from the mountain, we saw lots of cows that were grazing on the meadows.
5. After Nick had finished school, he got a job at a shop that sells computers.
6. While Sue was sitting on a park bench, she observed a man who was talking to some young girls.
7. As the room was in a mess, I picked up all the things from the floor.
8. As Joe did not know what to do with them, he threw away the photos that were hanging on the walls.
9. When the party was over, the people got in the cars that were waiting outside and drove away.
10. When you get off the bus, you will see the birds that are nesting in the trees.

18. KAPITEL *THE PRESENT PERFECT TENSE* – DIE VERGANGENHEIT

A BILDUNG VON *PRESENT PERFECT TENSE*

present perfect simple		*present perfect progressive*	
I, you, we, they	***have worked***	*I, you, we, they*	***have been working***
he, she, it	***has worked***	*he, she, it*	***has been working***
▼		▼	
have/has + 3rd form		***have/has been + ing-form***	

- **Fragen und Verneinung** *(questions and negation)* werden mit ***have*** **oder** ***has*** gebildet. Die Frage nach dem **Subjekt** heißt immer ***"Who has ...?"***

B ANWENDUNG VON *PRESENT PERFECT SIMPLE*

1 Grundsätzliches

- ***Present perfect simple*** wird häufig mit der deutschen Vergangenheit (Perfekt) gleichgesetzt. Im Aussehen gibt es diese Ähnlichkeit („Ich habe gewartet." ▶ ***"I have waited."***), aber in der Anwendung gibt es große Unterschiede. Manchmal kann *present perfect simple* genauso verwendet werden wie das Perfekt im Deutschen, in vielen Fällen aber nicht!

- ***Present perfect simple*** beschreibt **Handlungen**, die – meist kurz – vor dem „Hier und Jetzt" geschehen sind und die **Auswirkungen und/oder Folgen auf das „Hier und Jetzt"** haben.

- Es ist **nicht wichtig, wann** die Dinge geschehen sind, **sondern dass oder ob** sie geschehen sind. Wir erhalten eigentlich Informationen über das „Hier und Jetzt" und nicht so sehr über die Vergangenheit.

*The guests **have come**.*	▶	Die Gäste sind da! Und wir können („hier und jetzt") essen, tanzen, Fotos anschauen, usw. Es ist egal, wann sie kamen; wichtig ist, dass sie gekommen sind! Deshalb fehlt auch die Zeitangabe.
*Harry **has gone** out.*	▶	Er ist („hier und jetzt") nicht da! Wieder ist es uns egal, wann er wegging; wichtig ist, dass er fort ist.
***Have** you **seen** Mary?*	▶	Weißt du also („hier und jetzt"), wo sie ist? Hast du sie schon gesehen?
*Jill **hasn't called**.*	▶	Ich kann dir also („hier und jetzt") nicht sagen, wie es ihr geht; sie hat noch nicht angerufen.

A 117 **Bilde *present perfect simple* und *present perfect progressive* mit den folgenden Personen und Verben.**

1. I – ask
2. you – buy
3. Tom – cry
4. Sandy – drink
5. the cat – eat
6. we – fish
7. you – grow
8. the boys – hide
9. Joe – install
10. I – jump
11. we – keep
12. you – live
13. Jane – make
14. the girls – order
15. you – plant
16. I – read
17. Mary – sing
18. Mr. Jones – try
19. the bus – wait
20. Cynthia – yearn

Additional exercise Seite 167

A 118 **Setze *present perfect simple* in die Sätze 1 bis 5 und *present perfect progressive* in die Sätze 6 bis 10 ein.**

1. Look, the birds (*build*) ... a nest again!
2. I'm hungry. I (*not eat*) ... since this morning.
3. Jill (*call*) ... her parents, but they are not at home.
4. (*you, hear*) ... from James lately? – No, I haven't.
5. (*Joe, take*) ... the books back to the library? – I really don't know.
6. It (*rain*) ... for three days. I hope it stops soon.
7. Dad and I (*work*) ... on this model car since Christmas.
8. The baby (*sleep*) ... for eight hours. He'll wake up soon.
9. I (*go*) ... to this school since we moved to this town.
10. What (*you, talk*) ... about? – Don't worry, not about you.

Additional exercise Seite 167

A 119 **Bilde die Entscheidungsfrage und die Verneinung (nur bei Satz 1) und stelle die Fragen nach den unterstrichenen Satzteilen.**

1. <u>Kevin</u> has found <u>important documents</u> <u>in a trash can</u>.
2. <u>The girls</u> have been playing <u>on the beach</u>.

B 1 120 **Wie ist es dazu gekommen? Bilde Sätze in *present perfect simple* mit den in Klammer angeführten Wörtern.**

1. Peter is not in his room. (*he – go – park*)
2. We can go now. (*I – tidy – my room*)
3. Our neighbours are selling their house. (*they – find – bigger one*)
4. I know everything about it. (*I – watch the story – on TV*)
5. Daniel is very sad. (*his girlfriend – leave him*)
6. Sally can't come skiing with us tomorrow. (*she – hurt – leg*)
7. Look, Mike's hair is purple! (*he – dye it – again*)
8. Dad has to walk to work the next few days. (*he – sell – his car*)
9. I don't feel too good. (*I – eat – too much*)
10. You can go in now. (*Mr. Jackson – arrive*)
11. Gillian wants to speak with you. (*she – hear – about your accident*)
12. Why is it so cold in here? (*someone – leave – windows open*)

Additional exercise Seite 167

2 Bezug zur Gegenwart („Hier und Jetzt“)

Bestimmte Wörter stellen den Bezug zur Gegenwart her. Dazu zählen:

just	*already*	*ever?*	*never*	*so far*
soeben, gerade	schon, bereits	schon (einmal)? jemals?	nie(mals), noch nie	bis jetzt

- *Dad **has just arrived**. We can have dinner now.*
  *Somebody **has just asked** for you, Tom. I think it was a girl.*
- *That's a great film! We**'ve already seen** it several times.*
  *Would you like a Coke? – No, thanks. I**'ve already had** three.*
- ***Have** you **ever danced** with Julia? – No, never, but I'd like to.*
  *Llangollen? Who **has ever heard** of this place before?*
- *I **have never tried** to write a poem.*
  *Can you imagine? Nancy **has never visited** a museum!*
- *We**'ve been** very satisfied with our car **so far**.*
  *I asked Joe to get in touch with us, but **so far** he **hasn't called**.*

in the last few (days, hours ...)	*recently, lately*	*this (week, morning, year ...)*	*today, all day*
in den letzten paar (Tagen, Stunden ...)	vor kurzem, unlängst	diese/s/n (Woche, Jahr, Vormittag ...)	heute, den ganzen Tag

Present perfect simple verlangt in den meisten Fällen keine Zeitangabe. Will man aber den Zeitraum einengen, der bis an die Gegenwart (das „Hier und Jetzt“) heranreicht, kann man diese Zeitangaben nennen.

- *Rita **has sent** five emails **in the last two hours**.*
  ***In the last few days** I **haven't seen** or **heard** from James.*
- ***Have** you **talked** to Frank **recently**? – No, I haven't.*
  *I**'ve met** some very interesting people **lately**.*
- *My dad **has been** to China three times **this year**.*
  ***This week**, we**'ve had** three written exams already.*
- *What **have** you **learned** in school **all day**?*
  ***Today**, I**'ve fed** the dog, **watered** the flowers and **done** the dishes.*

yet? – already	*not yet*
schon? bereits?	noch nicht

Für die Frage „Hast du **schon ...?**“ und die Antwort „Ich habe **noch nicht**!“ verwendest du *present perfect simple* mit *“yet/already”* und *“not yet”*.

- ***Has** Dominic **called yet**?*
  ***Have** they **written yet**?*
- *He **hasn't called yet**.*
  *They **have already written**.*

Bei den folgenden Übungen geht es um die Anwendung der Wörter, die einen Bezug zur Gegenwart – zum „Hier und Jetzt" – herstellen.

B 2 121 **Bilde passende Antworten mit *"just"* und/oder *"already"*. Meist passen beide!**

example: *Have you watered the flowers? (do)* ▶ *Yes, I've just done it.*
▶ *No, but Dad has already done it.*

1. Don't worry about your keys, Dad. (*I – find them*)
2. Have you forgotten to call Grandma, boys? – No, (*we – speak with her*)
3. Let's go to the movies. They're showing "King Kong". (*I – see it twice*)
4. Is Joe in? – No, (*he – go to town – brothers*)
5. Are you tired, Anne? – No, (*I – take a rest*)
6. How horrible! What shall we do now? – Don't worry, (*I – call – police*)

B 2 122 **Bilde Fragen mit *"ever"* und *"yet"* und passende Antworten mit *"never"*, *"not yet"* oder *"already"*.**

example: *(you, see) Rome? – No, I (be) there.* ▶
Have you ever seen Rome? – No, I haven't been there yet.
Have you seen Rome yet? – No, I've never been there.
– Yes, I've already been there.

1. (*you, smoke*) a cigar? – Yes, I (*try*) it, but I didn't like it.
2. (*your dad, work*) in another country? – No, he (*want*) to do it.
3. (*the boys, do*) jazz dancing? – No, they (*be*) asked.
4. (*Brian, be*) to a foreign country? – Yes, he (*visit*) Sweden and Norway.
5. (*you, try*) Indian food? – No, we (*be*) to an Indian restaurant.
6. (*you, see*) Eric Clapton in concert? – No, we (*have*) the chance.
7. (*Marilyn, play*) field hockey? – Yes, she (*play*) on the school team.
8. (*you, meet*) a prettier girl? – No, I (*see*) anyone as pretty.

B 2 123 **Bilde Fragen und Antworten mit *present perfect simple* und einer passenden „Zeitangabe". (+ bedeutet *yes*, – bedeutet *no*)**

example: *you, call Rosie (diese Woche)? / + talk to her (heute)* ▶
Have you called Rosie this week? – Yes, I've talked to her today.

1. you, see Harry (*vor kurzem*)? / – we, not see or talk to him (*diese Woche*)
2. your grandparents, visit you (*diesen Monat*)? / + they, be here (*kürzlich*)
3. Josie, call (*heute Nachmittag*)? / – we, not hear from her (*bis jetzt*)
4. you, touch this button (*vor kurzem*)? / – we, not be here (*den ganzen Tag*)
5. Tessa, talk to Jim (*heute*) / + she, call him (*heute Morgen*)
6. Uncle Tom, buy a car (*vor kurzem*) / – he, not sell, old one (*bis jetzt*)
7. you, watch TV (*heute*) / – I, not leave my room (*in den letzten paar Stunden)*
8. Tina, have lunch (*heute*) / – she, not come home from school (*bis jetzt*)

C ANWENDUNG VON *PRESENT PERFECT PROGRESSIVE*

1 Grundsätzliches

- *Present perfect progressive* beschreibt **zwei Arten von Handlungen:**

längere Handlungen, die erst vor kurzem zu Ende gingen	**längere Handlungen, die** „hier und jetzt" noch andauern
auf Deutsch: **„die ganze Zeit"** (Verb ▶ Perfekt)	auf Deutsch: **„schon seit"** (Verb ▶ Präsens)
*You look horrible! What **have** you **been doing**? – I've **been working** all day.*	*You look horrible! What **have** you **been doing**? – I've **been working** for ten hours.*
Was hast du denn [die ganze Zeit] gemacht? – Ich habe [die ganze Zeit] gearbeitet [aber jetzt arbeite ich nicht mehr].	Was hast du denn [die ganze Zeit] gemacht? – Ich arbeite schon seit zehn Stunden [und ich bin noch immer nicht fertig].

- Achtung bei der **Frage**!

*What **have** you **been doing?*** ▶ Was hast du denn die ganze Zeit gemacht (seit wir das letzte Mal miteinander sprachen)?

*What **have** you **done** (with your hair)?* ▶ Was hast du denn (mit deinen Haaren) gemacht (so dass ich „hier und jetzt" Auswirkungen und Folgen bemerken kann)?

2 „schon seit" mit *"since"* oder *"for"*?

Present perfect progressive sagt uns in bestimmten Fällen, **seit wann/wie lange schon** eine Handlung andauert. Wir brauchen dafür also eine Zeitangabe („schon seit ..."). Zwei Wörter stehen dafür zur Verfügung:

since	*for*
since 3 o'clock	*for three minutes*
since this morning	*for six hours*
since yesterday	*for two days*
since Christmas	*for half a year*
since 2001	*for a long time*
since the Middle Ages	*for ever*
▼	▼
seit einer bestimmten Zeit bis „hier und jetzt" (**Zeitpunkt**)	eine bestimmte Zeit lang bis „hier und jetzt" (**Zeitspanne**)

C 1 124 **Was ist passiert? Stelle die Frage auf Englisch und beantworte sie so wie im Beispiel. In beiden Fällen – Frage und Antwort – musst du *present perfect progressive* verwenden.**

example: *Vanessa looks very happy! (dance with Harry)* ►
What has she been doing? – She's been dancing with Harry.

1. Your clothes are absolutely dirty! – (*I, roll around on the ground*)
2. You look tired! – (*we, help Grandpa in the garden*)
3. The boys have bloody noses. – (*they, fight*)
4. You look like a fried chicken, Doris! – (*I, sunbathe, too long*)
5. Your dad seems to be very angry, Jill. – (*he, talk to my maths teacher*)
6. Tony says he can't sleep. – (*he, watch too much TV*)
7. Sally looks awful! – (*she, cry over her boyfriend*)
8. Children, why are your gloves all wet? – (*we, have a snowball fight*)
9. Dad is sleeping like a log. – (*he, working very hard lately*)
10. Look at the faces of the girls! – (*they, play around with Mum's lipsticks*)
11. Your mum looks excited! – (*she, talk to her boss about a new job*)
12. You look very slim and healthy, Jane. – (*I, do a lot of sport*)

C 2 125 ***"since"* oder *"for"*? Setze das passende Wort ein.**

1. ... my birthday
2. ... 1955
3. ... a short time
4. ... last night
5. ... ages
6. ... several years
7. ... we came here
8. ... as long as you like
9. ... an hour
10. ... Easter
11. ... hundreds of years
12. ... five minutes
13. ... midnight
14. ... a moment
15. ... I can remember

C 2 126 **Wie lange geht das schon so? Bilde Sätze in *present perfect progressive* und setze *"since"* oder *"for"* ein.**

example: *I am waiting for the train. I came here twenty minutes ago.* ►
I've been waiting for the train for twenty minutes.

1. The Bakers live next door to us. They bought the house in 2002.
2. Max and Mona are learning to drive. They started driving school in October.
3. Fred's uncle works in Australia. He went there a long time ago.
4. Lucy plays the violin. She started taking lessons when she was ten.
5. Betty is studying for her chemistry exam. She began a week ago.
6. Grandma is staying with us. She came on Easter Sunday.
7. Frank writes books. He started in 1980.
8. The boys are surfing the internet. They switched on the computer at 2 p.m.
9. I'm thinking of you. I started thinking of you when I first met you.
10. Grandpa drives only Opels. He bought his first Opel fifty years ago.
11. Sue is looking for her earrings. She started looking when she came home.
12. It is snowing. It started snowing five hours ago.

D UNTERSCHIED ZWISCHEN *PRESENT PERFECT SIMPLE* UND *PRESENT PERFECT PROGRESSIVE*

Die zwei Formen derselben Zeitstufe unterscheiden sich in einigen wichtigen Bereichen. Die folgende Gegenüberstellung zeigt dir, in welchen:

present perfect simple	*present perfect progressive*
have/has + 3rd form	***have/has been + ing-form***
Zustände	**Handlungen**
*How long **have** you **been** here? – We**'ve been** here for a week.*	*How long **have** you **been waiting** for us? – I**'ve been waiting** for an* hour.
*Since when **has** Bill **known** your sister? – He **has known** her since they were in kindergarten together.*	*Since when **has** Ruth **been going** out with Bill? – She**'s been going** out with him since January.*
▶ Wie lange **seid** ihr schon hier? Seit wann **kennt** er sie schon? ▼ **Zustand**	▶ Wie lange **wartet** ihr schon? Seit wann **geht** sie mit ihm aus? ▼ **Handlung**
Handlungen, die schon sehr lange andauern	**Handlungen, die noch nicht so lange andauern**
*The Windsors **have lived** here since the Middle Ages.*	*We **have been living** here for two years now.*
*Brigid **has danced** with John for as long as I can remember.*	*Brigid **has been dancing** with John all evening. I think she likes him.*
Auswirkung, Ergebnis, Folge mit oder ohne Zeitangabe	**Handlung** mit oder ohne Zeitangabe
*Look, someone **has left** the lights on!*	*People **have been leaving** their homes in the Third World for years.*
*We**'ve read** four books this semester.*	*Sam **has been reading** since he came home. He is getting tired now.*
Ausschließlich ***present perfect simple*** ist möglich …	
… wenn etwas **seit … nicht/noch nie/ so lange schon nicht** geschehen ist	… bei **bestimmten Verben** (siehe Liste auf Seite 115)
*We **haven't seen** her for …/since … Jack **has never eaten** snails before.*	*I**'ve known** Richard for …/since … Ian **has liked** my cakes since …*

D 127 ***Present perfect simple* oder *present perfect progressive*? Entscheide dich und setze ein.**

1. Aunt Eleonor (*take*) … pictures of her family since I can remember.
2. What's the matter with you? You look sad! – I (*cry*) … for hours because my cat (*die*) … .
3. Police (*look*) … for the money for hours, but they (*not find*) … it yet.
4. Dad, you (*work*) … too much lately. You (*not have*) … any time for yourself.
5. Leave some cake for the others, Bob! You (*eat*) … four pieces already!
6. My parents (*learn*) … Spanish for three years now, and they still like it.
7. Dad (*work*) … for the same company for twenty years, but now he (*find*) … a better job.
8. Look at your shoes, Joe! What (*you, do*) …? – I (*run*) … around in the mud!
9. Danny is worried about Cathy, but he (*not call*) … her yet.
10. Here you are! I (*try*) … to call you ten times today! What (*you, do*) …?
11. How boring! Mr. Jones (*speak*) … for over an hour, and he (*not finish*) … yet!
12. Inuit (*live*) … in Alaska and Northern Canada for more than 5000 years.
13. You must be hungry, boys! You (*not eat*) … all afternoon! Here, I (*make*) … some sandwiches for you!
14. How long (*you, have*) … this car? – For fifteen years, and there (*not be*) … a single problem!
15. My brother and I (*play*) … in a rock band since last summer, and we (*have*) … four concerts so far.
16. Girls, (*you, speak*) … with your parents about the skiing week yet?
17. Those poor people (*wait*) … for the bus in this cold for twenty minutes!
18. Why is Roman such a good dancer? – Well, he (*take*) … lessons for years!
19. I can't find my trainers! I'm sure my friends (*hide*) … them somewhere!
20. Are you blind? Your trainers (*be*) … in your locker all the time!
21. My mum (*be*) … a teacher for fifteen years, but she (*never, teach*) … any of her many nieces and nephews.
22. Let's go home now! We (*wait*) … long enough. They won't come any more.
23. Why is it so cold in here? – Look, someone (*leave*) … the windows open and the fire (*go*) … out.
24. We are ready to go, Dad. (*you, finish*) … reading the paper?
25. I've got a headache now because I (*sit*) … in front of the computer all day.

Additional exercise Seite 168

E *PAST SIMPLE* ODER *PRESENT PERFECT SIMPLE*?

- Bei diesen zwei Zeitstufen herrscht **Verwechslungsgefahr** – besonders für Deutsch Sprechende. Uns ist es nämlich ziemlich egal, ob jemand sagt:

  „Wir **haben** uns in der Stadt **getroffen**." oder
  „Wir **trafen** uns in der Stadt."

Uns ist klar, was gemeint ist. Wir erkennen bestenfalls an Ausdrucksweise und Wortwahl, aus welchem Teil des deutschsprachigen Gebietes der Sprecher kommt. Vielleicht bemerken wir auch noch einen Unterschied im Stil. Aber das ändert nichts an der Aussage oder am Inhalt.

Im Englischen ist das ganz anders. Hier gibt es große Unterschiede zwischen:

past simple	*present perfect simple*
*"We **saw** this film."*	*"We **have seen** this film."*
Dieser Satz sagt uns, dass jemand **irgendwann einmal** (zB gestern, vorige Woche, vor einem halben Jahr ...) den Film gesehen hat. Wir wissen nicht, ob sie sich noch daran erinnern können oder ob sie den Inhalt schon wieder vergessen haben oder ob sie inzwischen schon wieder im Kino waren oder nicht. Wir erfahren also etwas über das „Damals", nicht über das „Jetzt".	Dieser Satz sagt uns etwas über das „Hier und Jetzt". Wir wissen, worum es in dem Film geht, weil wir ihn irgendwann einmal gesehen haben (zB gestern, vorige Woche, vor einem halben Jahr ...). Uns interessiert dabei **nicht**, **wann** das war, **sondern dass** es passiert ist.

- Dieser grundsätzliche Unterschied zeigt sich auch in den folgenden Fällen:

irgendwann einmal	gilt aber „jetzt" nicht mehr, weil ...
*Jeremy **bought** a DVD player,*	*but he **has not used** it yet.* (▶ Er steht noch immer verpackt herum.)
*Emily **left** the party at 10 p.m.*	*and nobody **has seen** her since then.* (▶ Wir wissen nicht, wo sie jetzt ist.)
„historische" Ereignisse ohne Bezug zu „Jetzt und Hier"	**Ereignisse** mit Bezug zu „Jetzt und Hier"
*James Dean **made** only four films.* (James Dean starb 1955. Er kann keine Filme mehr machen. Daher: „historisches" Ereignis!)	*Brad Pitt **has made** forty films (so far).* (Brad Pitt lebt und hat es bis jetzt auf rund 40 Filme gebracht; weitere werden folgen. Daher: Bezug zu „hier und jetzt".)
vergangener Zeitpunkt **abgeschlossener Zeitrahmen**	**Zeit reicht bis „Jetzt und Hier"**
*The Smiths **came** here **in 1999**.*	*They **have been** here **for seven years**.*

E 128 **Bilde mit den gegebenen Personen und Verben *past simple* und *present perfect simple.***

example: *Maureen – write poems* ▶
Maureen wrote poems – Maureen has written poems

1. the man – ask a question
2. Joe – buy an MP3 player
3. Dad – catch a big fish
4. Sally – dance with Simon
5. Max – eat all the sweets
6. we – find the map
7. nobody – get a letter
8. I – hear a loud noise
9. Nelly – jump into the river
10. Mum – keep the photos
11. the girls – learn to dance
12. Grandma – make cookies
13. someone – open the doors
14. who – press the button – ?
15. Edward – quit smoking
16. two men – rob a bank
17. Richard – see the doctor
18. we – tell the headmaster
19. somebody – use my towel
20. Tina – write a nice story

E 129 ***Past simple or present perfect simple?* Überlege die Zusammenhänge und setze die richtige Zeitstufe ein.**

1. I (*try*) … to call you five times yesterday. Where (*you, be*) …? – I (*be*) … at the cinema with my friends. We (*see*) … some very good films this month.
2. Is Joe at home? – I'm sorry, he isn't. He (*just, leave*) … the house.
3. My dad (*have*) … a bad skiing accident when he (*be*) … twenty-five. He (*have*) … to stay in hospital for three months.
4. (*you, ever, see*) … the Rolling Stones in concert? – They are too old for me! But my parents (*see*) … them when they (*be*) … in Austria in 1999.
5. Dad (*buy*) … a Harley Davidson last year, but he (*not use*) … it much so far.
6. Karl May (*write*) … more than a hundred books, and I (*read*) … them all.
7. It (*rain*) … a lot this summer. – Yes, hasn't it? Last summer it (*not rain*) … so much. The weathermen say it (*not rain*) … so much since 1925.
8. Cindy and Bert (*begin*) … singing as a duo in 1961. – Wow! This means they (*be*) … together for more than forty years!
9. Dad (*like*) … to watch westerns when he (*be*) … a boy, but he (*not watch*) … one in a long time now. He says there aren't any good ones any more.
10. Grandma (*give*) … me a snowboard for Christmas, but I (*try*) … it only three or four times so far.
11. (*you, ever, hear*) … about the Incas? – Oh yes. We (*talk*) … about them in our history lessons. They (*control*) … most of South America before the Spanish (*arrive*) …, and last week Mrs. Jones (*show*) … us a film about them.
12. Look, Grandpa (*send*) … us a postcard again! It's from Rome. Last week he (*write*) … us from Sicily.
13. This week, Jack (*win*) … all his tennis games so far. – That's great, because last week he (*lose*) … them all.

Additional exercise Seite 169

19. KAPITEL	*THE PRESENT TENSE –* DIE GEGENWART/DAS PRÄSENS

A FORMEN VON *PRESENT TENSE*

present simple		*present progressive*		
		I	***am***	***coming***
I, you, we, they	***come***	*you, we, they*	***are***	***coming***
he, she, it	***comes***	*he, she, it*	***is***	***coming***

Das ***-s*** der 3. Person Einzahl *(3rd person s)* – bei *he, she, it* – darfst du auf keinen Fall vergessen.
Wenn der Infinitiv *(base form)* auf einen Zischlaut endet, hängst du in der 3. Person meist ***s*** oder ***es*** an und sprichst [iz]:

*wash**es** – ris**es** – splash**es** – fix**es***

B FRAGEN UND VERNEINUNG – *QUESTIONS AND NEGATION*

Die Fragebildung und die Verneinung folgen in *present tense* den „üblichen" Regeln: Du brauchst **für jede Frage** (außer für die Frage nach dem Subjekt in *present simple*) **und für die Verneinung ein Hilfs(zeit)wort**.

present simple	*present progressive*
Joe plays basketball after school.	*Joe is playing basketball in the park.*
***Does** Joe **play** basketball after school?*	***Is** Joe **playing** basketball in the park?*
*What **does** Joe **play** after school?*	*What **is** Joe **playing** in the park?*
*When **does** Joe **play** basketball?*	*Where **is** Joe **playing** basketball?*
*Joe **does not play** basketball ... .*	*Joe **is not playing** basketball ... .*
▶ ***Who plays** basketball after school?*	▶ ***Who is playing** basketball ...?*

Achtung – Falle!
Die Frage nach dem Subjekt steht immer in *3rd person singular*; daher lautet sie in *present progressive* immer ***"Who is ...?"*** oder ***"What is ...?"***

A 130 **Setze die Beispiele in *present simple.* Achte dabei auf die vorgegebene Person.**

1. My older brother (*want*) … to buy a car as soon as he is eighteen.
2. Dominic's parents (*own*) … a music shop. They (*sell*) … instruments.
3. Dominic (*play*) … the trumpet and the trombone.
4. The boys often (*build*) … igloos when there is enough snow.
5. James (*like*) … winter best because his parents always (*take*) … him skiing. James (*love*) … skiing, and he (*ski*) … very well.
6. A good teacher never (*get*) … angry or (*shout*) … at his pupils.
7. Intelligent drivers (*drive*) … carefully.
8. My dad (*know*) … many interesting people and they (*know*) … him.
9. Frank (*read*) … one or two books per week. I never (*read*) … so much.
10. The sun (*rise*) … in the east and (*set*) … in the west.

A 131 **Setze die Beispiele in *present progressive.* Achte wieder auf die vorgegebene Person.**

1. Look, somebody (*try*) … to take off on your bike!
2. Joe says he can't come with us because he (*study*) … for his exams.
3. Mum and Dad are in the garden. They (*plant*) … some flowers.
4. Boys, where are you? – In Mike's room. We (*play*) … games.
5. Hurry up, Mary! I (*wait*) … for you!
6. Hey, you (*write*) … with my pen again! Give it back!
7. Listen, someone (*knock*) … at the door.
8. Jill and Jodie (*have*) … a party on Saturday. I think I'll go.
9. Please turn off the TV. I (*think*) …!
10. There's Mr. Smith. He (*run*) … to catch his bus again.

Additional exercise Seite 170

B 132 **Bilde die Entscheidungsfrage und die Verneinung und frage nach den unterstrichenen Satzteilen.**

1. <u>The guests</u> are leaving <u>because it is late</u>.
2. <u>Michelle</u> is watching <u>a film</u> <u>in her room</u>.
3. I am watering <u>the flowers</u> <u>in the living room</u>.
4. <u>Francis</u> lives <u>near London</u>.
5. <u>Linda</u> works <u>in a flower shop</u> <u>every Friday afternoon</u>.
6. <u>Many tourists</u> visit <u>St. Paul's Cathedral</u> <u>every day</u>.
7. <u>Young people</u> love <u>snowboarding</u> <u>because it's easy to learn</u>.
8. <u>Joe and his friends</u> enjoy watching <u>horror films</u>.
9. Miriam is <u>in bed</u> <u>because she is ill</u>.
10. <u>Many people</u> come <u>to Britain</u> <u>to study English</u>.
11. <u>The girls</u> sing <u>beautifully</u>.
12. I am painting <u>my room</u> <u>orange and pink</u>.
13. Eric is studying <u>history</u> <u>because he wants to pass tomorrow's test</u>.
14. <u>You</u> are sleeping <u>in our beds</u>.

Additional exercise Seite 170

C ANWENDUNG VON *PRESENT SIMPLE* UND *PRESENT PROGRESSIVE*

present simple	*present progressive*
① **zeitlose Zustände und allzeit gültige Tatsachen**	④ **Handlungen, die im Augenblick des Sprechens geschehen**
② **regelmäßige oder wiederholte Handlungen**	⑤ **Handlungen, die von der „Norm" abweichen**
③ **zukünftige Ereignisse, die zeitlich genau festgelegt sind**	⑥ **zukünftige Handlungen (mit Zeitangabe)**

① *Water **freezes** at 0°C or 32°F.*
② *Maria always **rides** her bike to school, but ⑤ today she **is walking**.*
③ *Elena's train **leaves** at 5 o'clock this afternoon.*
④ *I can't hear you! **I'm listening** to a rock concert.*
⑥ *Elsie and Oliver **are driving** to Salzburg at the weekend.*

D VERBEN, DIE NORMALERWEISE NUR IN *SIMPLE FORM* VORKOMMEN

Einige Verben werden fast ausschließlich in ***simple form*** verwendet.
Die wichtigsten findest du in dieser Liste. Allerdings gibt es auch Ausnahmen (*).

believe	***have****	***love***	***realise***	***see****
belong	***hear***	***mean***	***recognise***	***seem***
forget	***know***	***need***	***remember***	***want***
hate	***like***	***prefer***	***understand***	***wish***

Es muss so heißen:

*We **need** your help now, Dad!*
*Do you **understand** me?*
*I **love** hamburgers.*

und nicht so:

We are needing your help now, Dad.
Are you understanding me?
I am loving hamburgers.
(Auch wenn's die Werbung behauptet!)

Ausnahmen: *have* und ***see*** kennen sowohl ***simple form* als auch *progressive form***, wenn auch bei geänderter Bedeutung.

*Marcus **has** no time for hobbies.*
(haben, besitzen, verfügen)

*I **see** my friends every day.*
(sehen, treffen)

*He **is having** lunch right now.*
(essen)

*I'**m seeing** the doctor tomorrow.*
(aufsuchen)

*We **are seeing** you to the station.*
(begleiten, hinbringen)

C 133 ***Present simple* oder *present progressive?* Wähle die richtige Form!**

1. Gorillas (*live*) … in the wild only in Africa.
2. Look, Adrian (*talk*) … to Suzie!
3. Dad usually (*drive*) … to work, but today he (*walk*) … because the car is at the mechanic's.
4. Our plane (*leave*) … at 4 o'clock tomorrow afternoon, and it (*arrive*) … at 6.
5. Next Sunday, Gloria and I (*go*) … to a concert.
6. The earth (*turn*) … around the sun, and the moon (*turn*) … around the earth.
7. Listen, the neighbours (*fight*) … again!
8. Mum never (*bake*) … a cake, but Grandma (*do*) … it every weekend.
9. Hurry up! The film (*start*) … in five minutes!
10. Something's wrong with Charlie! He (*look*) … very sad today.
11. Helen and Joe (*drive*) … to the mall this afternoon. I'd like to go with them.
12. Grapes (*grow*) … best in dry and sunny places.
13. Look, Mr. Jackson (*grow*) … a beard! I think he (*look*) … strange.
14. Normally, Mum (*go*) … to bed early, but today she (*watch*) … the late show.
15. The train to Hogwarts (*leave*) … from platform 9¾.
16. Most of my friends (*enjoy*) … the Harry Potter books.
17. Look at Dad! He (*lie*) … in the sun while we (*work*) … .
18. Mrs. Collins always (*give*) … us a lot to do over the weekend.
19. Listen, somebody (*ring*) … the bell! – That's Judy. She always (*visit*) … us at this time of the day.
20. We usually (*see*) … a video in our Friday physics lesson, but this week Mr. Peters (*show*) … us an exciting experiment.

D 134 ***Present simple or progressive?* Entscheide, aber achte auf die Verben, die normalerweise nur in *simple form* vorkommen.**

1. This wonderful dress (*belong*) … to me now! I'm so happy!
2. Listen, Nancy (*talk*) … about her boyfriends again, but I (*not believe*) … her.
3. You (*eat*) … a hamburger, Jenny. (*you, like*) … fast food? – I (*love*) … it!
4. Now I (*understand*) … why you (*not like*) … this cheese. It (*taste*) … horrible!
5. Oliver (*say*) … that he (*own*) … three cars, but I'm sure he (*lie*) … .
6. Look, that man over there (*watch*) … us! I (*not want*) … him to do this!
7. What (*you, normally, have*) … for breakfast? – Only toast and coffee.
8. Every day, I (*see*) … the same people and I (*hear*) … the same stories.
9. Thanks for telling me everything. Now I (*know*) … the whole story.
10. Vanessa can't come to the phone. She (*have*) … dinner with her family.
11. Dad (*work*) … six days a week, but today he (*not work*) … because he's ill.
12. Where (*you, go*) …, Raymond? – To the station. I (*see*) … Linda to her train.

Additional exercise Seite 170

20. KAPITEL — PROGRESSIVE FORM AND SIMPLE FORM – ZWEI „TYPISCH ENGLISCHE“ FORMEN DES ZEITWORTES

Diese zwei Seiten sind eine **Zusammenfassung.** Detaillierte Auskünfte über diese beiden wichtigen Zeitwortformen findest du in den Kapiteln zu den einzelnen Zeitstufen:

present tense (Seite 110)
past tense (Seite 86)
present perfect tense (Seite 100)
past perfect tense (Seite 82)
future tense (Seite 34)

simple form	*progressive form*
Simple form bedeutet einfache Form. Sie heißt deshalb so, weil sie ganz „einfach“ – **ohne Erweiterungen** – gebildet wird.	*Progressive* lässt sich mit fortlaufend, fortschreitend übersetzen. Damit bezeichnen wir Vorgänge, die **noch nicht abgeschlossen** sind und daher **noch andauern.** Der deutsche Name ist „Dauerform“ oder „Verlaufsform“. Neben *“progressive form”* finden sich auch die Bezeichnungen *“expanded form”* oder *“continuous form”*.
Beispiele für *simple form* sind: *I **dance** – you **work** – he **studies*** *she **asked** – it **rained** – they **ate***	
“(e)s” und *“(e)d”* sind keine Erweiterungen, sondern Endungen: *3rd person -(e)s; past tense -(e)d.*	Beispiele für *progressive form*: *I **am dreaming** – you **were lying** – he **has been waiting***

Grundsätzliche Anwendung	
Simple form wird immer dann verwendet, wenn es um die **Handlung an sich** geht. Man erfährt durch *simple form* einfach, was geschieht, geschah oder geschehen wird.	*Progressive form* beschreibt den **Verlauf der Handlung.** Man erfährt, was **zu einem bestimmten Zeitpunkt** gerade geschieht, geschah oder geschehen wird.
*Dad **reads** the paper every day.* *Dad **read** the paper an hour ago.* *Dad **has read** the paper. You can have it now.*	*Dad **is reading** the paper right now.* *Dad **was reading** ... when you rang.* *Dad **has been reading** the paper for over an hour!*

Der folgende **Überblick** zeigt, wie ***simple form*** und ***progressive form*** **in den verschiedenen Zeitstufen** gebildet werden. Als „Verb für alle Zwecke" dient ***to ask***.

simple form		*progressive form*	
present tense simple		*present tense progressive*	
I, you, we, they	***ask***	*I*	***am asking***
he, she, it	***asks***	*you, we, they*	***are asking***
		he, she, it	***is asking***
present perfect tense simple		*present perfect tense progressive*	
I, you, we, they	***have asked***	*I, you, we, they*	***have been asking***
he, she, it	***has asked***	*he, she, it*	***has been asking***
past tense simple		*past tense progressive*	
(all persons)	***asked***	*I, he, she, it*	***was asking***
		we, you, they	***were asking***
past perfect tense simple		*past perfect tense progressive*	
(all persons)	***had asked***	*(all persons)*	***had been asking***
future with "will" simple		*future with "will" progressive*	
(all persons)	***will ask***	*(all persons)*	***will be asking***

Über Bildung und Anwendung von ***conditional present*** und ***conditional perfect*** informierst du dich in Kapitel 4, ab Seite 30. In diesen Zeitstufen kommt *progressive form* so selten vor, dass wir uns hier nicht näher darum kümmern müssen.

Achtung – Falle!
Es gibt Gruppen von **Verben, die nicht in *progressive form*** auftreten.
Dazu zählen:

believe	***have***	***love***	***realise***	***see***
belong	***hear***	***mean***	***recognise***	***seem***
forget	***know***	***need***	***remember***	***want***
hate	***like***	***prefer***	***understand***	***wish***

21. KAPITEL *PRONOUNS* – FÜRWÖRTER/PRONOMEN

A PERSÖNLICHES FÜRWORT – *PERSONAL PRONOUN*

1 Das persönliche Fürwort als Ersatzwort

Es steht anstelle eines Hauptworts (Nomen) oder eines Namens.
Dazu einige Beispiele:

__The girls__ listen to their CDs. ► *__They__ listen to their CDs.*
Joe likes __Tina__ very much. ► *Joe likes __her__ very much.*
__Tim and I__ will read __the story__ later. ► *__We__ will read __it__ later.*

2 Das persönliche Fürwort als Subjekt oder Objekt

Bei Bill, dem Obsthändler, sieht das dann so aus:

personal pronoun as subject	Person	*personal pronoun as object*
I *like green apples.*	*1st singular*	*Joe gave* ***me*** *one.*
You *like red apples.*	*2nd singular*	*Joe gave* ***you*** *two.*
He *likes oranges better*		*Joe gave* ***him*** *one.*
She *likes oranges, too.*	*3rd singular*	*Joe gave* ***her*** *two.*
It *doesn't like oranges.*		*Joe didn't give* ***it*** *any.*
We *like bananas.*	*1st plural*	*Joe gave* ***us*** *some.*
You *like pineapples better.*	*2nd plural*	*Joe gave* ***you*** *one.*
They *like kiwis best.*	*3rd plural*	*Joe gave* ***them*** *some.*

Achtung bei ***3rd person singular*:**

► ***he, she*** und ***it*** entsprechen **nicht ganz** „unserem" **er, sie** und **es.**
he **und** ***she*** darfst du **nur für Personen** (und Haustiere) verwenden;
it steht **für Dinge und** (alle übrigen) **Tiere.**

Daher:

Sie (die Suppe) ist zu heiß! ► ***It****'s too hot!*
Er (der Salat) schmeckt gut. ► ***It*** *tastes good.*
Es (das Frühstück) ist serviert! ► ***It*** *has been served!*

Aber:

Es (das Mädchen) lächelt wieder. ► ***She*** *smiles again.*

A 1 135 **Ersetze die unterstrichenen Wörter durch ein *personal pronoun*.**

Additional exercise Seite 171

1. Don't ask Walter! He doesn't know the answer.
2. Cathy and I are waiting for the boys.
3. Let's buy the bracelet for Mum!
4. Mary's parents want to speak with you and me.

A 2 136 **Die folgenden Sätze verlangen ein *personal pronoun* als Subjekt. Setze das passende *personal pronoun* ein.**

1. Can ... show me the way to the park, please?
2. Are these your trainers, Caroline? – No, miss, ... don't have black trainers.
3. Thanks for the tea, Mary. ... was excellent.
4. Do you know Jack Williams? – Oh, yes! ... is a very good friend.
5. Gina and Tina are sisters, but ... look very different.
6. Look, there's Emily! I think ... wants to go shopping.
7. This is Steven's new car. ... was very expensive.
8. Steven likes his new car. – Yes, ... is very proud of it.
9. Benjamin, are ... in your room? – No, Mum, ...'m in the living room.
10. I like your new skis, Tony! – Yes, ... are great.

Additional exercise Seite 171

A 2 137 **Für diese Sätze brauchst du ein *personal pronoun* als Objekt.**

1. When Jack calls, please tell ... to call again later.
2. Have you seen Dad's car keys? He can't find ... .
3. Look, there's Amelie! – I don't want to speak with ...!
4. I'm sorry, Sue, but I can't help ...! I'm busy.
5. We saw "Fast & Furious" yesterday, and we liked ... a lot.
6. Boys, where are ...? I can't see or hear ...!
7. When my brother and I make model planes, Dad always helps ... .
8. Are the new neighbours nice? – Oh, yes! We like ... very much.
9. When Mum comes home, let's ask ... about the party on Friday.
10. Bill, do you want to go to the cinema with ... and my friends?

A 2 138 **Setze das *personal pronoun* entweder als Subjekt oder als Objekt ein.**

1. Look, there's a fly in your soup! – Take ... out! I don't want to see ...!
2. Where is Eric? I must speak with ...! – ... is in the garden, I think.
3. Jessica and Philip are okay. ... are in my class this year, but I don't often speak with ... .
4. Terry and I live in the same house, but ... go to different schools.
5. Is Judy nice? – I don't like ...; I think ... is very arrogant.
6. Thanks for the cake, Grandma. ... is delicious!
7. Boys, can ... come here, please? – In a minute, Mum. ... are busy right now.
8. Are the girls in the house? – No, ... are in the garden. Can't you see ...?
9. Frank really likes his new jeans. He wears ... every day!
10. I really fancy Monica. Do you know ...? – Of course! ... is tall and pretty and ... has dark hair and blue eyes.

B BESITZANZEIGENDES FÜRWORT – *POSSESSIVE PRONOUN*

Das besitzanzeigende Fürwort gibt an, **wem oder zu wem** etwas gehört. Es kommt **mit oder anstelle** eines Hauptworts vor. Das sieht dann so aus:

mit Hauptwort			Person	anstelle des Hauptworts	
This is	***my***	*room.*	*1st singular*	*It is*	***mine.***
Is this	***your***	*bike?*	*2nd singular*	*Is it*	***yours?***
This is	***his***	*CD.*		*It is*	***his.***
Is this	***her***	*jacket?*	*3rd singular*	*Is it*	***hers?***
This is	***its***	*food.*		*(It is*	***its.)***
They are	***our***	*toys.*	*1st plural*	*They are*	***ours.***
Is this	***your***	*house?*	*2nd plural*	*Is it*	***yours?***
They are	***their***	*books.*	*3rd plural*	*They are*	***theirs.***

Vorsicht – Falle!

- „Ist das **ihr/Ihr** Auto?"
  - ► *Is this **her** car?* (das Auto einer Frau oder eines Mädchens)
  - ► *Is this **their** car?* (das Auto mehrerer Personen)
  - ► *Is this **your** car?* (höflich: das Auto einer Person)
- ***its*** ≠ ***it's***
  Besitzanzeiger — **Kurzform von *"it is"***

C HINWEISENDES FÜRWORT – *DEMONSTRATIVE PRONOUN*

Das hinweisende Fürwort **hebt eine Person** (oder Personen) **oder eine Sache** (oder Sachen) **aus einer Menge heraus**, indem es auf sie „hinweist". Die wichtigsten Fürwörter dieser Gruppe sind:

this ***these*** ► **der, die, das hier; dieser, diese, dieses (hier)**
that ***those*** ► **der, die, das dort; jener, jene, jenes (dort)**
▼ ▼
singular ***plural***

this und ***these*** bezeichnen das, was **näher** beim Sprecher liegt;
that und ***those*** bezeichnen das, was **weiter weg** vom Sprecher liegt.

Die Wortwahl hängt also vom Standpunkt des Sprechers ab. Was für den einen ***"this door"*** heißt, ist für den anderen ***"that door"***.

D BEZÜGLICHES FÜRWORT – *RELATIVE PRONOUN*

Das bezügliche Fürwort wird in Kapitel 23, ab Seite 132 ausführlich besprochen.

B 139 **Setze das passende *possessive pronoun* ein.**

1. Betty is okay, but … sister is awful!
2. … brother and I are lucky – we have … own rooms!
3. Karla, is this … T-shirt? – No, it isn't. … T-shirt is pink, not yellow.
4. Can you come to … place this afternoon? Mum says it's okay.
5. Girls, go and wash … hands! They are full of paint.
6. Sir, you can't park … car here! Don't you see the sign?
7. I like Uncle Albert. He often lets me drive … tractor.
8. My sister and I have to ask … parents before we go out.
9. I once saw an interesting film about the Mayas, but I forgot … name.

Additional exercise Seite 171

B 140 **In den folgenden Sätzen wird nach den *possessive pronouns* anstelle eines Hauptworts gesucht. Setze die passenden Wörter ein.**

example: *Are these Alice's jeans?* ▶ *Yes, they are hers./No, they aren't hers.*

1. Whose books are these? – Well, they've got Monica's name on them, so they must be … .
2. Boys, don't touch this computer. It's not …!
3. Alex, is this your biro? – Let me see! Yes, it's … . Where did you find it?
4. My bike has got a flat tyre. Can I use … today, Mum?
5. Children, is that your house over there? – Yes, Mr. Higgins, it's … .
6. Gina and I have the same taste in clothes, so sometimes I wear … and sometimes she wears … .
7. This looks like Dominic's sweater. – Yes, I think it's … .
8. Can I borrow these scissors, please? – I don't know. They aren't …!
9. Whose T-shirt is this, Nathan? … or your brother's? – It must be …, because I don't wear heavy metal T-shirts.

Zum raschen Nachschlagen – ein **Überblick über alle *personal and possessive pronouns*.**

personal (subject)	*possessive (with noun)*	*possessive (without noun)*	*personal (object)*
I	***my***	***mine***	***me***
you	***your***	***yours***	***you***
he	***his***	***his***	***him***
she	***her***	***hers***	***her***
it	***its***	***its***	***it***
we	***our***	***ours***	***us***
you	***your***	***yours***	***you***
they	***their***	***theirs***	***them***

E RÜCKBEZÜGLICHES FÜRWORT – *REFLEXIVE PRONOUN*

- Das rückbezügliche Fürwort gleicht in vielem seinem deutschen Gegenstück, doch gibt es auch Unterschiede, die zu Fehlern verleiten können. Das ***reflexive pronoun*** wird manchmal auch ***"self-pronoun"*** genannt.

singular					*plural*			
I	*saw*	***myself***	*in the mirror.*	1st	***We***	*saw*	***ourselves***	*in the mirror.*
You	*saw*	***yourself***	*in the mirror.*	2nd	***You***	*saw*	***yourselves***	*in the mirror.*
He	*saw*	***himself***	*in the mirror.*					
She	*saw*	***herself***	*in the mirror.*	3rd	***They***	*saw*	***themselves***	*in the mirror.*
It	*saw*	***itself***	*in the mirror.*					

- Es heißt ***-self***, wenn du von einer **einzelnen Person** *(singular)* sprichst, und ***-selves***, wenn du von **mehreren Personen** *(plural)* sprichst.
- Es heißt daher ***yourself*** im ***singular*** und ***yourselves*** im ***plural***.
- Es heißt ***himself*** und <u>nicht *hisself*</u>, und ***themselves*** und <u>nicht *theirselves*</u>.

- Zur **Anwendung** des *reflexive pronoun* kommt es in folgenden Situationen:

1 Dann, wenn man auf Deutsch sagt:
ich ... mich/mir; du ... dich/dir; er ... sich; wir ... uns und **ihr ... euch.**

I *taught* ***myself*** *to ride the bike when I was three.*
Ich brachte **mir** das Radfahren bei, als ich drei Jahre alt war.

They *locked* ***themselves*** *into their room.*
Sie sperrten **sich** in ihrem Zimmer ein.

2 Wenn man sagen will, dass jemand etwas selbst gemacht hat (daher auch die Bezeichnung *"self-pronouns"*).

Nobody wanted to do it, so ***we*** *did it* ***ourselves.***
Niemand wollte es tun, also machten **wir** es **selbst.**

An old saying goes like this, "Help ***yourself****, and God will help you."*
Ein altes Sprichwort sagt: „Hilf **dir selbst**, dann hilft dir Gott."

3 Wenn man eine Person oder eine Sache hervorheben will:

Helena was very courageous. ***She herself*** *chased away the burglars.*
Helena war sehr mutig. **Sie selbst** verjagte die Einbrecher.

The film itself *was okay, but some of the actors were very bad.*
Der Film selbst war in Ordnung, aber manche der Schauspieler waren sehr schlecht.

E 1 141 **Setze die passenden *reflexive pronouns* ein: „ich … mir/mich", „du … dir/dich", „er … sich" und so weiter.**

1. Do you sometimes talk to … in your dreams?
2. Boys, be careful, or you will hurt …!
3. Good parents think of their children first and of … last.
4. Marcus is a problem. He can't control … when he something worries him.
5. Most young people ask … what the future will be like.
6. Florian is so clever! He taught … to read and write when he was only five.
7. Look at Christine! She's admiring … in the mirror again!
8. I often tell … that I shouldn't eat so much chocolate.
9. The summer holidays were great! We enjoyed … very much.
10. Do you ever ask … why nobody likes you?
11. Sometimes we have to remind … to work a little harder.
12. That wasn't a nice thing to do, girls! Don't you know how to behave …?

E 2 142 **Setze die passenden *reflexive pronouns* ein: „selbst (gemacht)"**

1. No thanks, I don't need your help. I can do it … .
2. One day they will build computers that can program … .
3. Jack is old enough. He can brush his shoes …!
4. Nobody was there, so we had the house to … .
5. The President answered our letter … . I think that was nice of him.
6. Some old people cannot look after … any more, so they need our help.
7. The rocket will destroy … if there is a problem with the engine.
8. You mustn't copy your homework, Joe! You must do it …!
9. Who has painted these pictures? – I did it …, but I had some help.
10. Boys, did you answer these questions … or did somebody help you?
11. Maria, did you drive … or did you come by taxi?
12. Don't tell me where the Easter eggs are. Let me try to find them …!

E 3 143 **Setze die passenden *reflexive pronouns* ein: „Das gehört hervorgehoben!"**

1. We're going to build a tree house. Dad … said so.
2. Charlie likes his new bike. I … think his old one was much better.
3. The Queen … will open the new bridge across the Thames.
4. Skiing … is fun, but I really hate the cold weather.
5. What a nice surprise! The children … had the idea.
6. Someone has left the windows open! – It was you …! Don't you remember?
7. What a perfect game! We … couldn't play better!
8. Look at this photo! David Alaba … signed it for me!
9. The party was a great success. The guests … told me it was great!
10. Did you like Rita's new house? – Well, the house … is very nice, but the neighbourhood is not so good.
11. Everybody liked the show, but I … thought it was terrible.
12. Grandma will leave the hospital tomorrow. She … said so.

Additional exercise Seite 172

4 Wenn man sagen will, dass man allein ist oder war: *by + ...self/...selves*

Let's go there together. ***We*** *don't want to go* ***by ourselves****.*
Gehen wir gemeinsam hin. **Wir** wollen nicht **allein** gehen.

I often see this old lady. ***She****'s always* ***by herself****.*
Ich sehe diese alte Dame oft. **Sie** ist immer **allein**.

5 Man darf die *self-pronouns* nicht mit *"each other"* oder *"one another"* (einander, gegenseitig) verwechseln.

When ***we*** *saw* ***ourselves*** *in the mirror, we couldn't help laughing.*

We *looked at* ***each other*** *and couldn't help laughing.*

6 Achtung – Falle!

Es gibt eine Reihe von **Verben**, die im Deutschen mit einem rückbezüglichen Fürwort verwendet werden, im Englischen aber nicht! Die wichtigsten sind:

We cannot ***afford*** *a hotel.*	**Wir** können **uns** kein Hotel leisten.
Joe ***apologised*** *for his mistake.*	**Joe** entschuldigte **sich** für seinen Fehler.
Jeremy has ***broken*** *his arm.*	**Jeremy** hat **sich** den Arm gebrochen.
Have you ever ***fallen in love****?*	Hast **du dich** schon einmal verliebt?
How do you ***feel****?*	Wie fühlen **Sie sich**?
The cat often ***hides*** *under the bed.*	**Die Katze** versteckt **sich** oft unter dem Bett.
I must ***hurry****.*	**Ich** muss **mich** beeilen!
You should ***lie*** *down now.*	**Du** solltest **dich** jetzt hinlegen.
Look around *the room carefully.*	Blicke **dich** sorgfältig im Zimmer um!
I'm so tired I can't ***move****.*	... müde, dass **ich mich** nicht bewegen kann.
They ***meet*** *twice a month.*	**Sie** treffen **sich** zweimal pro Monat.
The door did not ***open****.*	**Die Tür** ließ **sich** nicht öffnen.
He can't ***remember*** *us.*	**Er** kann **sich** nicht an uns erinnern.
Sit down *and be quiet!*	Setzt **euch** hin uns seid ruhig!
You should ***wash*** *your hair.*	**Du** solltest **dir** die Haare waschen!
She often ***worries*** *about us.*	**Sie** macht **sich** oft Sorgen um uns.

E 4 144 **Setze das passende *self-pronoun* im Sinne von „allein" ein.**

1. What's George doing … in the garden?
2. I hate to be … when all my friends go out.
3. Little children are not allowed to ride a lift … .
4. Grandma has been living all … for ten years now.
5. Mum says we can go skating … if we are careful.
6. Can I sit with you, boys, or do you want to be …?
7. Philip prefers working … to working in a team.
8. Sandra often plays … . I think she hasn't got any friends.
9. The fever doesn't go away …, Tom. You should see a doctor.
10. "What am I doing here all …?" Fred asked himself.

E 5 145 **Verwechslungsgefahr! *"self-pronouns"* oder *"each other"/"one another"*?**

1. Linda and Anna are good friends, but at the moment they do not speak with *themselves/each other.*
2. Linda and Anna are proud of *themselves/each other* because they won the tournament again this year.
3. My classmates ask *themselves/one another* questions before an exam.
4. The tourists did not speak German and we did not speak their language, so we spoke English with *ourselves/one another.*
5. Alice and I have been friends since we first saw *ourselves/each other.*
6. Many people talk to *themselves/one another* in their sleep.
7. You and I must speak with *ourselves/each other* before the end of the day.
8. If we help *ourselves/one another*, everything will be easier.
9. Bob and Sam hurt *themselves/each other* when their igloo collapsed.
10. Boys, you should be ashamed of *yourselves/one another* for what you have done!

Additional exercise Seite 172

E 6 146 **Übersetze die folgenden Sätze in gutes Englisch. Achte darauf, wo du ein *reflexive pronoun* brauchst und wo nicht!**

1. Am Abend mache ich mir oft Ham and Eggs.
2. Schnell, ruf die Rettung! Veronica hat sich verletzt!
3. Wir müssen uns beeilen! Unser Zug fährt (*leaves*) in zehn Minuten.
4. Kannst du dich an Rupert erinnern? Rosie hat sich in ihn verliebt.
5. Julius wird sich eines Tages umbringen, wenn er so schnell fährt!
6. Nicht vergessen, ihr müsst alle Fragen selbst beantworten!
7. Wir setzten uns auf die Bank und schauten aufs Meer hinaus.
8. Lucky brach sich beim Eislaufen den Arm.
9. Sandra fühlt sich heute nicht gut. Sie möchte alleine sein.
10. Treffen wir uns nach der Schule im Park.
11. Ich habe die Hotdogs nicht für mich gekauft, sondern (*but*) für uns alle.
12. Wir kennen das Ende der Geschichte. Robert selbst hat es uns erzählt.
13. Komm her und hilf mir! Ich kann mich nicht bewegen!
14. Fred ist ein Egoist! Er denkt nur an sich!

Additional exercise Seite 172

22. KAPITEL — *QUESTION AND NEGATION –* FRAGE UND VERNEINUNG

Wichtigste Regel: Jede Frage (mit Ausnahme der Frage nach dem Subjekt) **und jede Verneinung muss ein Hilfsverb enthalten!**
Hilfsverben sind Verben, die für sich allein keine Handlung ausdrücken. Sie treten daher gemeinsam mit einem Vollverb (Hauptzeitwort) auf.

Hilfsverben sind: **alle Formen von** ***be (am, is, are; was, were)***
alle Formen von ***have (have, has; had)***
can – could
may – must – shall
will – would
(do – does – did)

*William **can/must/will/could/shall/... play** the violin.*
*William **has/had played** the violin.*
*William **is/was playing** the violin.*

Wenn der Satz **kein Hilfsverb** enthält, bildet man Frage und Verneinung mit ***do, does*** oder ***did***.

A FRAGE UND VERNEINUNG MIT EINEM HILFSVERB

1 Entscheidungsfrage

Die Entscheidungsfrage (oder ***general question***) lässt sich mit **JA** oder **NEIN** beantworten.
Sie dient als Ausgangspunkt für alle anderen Fragen (außer der Frage nach dem Subjekt).

*English **is** my favourite subject.* — *It **will** rain soon.*
***Is** English your favourite subject?* — ***Will** it rain soon?*

2 Verneinung

*English **is** my favourite.* ► *English **is not** my favourite.*
*It **will** rain soon.* ► *It **will not** rain soon.*

Ausnahme: ***may*** und ***must***

- *You **may** watch this film.* ► Erlaubnis oder Möglichkeit
  *You **may not** watch it.* ► mildes Verbot („lieber nicht")
  *You **must not** watch it.* ► strenges Verbot („auf keinen Fall")
- *We **must** wait for Joe.* ► Gebot, Befehl („du musst")
  *We **need not** wait for Joe.* ► „du musst/brauchst nicht"

A 147 **Bilde von den folgenden Sätzen die Entscheidungsfrage und die Verneinung.**

1. Jackie is in her room.
2. Ginger and Fred were at the party.
3. I am late again.
4. Doris was in London last week.
5. Apples are cheap at the moment.
6. Celine was crying.
7. I am in your group this year.
8. Joe's parents were angry.
9. Linda is Anna's best friend.
10. The mountains are very steep.

11. Max can speak Russian.
12. We will tell you a nice story.
13. My friends could solve the riddle.
14. George would like to go now.
15. I have seen this film before.
16. Sam could hear everything.
17. Jessica will be here soon.
18. We would do it if we could.
19. Eric has written the best essay.
20. They will show the film next week.

21. Sammy has found a gold coin.
22. You may take the book. (*2 Verneinungen*)
23. Rudy is studying for his exam.
24. We have lost the match.
25. You must speak with the headmaster.
26. It was snowing heavily.
27. I have got enough money.
28. They are painting the walls.
29. I can stay out all night.
30. People were waiting for the beginning of the concert.

31. You must answer this question.
32. Grandpa is going to fix my bike.
33. Walter has gone to town.
34. Our friends can see us here.
35. We should ask Elvis for advice.
36. You may leave the room.
37. They will ask us lots of questions.
38. We may talk to Gina tomorrow.
39. The rooms were empty.
40. You would do it again.

3 Bildung der Ergänzungsfrage

- Ziel der Ergänzungsfrage ist immer **ein bestimmter Satzteil.**
- Sie lässt sich leicht **aus der Entscheidungsfrage ableiten.**
- Sie wird immer **mit einem Fragewort eingeleitet.**

*The boys **are** in the park every afternoon.*					
	Are	*the boys*	*in the park*	*every afternoon?*	▶ ***general question***
Where	***are***	*the boys*	—	*every afternoon?*	▶ ***place***
When	***are***	*the boys*	*in the park*	— ?	▶ ***time***
Who	***is***	—	*in the park*	*every afternoon?*	▶ ***subject***

*My friends **have** lost the match again.*						
	Have	*my friends*	*lost*	*the match*	*again?*	▶ ***general question***
What	***have***	*my friends*	*lost*	—	*again?*	▶ ***object***
Who	***has***	—	*lost*	*the match*	*again?*	▶ ***subject***

Achtung – Falle!
Die Frage nach dem Subjekt verlangt **immer *3rd person singular*!**

*The girls **are** in the garden.* ▶ *Who **is** in the garden?*
*My parents **were** happy.* ▶ *Who **was** happy?*
*I **am** hungry.* ▶ *Who **is** hungry?*
*We **have** all heard of you.* ▶ *Who **has** heard of me?*

Die **Fragewörter** für die Ergänzungsfragen sind:

who?	▶	**Subjekt**	*Who has seen this man?*	**(wer?)**
who(m)?	▶	**Objekt**	*Who(m) can we interview?*	**(wem? wen?)**
whose?	▶	**Besitz**	*Whose house is this?*	**(wessen?)**
what?	▶	**Objekt**	*What will we do next?*	**(was?)**
	▶	**Subjekt**	*What grows on trees?*	**(was?)**
where?	▶	**Ort**	*Where have I put my keys?*	**(wo?)**
when?	▶	**Zeit**	*When can we see Mary?*	**(wann?)**
why?	▶	**Grund**	*Why were you not there?*	**(warum?)**
how?	▶	**Art**	*How may I help you?*	**(wie?)**

A 148 **Bilde die Entscheidungsfrage und die Verneinung und stelle möglichst viele Ergänzungsfragen.**

1. Janet can play the guitar very well.
2. Sarah has got an aquarium in her room.
3. The boys are in the locker room.
4. Gina and Susan are listening to their CDs in Gina's room.
5. We must read the book at home.
6. The girls were tired because they had not eaten.
7. Lucy was in Liverpool last week.
8. Marcus could answer all the questions.
9. My parents will sell the car next year.
10. The children are going to see "West Side Story" at school.
11. Peter's car is at the mechanic's.
12. They are showing "Monk" tonight.
13. Monica's concert will be wonderful.
14. Mum has baked a cake because today is Dad's birthday.
15. We can sleep in Joe's room because he is not here.
16. The boys should go home because it's very late.
17. Our neighbours have built a new barbecue in their garden.
18. Mona was sleeping in Christopher's arms.
19. The guests have left the party because they are tired.
20. You will like Jimmy because he is very nice.
21. Bettina's necklace was very expensive.
22. We can ask Mr. Langdon everything.
23. Marie can sing well.
24. Laura must ask her parents because they are very strict.
25. Jack and Jill are going to buy the house on the hill.
26. We could leave because the concert was over.
27. Leo's father is working for Sandra's dad at the moment.
28. James will marry his girlfriend some day.
29. You must finish the report before the weekend.
30. Charlie has seen us in town.
31. The children are in Mr. Harrison's room.
32. Norah's parents should give her more pocket money.
33. Claire's Christmas tree has caught fire.
34. They have interviewed the Pope on TV.
35. Caroline will invite all her friends next week.
36. You must study hard because the next test will be difficult.
37. The papers are on Judy's desk.
38. Helen's holiday in Turkey was okay.
39. The spectators will freeze during the match because it is so cold.
40. Alex has given you the wrong telephone number.

Additional exercise Seite 173

B FRAGE UND VERNEINUNG MIT *"DO – DOES – DID"*

Wenn ein Satz **kein Hilfsverb** enthält, bildet man Frage und Verneinung auf folgende Weise:

- ***present tense*** ► ***"do (not)"*** oder ***"does (not)"***
- ***past tense*** ► ***"did (not)"***

"do", "does" und ***"did"*** werden damit zu Hilfsverben. Sie treten immer gemeinsam mit einem Vollverb auf. Dieses **Vollverb** steht immer in ***base form*** (Infinitiv, *1st form*).

1 Entscheidungsfrage und Verneinung

Entscheidungsfrage und Verneinung dienen auch hier als Ausgangspunkte für die Bildung der Ergänzungsfragen.

	The girls		***play***	*volleyball in school.*	
Do	*the girls*		***play***	*volleyball in school?*	**keine Änderungen** des Vollverbs **bei *do***
	The girls	***do not***	***play***	*volleyball in school.*	
	Jessica		***goes***	*to school in Austria.*	
Does	*Jessica*		***go***	*to school in Austria?*	***3rd person "s"*** geht vom Vollverb zu ► ***does*** Vollverb = *base form*
	Jessica	***does not***	***go***	*to school in Austria.*	
	Simon		***found***	*a $ 5 note.*	
Did	*Simon*		***find***	*a $ 5 note?*	***past tense*** geht vom Vollverb zu ► ***did*** Vollverb = *base form*
	Simon	***did not***	***find***	*a $ 5 note.*	

2 Ergänzungsfragen mit *"do – does – did"*

Wenn man die Entscheidungsfrage „gefunden" hat, lassen sich die Ergänzungsfragen leicht bilden: Man stellt die **Fragewörter** **vor *do – does – did***.

		Malcolm	***plays***	*the trumpet*	*in his room*	*every day.*
	Does	*Malcolm*	***play***	*the trumpet*	*in his room*	*every day?*
What	***does***	*Malcolm*	***play***	—	*in his room*	*every day?*
Where	***does***	*Malcolm*	***play***	*the trumpet*	—	*every day?*
		Who	***plays***	*the trumpet*	*in his room*	*every day?*
		Malcolm ***does not***	***play***	*the trumpet*	*in his room*	*every day.*

Achtung – Fallen!
- **Subjektfrage** ► **immer *3rd person singular*** ► *Who plays ...?*
- **Objektfrage mit *"who"*** ► **immer mit *"do", "does", "did"*** ► *Who(m) did you show the room?*

B 1 149 **Bilde die Entscheidungsfrage und die Verneinung.**

1. Joe's grandparents live on a farm.
2. Joe visits them every month.
3. Mr. Miller bought the farm after the war.
4. He grows wheat and sugar beets.
5. Joe keeps a horse on his granddad's farm.
6. In summer, the Millers rent rooms to tourists.
7. Some tourists help Mr. Miller with his work.
8. I stayed at the farm two years ago.
9. We liked it because there are some cows and sheep.
10. Mrs. Miller cooks wonderful dinners.
11. In spring, the doctor sent her to hospital because she had the flu.
12. Joe wants to be a farmer when he is older.
13. His dad left to study at the university.
14. Joe's mum and dad met at university.
15. Ten years later they bought a nice little house in the town.

B 1 150 **Bilde mit den Sätzen aus Übung 149 möglichst viele Ergänzungsfragen.**

B 2 151 **Stelle die Fragen nach dem Subjekt und nach den Objekten. Achte bei der Objektfrage auf das Fragewort: *"who?"* für Personen und *"what?"* für Sachen.**

1. Frank helps his friends with their homework.
2. The boys liked reggae music.
3. Betty sent her grandma a birthday telegram.
4. Fred showed me his hamster.
5. Lydia gave Harry a kiss.
6. Gina writes me a letter every week.
7. I buy her flowers.
8. The tourist asked us lots of questions.
9. We called the doctor and the ambulance.
10. My parents know everybody in this town.
11. We see the new students every day.
12. Jack's dad plans and builds houses.
13. Many people like Italian wines and cheeses.
14. Mrs. Smith watched the burglars leaving the house.

C „NICHT WAHR?"-FRAGE

Die „Nicht wahr?"-Frage stellt man, wenn man sich seiner Sache nicht ganz sicher ist. Man hängt sie einfach an die Aussage an.
Im Englischen geht das nicht ganz so einfach. Es gibt zwar dieses „Frage-Anhängsel" – ***question tag*** oder ***tag question*** genannt –, aber es sieht von Fall zu Fall anders aus.

Wir sind zu spät dran, nicht wahr? ▶ *We **are** late, **aren't** we?*
Das ist sehr kompliziert, nicht wahr? ▶ *This **is** very complicated, **isn't** it?*
Ihr wart einkaufen, nicht wahr? ▶ *You **were** shopping, **weren't** you?*
Es hat geregnet, nicht wahr? ▶ *It **has** rained, **hasn't** it?*
Joe wird wieder kommen, nicht wahr? ▶ *Joe **will** come again, **won't** he?*
Wir arbeiten schnell, nicht wahr? ▶ *We **work** fast, **don't** we?*
Ich habe gewonnen, nicht wahr? ▶ *I **won**, **didn't** I?*

Die folgenden **Hauptregeln** musst du bei der Bildung dieser Frage beachten:

- Wenn die Aussage ein **Hilfsverb** enthält, wird es im Frage-Anhängsel **weiterverwendet** (und auch in der Kurzantwort):

  *The film **was** great, **wasn't** it? – Yes, it **was**./No, it **wasn't**.*

- Wenn die Aussage ein **Vollverb** enthält, wird im Frage-Anhängsel entweder ***do – don't*** oder ***does – doesn't*** oder ***did – didn't*** verwendet.

  *Peter **likes** pizza, **doesn't** he? – Yes, he **does**./No, he **doesn't**.*
  *You **know** very much, **don't** you? – Yes, I **do**./No, I **don't**.*
  *Lisa **kissed** you, **didn't** she? – Yes, she **did**./No, she **didn't**.*

- Wenn die **Aussage positiv** (das heißt nicht verneint) ist, wird das **Frage-Anhängsel verneint**; wenn die **Aussage negativ** (also verneint) ist, wird das **Anhängsel positiv**.

Es gibt aber auch ein paar **„Nebenregeln"**, auf die du nicht vergessen darfst:

- Aussage und Anhängsel stehen in **derselben Zeitstufe** (siehe oben);
- Das Subjekt der Aussage wird durch das passende **persönliche Fürwort** ersetzt (siehe oben).
- Das Scheinsubjekt ***"there"*** (wie zB in *"There is ...", "There are ..."* usw.) wird weiterverwendet.

  ***There isn't** any orange juice left, **is there**? – Yes, **there is**./...*

Und es gibt natürlich auch **„Ausnahmen"** von diesen Regeln:

- Man sagt: *I'm **not** the last, **am** I?* **Aber:** *I'm the last, **aren't I?***
- Nach der Aufforderung ***"Let's ...!"*** sagt man ***"..., shall we?"***
- Nach der Befehlsform (zB ***"Take it!"***) sagt man ***"..., will you?"***

C 152 **Du bist dir deiner Sache nicht ganz sicher und möchtest dich vergewissern. Bilde also die *tag questions* (Frage-Anhängsel) und beantworte sie in Form von Kurzantworten (so weit vorgesehen).**

example: *You have all seen this video, ...? – Yes, we ... ./No, we ... .*
You have all seen this video, haven't you?
Yes, we have./No, we haven't.

1. Max is in his room, ...? – Yes, .../No, ...
2. Your new neighbours are nice, ...? – Yes, .../No, ...
3. Your dad was in China last month, ...? – No, ..., he was in Japan.
4. The summer holidays were too short, ...? – Yes, ... They always are.
5. We have lost again, ...? – No, ...! We've won our first game!
6. Julia will be at your party, ...? – Yes, ... And Tina will be there, too.
7. All your friends sing in a choir, ...? – Yes, ..., but I don't like singing.
8. Emily can be very arrogant, ...? – Oh, yes, ..., and that's not nice.
9. Andy has been here before, ...? – No, ... This is his first visit.
10. You won't call the police, ...? – No, I ... . Don't worry!
11. Columbus discovered America in 1492, ...? – Yes, ..., but the Vikings were there 500 years before him!
12. Jenny doesn't like Hip Hop, ...? – No, ... She prefers classic rock.
13. There is a strong smell in this room, ...? – Yes, ..., and I don't like it.
14. Stephanie hasn't answered your email, ...? – No, .../Oh yes, ...!
15. There aren't any sweets left, ...? – Oh yes, ... I didn't eat them all.
16. You haven't read this book, ...? – No, ..., but I'd like to read it now.
17. There were a lot of people at the concert, ...? – Yes, ... More than 1,000.
18. Gerald got hurt in the car crash, ...? – Yes, ..., but only a little.
19. You don't believe me, ...? – No, ... This sounds crazy.
20. I'm not on your address list, ...? – Yes, .../No, ...
21. Stop that noise, ...? – Okay, sorry!
22. Let's play "Warhammer", ...? – Oh yes, let's! Good idea!
23. I'm still your best friend, ...? – Yes, ..., and you always will be.
24. There weren't any problems, ...? – No, ..., but it wasn't easy.
25. Your mother works at the hospital, ...? – Yes, ... She's a nurse.
26. You didn't speak with Martin, ...? – No, ... Let's call him now, ...?
27. Hold this ladder for me, ...? – Sorry, I can't. I'm busy.
28. There are many pretty girls in Florida, ...? – Oh yes, ...!
29. Let's go there, ...?
30. Your dog eats carrots, ...? – No, ...! Who told you that?

Additional exercise Seite 173

23. KAPITEL | *RELATIVE CLAUSES* – RELATIVSÄTZE

Relativsätze sind Gliedsätze, die Bezüge zwischen einzelnen Teilen des Satzes herstellen und erklären. Sie werden von bezüglichen Fürwörtern eingeleitet (auch Relativpronomen oder ***relative pronouns*** genannt).

Relativpronomen sind Fürwörter, die sich auf etwas beziehen, was schon **vorher im Satz genannt** wurde. Sie folgen sofort auf dieses Bezugswort, das sieht dann so aus:

*Do you know **the man who** is watching our house?*

Zur Gruppe der ***relative pronouns*** zählen:

who – which – that – (whom) – whose – what – where – why

A *RELATIVE PRONOUNS* BEI PERSONEN

Wenn sich der Relativsatz auf eine Person bezieht, kommen die folgenden ***relative pronouns*** in Frage:

who (that)	Wenn das Bezugswort das **Subjekt** des Satzes ist, zieht man eher ***"who"*** heran; ***"that"*** ist ebenfalls denkbar.
	The people who *bought our car were lucky.* **Die Leute, die** unser Auto kauften, hatten Glück.
whose	weist auf den 2. Fall (Genitiv, *genitive*) hin und drückt **Zugehörigkeit oder Besitz** aus.
	The people whose *car has disappeared have called the police.* **Die Leute, deren** Auto verschwand, haben die Polizei gerufen.
who/whom that	Wenn das Bezugswort das **Objekt** des Satzes ist, verwendet man im modernen Englisch meist ***"who"*** oder ***"that"*** oder man lässt das Relativpronomen einfach ganz weg. (Siehe dazu auch Abschnitt 23G, Seite 136). ***"Whom"*** ist eine ältere Form, die man heute nur mehr selten antrifft, vor allem aber in Verbindung mit Präpositionen.
	The people who/that *you met last night are our friends.* *The people you met last night are our friends.* *(The people **whom** you met last night are our friends.)* ***The people (who/that)*** *you spoke **with** last night are ... .* *The people **with whom** you spoke last night are our friends.*

A 153 **Verwende *who* (auch statt *whom*) oder *whose* in den folgenden Sätzen.**

1. Mr. Frank is a teacher ... is very interested in his students.
2. "Snow White" is the story of a girl ... lives with seven dwarves.
3. The old man ... lives in this house gets angry easily.
4. The tall man ... is crossing the street over there is my new maths teacher.
5. A journalist is a person ... writes reports and interviews people.
6. I've never heard of anyone ... does not like pizza.
7. What was the name of the person ... discovered the X-rays?
8. Do you know the people ... have moved into the house next door?
9. Simon fancies a girl ... is new in his school.
10. This is the woman ... could be the first president of our country.
11. In my class, there are some kids ... home country is not Austria.
12. Are you the woman ... dog has bitten my dog? I think we must talk!
13. Do you know everybody ... will be at the party tonight?
14. You look like someone ... has just won in the lottery.
15. Is this the man ... house is for sale?
16. All the people ... were there say it was a fantastic show.
17. I don't know anybody ... smile is as pretty as yours, Judy!
18. All those pupils ... name starts with "A" or "B", please go to room 1.
19. People ... want to smoke must do so outside the building.
20. Who are you? – I am the boy ... bike has been stolen. I want to report it.
21. What do you think of the girls ... we met at Harry's party last night?
22. That's the man ... I would like to talk to.
23. Where are the passengers ... buses have not arrived yet?
24. The boy ... you are going to meet tonight is an excellent dancer.
25. I'm sorry, but nobody ... lives here knows a Mrs. James.
26. Is this the girl ... you told me about yesterday?
27. The woman ... Uncle Joe wants to marry is from Brazil.
28. I can't stand people ... idea of fun is to get drunk at the weekend.

Setze in den folgenden Sätzen das *relative pronoun* nur dort ein, wo es sein muss. Wo es möglich ist, lasse es weg.

29. The people ... live here are very poor.
30. Who is this woman? Is she somebody ... I should know?
31. I know a girl ... parents have houses in London, Paris and Rome.
32. Most of the teachers ... teach at our school are okay.
33. Is there anyone here ... name is Perkins? I've got a message for them.
34. I would like to speak with the people ... have made this stupid film.
35. The director ... new film you have just seen will now answer your questions.
36. The mechanic ... repaired my bike was very nice.
37. The mechanic ... you asked for help is my uncle.
38. Everybody ... I know thinks very much of you.
39. I like talking to people ... have the same interests as I.
40. Is this the person ... called the police and the ambulance?

Additional exercise Seite 174

B *RELATIVE PRONOUNS* BEI SACHEN

Wenn sich der Relativsatz auf eine **Sache** (ein Ding, ein Tier) bezieht, dann kommen die folgenden *relative pronouns* in Frage:

that (which)	Wenn sich der Relativsatz auf das **Subjekt** bezieht, zieht man im modernen Englisch ***"that"*** vor; ***"which"*** ist aber ebenfalls möglich.
	Birds that (which) *fly south in winter are called "migratory birds".* **Vögel, die** im Winter nach Süden fliegen, nennt man Zugvögel.
	Wenn sich der Relativsatz auf das **Objekt** bezieht, verwendet man gleichfalls eher ***"that"*** als ***"which"*** oder man lässt das *relative pronoun* ganz weg. (Siehe auch Abschnitt 23G, Seite 136.)
	The birds (that/which) *we saw at the zoo were cockatoos.* **Die Vögel, die** wir im Zoo sahen, waren Kakadus.
whose	Vertritt auch bei Sachen den Genitiv (2. Fall, *genitive*) und drückt somit **Zugehörigkeit oder Besitz** aus.
	After the tanker accident people cleaned ***the birds whose*** *feathers were covered in oil.* Nach dem Tankerunfall säuberten die Leute **die Vögel, deren** Federn voll Öl waren.

C *"THAT"*

Das Relativpronomen ***"that"*** ist ein besonderer Fall: Es kann sich sowohl auf **Sachen** als auch auf **Personen** beziehen. Und es gibt einige Fälle, in denen es besser ist, *"that"* zu verwenden.

- Wenn das „Bezugswort" aus **Personen und Nicht-Personen zugleich** besteht (was aber recht selten der Fall ist):

  Everyone watched ***the torero and the bull that*** *were fighting in the arena.*
  Alle beobachteten **den Torero und den Stier, die** in der Arena kämpften.

- Wenn das „Bezugswort" ein **Superlativ oder ein „Extremwort"** ist (wie zB *best, worst, fastest* ... oder *first, last, the only* ...):

  The Concorde is ***the fastest*** *airliner* ***that*** *was ever built.*
  Frank was ***the only*** *one* ***that*** *finished the test in time.*

D *"WHICH"*

- Wenn sich ein Relativsatz auf die **gesamte vorherige Aussage** bezieht, wird ***"which"*** als *relative pronoun* verwendet. Vor dem Relativpronomen steht dann ein **Komma** (Beistrich).

  They showed us how to bake bread in the old way. This was interesting.
  They showed us how to bake bread in the old way, which *was interesting.*

B C 154 **Setze das passende *relative pronoun* ein.**

1. They showed a picture of a calf ... had two heads and five legs.
2. The bridge ... they closed last month has been opened again.
3. They were looking for a city ... houses were made of gold.
4. Madagascar is a country ... I would like to visit one day.
5. Have you read the letter ... came today?
6. Missing the bus this morning was the best thing ... happened today.
7. Where are the books ... you borrowed last week? I need them badly.
8. Is this the horse ... parents have won so many races?
9. The first space ship ... landed on the moon was called "Eagle".
10. The flowers ... Dad bought for Mum last Friday still look good.
11. Coca Cola is a drink ... logo is known all over the world.
12. Mum says that "Cats" is the most wonderful musical ... she has ever seen.
13. I've seen all the films ... were made in these studios.
14. Children prefer books ... have lots of pictures.
15. The pictures ... we took of Fred and Gina can be seen on the internet.
16. This is not the answer ... I was waiting for.
17. They say you are the last person ... saw Mary before she disappeared.
18. A car ... brakes don't work is a dangerous thing.
19. Dad wants to sell the car ... he bought last year because it's too slow.

D 155 **Verbinde die folgenden Satzpaare mit Hilfe von *"which"*. Vergiss dabei nicht auf den Beistrich!**

example: *We spent three weeks in the mountains. This was quite expensive.* ►
We spent three weeks in the mountains, which was quite expensive.

1. Mona said she would come to my party. This was a great surprise.
2. Sometimes Dad tries to dance boogie. This looks rather funny.
3. Joe decided to stay at home on the day of the maths test. This was stupid.
4. Eric says that he is my boyfriend. This is not true!
5. They reached the top of the mountain after six hours. This was fantastic.
6. Ben ran the mile in less than four minutes. This was a new record for him.
7. Betty cannot find her favourite mascot. This makes her very sad.
8. They say Dennis has stolen some money. This I cannot believe!
9. Victor passed the test with 100 per cent. This is what we had all expected.
10. My brother broke Mum's favourite vase. This cost him a lot of money.
11. Henry often uses my things without asking. I don't like this.
12. I won the tournament. Nobody had thought that I could do it.
13. Peter said I should jump from the 10 m board. I refused to do it.
14. Norma had to write the whole text again. This made her very angry.
15. Gillian and Terry are getting married in May. This will be a shock to Jamie.
16. We've won four matches so far. This gives us the chance to win the series.
17. Cynthia told me she loved me. This is wonderful news.
18. Leslie is going back to Canada next month. Everybody feels sorry about it.
19. I got an "F" in my English test. I didn't want you to know about it.

E *"WHAT"*

Das Relativpronomen ***"what"*** leitet einen Objektsatz ein. Vor *"what"* steht kein Komma.

*I have no idea **what** this means.*	(... **was** das bedeutet.)
*Do you know **what** Judy wants?*	(... **was** Judy will?)
*Can you hear **what** I say?*	(... **was** ich sage?)

F *"WHERE" – "WHY"*

Wenn das Bezugswort eine **Ortsangabe** ist, verwendet man ***"where"*** als *relative pronoun*. Wenn man den **Grund** angibt, verwendet man ***"why"***.

*Last summer we visited Salzburg, **the city where** Mozart was born.*
*You are **the reason why** we are here. We must ask you some questions.*

G *CONTACT CLAUSES* – RELATIVSÄTZE OHNE RELATIVPRONOMEN

Unter bestimmten Bedingungen kann der Relativsatz auch ohne Relativpronomen auskommen. Man nennt diese Sätze *contact clauses*, weil der Relativsatz in direktem Kontakt mit dem Bezugswort steht, also ohne „dazwischen geschaltetes" Relativpronomen.

1 *Contact clauses*

sind immer dann möglich, wenn sich der Relativsatz auf das **Objekt** im Satz bezieht. Das ist sehr leicht zu erkennen – auf das Relativpronomen folgt **kein Verb**!

mit Relativpronomen:	*That's **the man who(m)** you met yesterday.* *Where's **the CD that (which)** I left on my desk?*
ohne Relativpronomen:	*That's **the man** ❖ you met yesterday.* *Where's **the CD** ❖ I left on my desk?*

2 Verbindung von zwei Sätzen:

***The girl** is my cousin Liz. I talked to **her** at the party.*
*The girl **who/whom/that** I talked to at the party is my cousin Liz.*
► *The girl ❖ I talked to at the party is my cousin Liz.*

*I like **the T-shirt**. You were wearing **it** yesterday.*
*I like the T-shirt **that/which** you were wearing yesterday.*
► *I like the T-shirt ❖ you were wearing yesterday.*

! Du darfst **nur *who(m), which* und *that*** weglassen.
Whose darfst du **niemals weglassen**!

E F 156 **Setze ein: *"which"* (mit Komma, auf den ganzen Satz bezogen), *"what"* (ohne Komma, anstelle eines Objekts), *"where"* (auf eine Ortsangabe bezogen) oder *"who"* (für einen Grund)?**

1. I have no idea ... 's in this box. Do you know?
2. Mum made steak for dinner last night ... was great.
3. Who can tell me ... *"Meinung"* means in English?
4. This is the place ... Mum and Dad met for the first time.
5. The reason ... I'm here is that I need your advice!
6. Believe me, I always mean ... I say; I don't lie!
7. Does anyone know ... the film is about? – I think it's about penguins.
8. The "White House" is the place ... the President of the USA lives and works.
9. Helen ate all the donuts ... was extremely unfair of her.
10. I can't remember ... we have to do for biology tomorrow. Can you?
11. Nobody knew ... to do when Felix collapsed during the match.
12. Greta has offered to help us with the decorations ... is very nice of her.
13. The penguin film was excellent ... surprised a lot of people.
14. Can you show me the shop ... you bought these jeans?
15. Tommy came back at 1 o'clock in the morning ... was too late.
16. The reason ... we are staying at this hotel is that all the others were full.
17. Luke wants to show us ... he has bought in his holidays.
18. Who has an idea ... we can go after the concert tomorrow?

G 1 157 **Relativsatz mit oder ohne *relative pronoun*? Setze es ein, wo es sein muss, und lasse es weg, wo es möglich ist.**

1. Are these the people ... children go to your school?
2. The person ... I like least is Mrs. Jackson. She is horrible!
3. The girl ... lives next door is my best friend.
4. Is this the song ... they played at the party? I think it's great!
5. The films ... are on at the cinema this week are not worth seeing.
6. Will the person ... car is blocking the street please drive it away?
7. Gina says the people ... she met at Joe's party were silly and arrogant.
8. Did you show Mike the place ... you had the accident last year?
9. I don't understand ... you are telling lies about me!
10. We don't like the stories ... people tell about you. Are they true?

G 2 158 **Verbinde die folgenden Sätze miteinander, indem du Relativsätze bildest. Lasse das Relativpronomen weg, wo es geht.**

1. Where did you put the books? They were lying on the table.
2. I liked the house. President Washington lived there.
3. Some of the books were very interesting. We read them at school last year.
4. I feel sorry for the people. Their dog ran away a few days ago.
5. We have just had a telephone call from a man. He wants to buy our car.
6. The film was really exciting. You told us about it.
7. Gloria has asked me to go to the dance with her. This is wonderful.
8. Frank has a new sweater. He wants to wear it day and night.

Additional exercise Seite 174

H EINSCHRÄNKENDE UND ERWEITERNDE RELATIVSÄTZE

Ein Relativsatz kann für das Verstehen eines Satzes unbedingt erforderlich sein, oder er liefert uns „nur" zusätzliche Informationen (die wir aber gar nicht wirklich benötigen, um den Sinn des Satzes zu begreifen).

1 Einschränkende Relativsätze

Where is the man?
The boys are here now.
I like the pictures.

▶ Wenn wir diese Sätze **so** stehen lassen, weiß niemand, welchen Mann, welche Buben oder welche Bilder wir meinen. Wir müssen also **genauer** sein und die Möglichkeiten **einschränken**.

*Where is **the man who lives here**?*
***The boys (who) we were talking about** are here now.*
*I like **the pictures that were painted by Klimt**.*

▶ Jetzt sind alle Aussagen eindeutig und verständlich.

Ein Relativsatz, der die Zahl der Möglichkeiten auf einen bestimmten Fall einengt, heißt **einschränkender Relativsatz**. Er ist **für das eindeutige Verstehen des Satzes erforderlich.**

„Regeln" für den einschränkenden Relativsatz – auf Englisch ***"defining relative clause"***:

- Er folgt **ohne Kommas** direkt auf das Bezugswort.
- ***"contact clauses"*** sind **möglich**. Das heißt, das *relative pronoun* kann wegfallen, wenn sich das Relativpronomen auf das Objekt des Satzes bezieht.

2 Erweiternde Relativsätze

Where is Mr. Smithers?
Randy and Mike are here now.
I like "The Kiss".

▶ Diese Sätze sind ohne Probleme zu verstehen, weil wir genau wissen, wer oder was gemeint ist. Wir brauchen also keine weitere Einschränkung der Möglichkeiten.

*Where is **Mr. Smithers, who lives in this house?***
***Randy and Mike, who(m) we were talking about,** are here now.*
*I like **"The Kiss", which was painted by Klimt**.*

▶ Hier liefern uns die Relativsätze nur zusätzliche (oder erweiternde) Informationen, die wir für das eindeutige Verstehen des Satzes nicht wirklich brauchen.

Ein Relativsatz, der zusätzliche Informationen bietet, heißt **erweiternder Relativsatz.** Er ist **für das Verstehen des Satzes nicht erforderlich.**

„Regeln" für den erweiternden Relativsatz – auf Englisch ***"non-defining relative clause"***:

- Er wird **durch Kommas** vom Hauptsatz getrennt.
- ***"contact clauses"*** sind **nicht möglich**. Das heißt, das *relative pronoun* darf unter keinen Umständen wegfallen.
- ***"that"*** kommt nicht vor; stattdessen werden ***"who"*** (für Personen) und ***"which"*** (für Sachen) verwendet.

H 159 **„Einschränkend" oder „erweiternd"? Kommas oder keine Kommas? Setze *relative pronouns* und Beistriche dort ein, wo sie sein müssen, und lasse sie dort weg, wo das sein kann oder muss.**

1. This is Mrs. Norris ... will cook for us tonight.
2. The people ... work in the hotel are from all over the world.
3. Hurricane Katrina ... hit the Gulf Coast in 2005 caused a lot of damage.
4. The woman ... answered the phone said that you were not at home.
5. My mum doesn't have a driving licence ... means she isn't allowed to drive.
6. The Battle of Hastings ... was fought in 1066 changed the history of Britain.
7. Do you know the children ... are playing in front of the house?
8. Mount Vernon ... was the home of President Washington is near the river.
9. George Washington ... home is called Mount Vernon was the first president.
10. The hospital ... my dad works is famous for its heart transplants.
11. I think they have found the girls ... have been missing since Saturday.
12. Joe lives in Oakdale ... is about 70 miles from San Francisco.
13. The sun ... was standing directly above us was very hot that day.
14. An old man ... English was very bad tried to tell us the way.
15. The person ... wins the jackpot will be very rich.
16. I have never visited Moscow ... is the capital of the world's largest country.

Additional exercise Seite 174

H 160 **Verknüpfe die folgenden Sätze durch die Bildung von Relativsätzen.**

example: *The song is called "Satisfaction". They are playing it right now.* ▶
The song they are playing right now is called "Satisfaction".
Toni Sailer won four gold medals in 1956. He lived in Kitzbühel. ▶
Toni Sailer, who lived in Kitzbühel, won four gold medals in 1956.

1. Mrs. Klein is my favourite teacher. She is my mother's best friend.
2. The mountain is called Vesuvius. It rises behind Naples.
3. What's the phone number of the girl? You've just talked to her.
4. Charlie hasn't answered any of my emails. This makes me quite mad.
5. Leo and Claire played Romeo and Juliet. They are both very good actors.
6. Police are looking for a man. His car was found near the lake.
7. Did you like the film? We talked about it last week.
8. The Volga is Europe's longest river. It empties into the Caspian Sea.
9. This must be the boy group. Their latest song is the current Number One.
10. The dress is from Paris. Mum is wearing it tonight.
11. Jamie bought an old motorbike. Its engine does not run properly.
12. The burglars took only an oil painting. It was worth thousands of dollars.
13. The oil painting was worth thousands of dollars. The burglars took it.
14. Tarzan was the king of the jungle. He grew up among wild animals.
15. John Grisham writes mostly thrillers. His books have been translated into several languages.

24. KAPITEL — *SINGULAR AND PLURAL* – EINZAHL UND MEHRZAHL

Das „Problem“ Einzahl oder Mehrzahl betrifft das Hauptwort (Nomen, *noun*).

A BILDUNG DER REGELMÄSSIGEN MEHRZAHL

- Die regelmäßige Mehrzahl ***(regular plural)*** bildest du, indem du ***"s"*** an das Hauptwort anhängst. Wenn das Hauptwort mit einem Zischlaut endet, hängst du ***"es"*** an. Zischlaute sind [s, z, ks, ʃ, tʃ, dʒ].

plural with -s	*plural with -(e)s* [iz]
book ▶ *book**s***	*cheese* ▶ *chees**es***
ring ▶ *ring**s***	*badge* ▶ *badg**es***
map ▶ *map**s***	*bus* ▶ *bus**es***
table ▶ *table**s***	*watch* ▶ *watch**es***

- Beim Anhängen von *"s"* oder *"es"* muss man allerdings die **Rechtschreibung** beachten. Hier sind die wichtigsten „Fallen“:

Konsonant + *y* ▶ *-ies*	*-f(e)* ▶ *-ves*	Konsonant + *o* ▶ *-oes*
lady ▶ *lad**ies*** *party* ▶ *part**ies*** *city* ▶ *cit**ies***	*calf* ▶ *cal**ves*** *leaf* ▶ *lea**ves*** *knife* ▶ *kni**ves***	*potato* ▶ *potat**oes*** *tomato* ▶ *tomat**oes*** *motto* ▶ *motto**(e)s***
	Achtung! – Gilt nicht für alle Wörter!	
	zB: *roof* ▶ *roof**s***	*ghetto* ▶ *ghett**os*** *photo* ▶ *phot**os***

B BILDUNG DER UNREGELMÄSSIGEN MEHRZAHL

Nicht alle Hauptwörter bilden die Mehrzahl mit *-(e)s*. In diesem Fall sprechen wir von der unregelmäßigen Mehrzahl ***(irregular plural)***. Diese Gruppe umfasst nicht sehr viele Wörter; die wichtigsten findest du hier. Du solltest sie auf jeden Fall kennen und anwenden können.

man	▶	***men***	*tooth*	▶	***teeth***	*mouse*	▶	***mice***
woman	▶	***women***	*foot*	▶	***feet***	*sheep*	▶	***sheep***
child	▶	***children***	*goose*	▶	***geese***	*fish*	▶	***fish***

A 161 **Setze die folgenden Sätze in die Mehrzahl. Beachte dabei besonders die unterstrichenen Wörter.**

1. On the wall of the room there was a photo of the sea.
2. New York is a large city. *(Tokyo and Mexico …)*
3. A book is often better than a film.
4. The hunter was attacked by a wolf.
5. Mum needs a potato and a tomato for the soup.
6. The desk is full of paper.
7. Please put the clothes in the box.
8. The bus and the train leave in ten minutes.
9. Our next door neighbour is an old lady. *(… two …)*
10. The snow must be removed from the roof.
11. A baby needs a lot of sleep.
12. A bird can fly. *(Most …)*

B 162 **Setze auch diese Sätze in die Mehrzahl. Achte wieder auf die unterstrichenen Wörter.**

1. This woman works in a factory.
2. The sheep ran away and the dog ran after it.
3. The nurse told the child a good-night story.
4. Don't cross this line with your foot.
5. The dentist pulled out my grandpa's last tooth.
6. The bush in our garden is full of raspberries.
7. I often put a berry in my yoghurt.
8. Do you know the man over there?
9. You can catch a mouse with this trap.
10. After the night frost, the last leaf fell from the tree.
11. Listen, the child is crying!
12. They say a horse can be quite stubborn.

C HAUPTWÖRTER OHNE EINZAHL – *NOUNS WITHOUT SINGULAR*

- Die englische Sprache kennt eine Reihe von Hauptwörtern, die **nur in der Mehrzahl** vorkommen, während sie im Deutschen in der Einzahl auftreten. Auch das Verb hat dann die Mehrzahlform. Wichtige Wörter aus dieser Gruppe sind:

glasses	*jeans*	*pants*	*pyjamas*	*scales*	*scissors*	*shorts*	*trousers*
Brille	Jeans	Hose	Pyjama	Waage	Schere	(kurze) Hose	(lange)

Diese Wörter kannst du auch mit ***"a pair of ..."*** verwenden:
I can't read this text. I think I need (a pair of) glasses.

- Außerdem gibt es Hauptwörter, die **auf *-s* enden, aber wie in der Einzahl verwendet** werden. Auch das Verb steht dann im Singular. Dazu gehören:

gymnastics	*maths/mathematics*	*news*	*physics*	*sports*
Gymnastik	Mathe/Mathematik	Nachricht(en)	Physik	Sport

I don't do much sports, but gymnastics is okay.
You can't come tonight? That's bad news!
The latest news is that Joe will leave hospital tomorrow.
Betty thinks maths is boring, but physics is her favourite this year.

Besonderheit:

person ► *singular*
people ► *plural*

*Jack Smith is **a** nice **person**.* ► *The Smiths are nice **people**.*
*Not **a single person** was there.* ► ***Lots of people** were there.*

D HAUPTWÖRTER OHNE MEHRZAHL – *NOUNS WITHOUT PLURAL*

- Hauptwörter, die keine Mehrzahl haben, bezeichnen **Sachen, die man nicht zählen kann**. Zu dieser Gruppe gehören etwa:

gold – iron – milk – money – music – water – wine – time – ...

- Die Gruppe schließt aber auch Wörter ein, die **im Deutschen schon zählbar** sind, wie zum Beispiel:

advice	*bread*	*furniture*	*information*	*work*
Rat	Brot	Möbel	Information	Arbeit

Ich brauche einen Rat! ► *I need some advice.*

- **Einige Hauptwörter** sind je nach Verwendung **entweder zählbar oder unzählbar**.
*Old Mr. Brown has only a few **hairs** left.* ≠ *Tina has dyed her **hair**.*

E "MUCH ≠ LITTLE" UND "MANY ≠ FEW"

- Ob man ***"much ≠ little"*** oder ***"many ≠ few"*** verwendet, hängt davon ab, ob etwas zählbar oder nicht zählbar ist.

much ≠ little	*many ≠ few*
■ heißt **viel ≠ wenig**	■ heißt **viele ≠ wenige**
■ bei **nicht zählbaren** Sachen	■ bei **zählbaren** Sachen
■ das nachfolgende Hauptwort steht immer in der **Einzahl**	■ das nachfolgende Hauptwort steht immer in der **Mehrzahl**

- Verwende ***"much"*** und ***"many"*** vor allem **in Verneinung und Frage** (besonders *"how much?"* und *"how many?"*).

  *Did you see **many** lions in Africa?*
  *Let's go! There is**n't much** time left.*

- Verwende ***"much"*** und ***"many"*** auch **nach *"too"* und *"so"***.

  *There was **so much** snow that we could not go skiing.*
  ***Too many** people have nothing to eat.*

- Verwende ***"a lot of"*** oder ***"lots of"*** in „normalen" Aussagesätzen, vor allem anstelle von *"much"*.

  ***Lots of** people spend their holidays in the mountains. (or: **Many** people ...)*
  *My parents paid **a lot of** money for our new house. (≠ ... much money ...)*

- Verwende ***"not enough"*** statt *"too few"*. Aber – ***"too little"*** ist in Ordnung.

  *There were **not enough** people to organise a football match.*
  *I have **too little** time (= not enough time) to finish the task today.*

E 163 **Setze *"much, many, a lot of, lots of"* ein (1 bis 8) und *"little/few"* (9 bis 12).**

1. We visited ... wonderful churches while we were in Rome last week.
2. There was so ... ice on the roads that Dad did not want to drive.
3. We have to read 25 pages for tomorrow! – Wow, that sounds like ... work!
4. There are ... discos in the town, so you can have ... fun if you like dancing.
5. I have ... friends, but not so ... time to see them during the week.
6. ... children are afraid of the dark.
7. How ... is this T-shirt, please? – It's 15 £. – What? That's too ...!
8. Grandpa has ... time for his hobbies because he doesn't work ... any more.
9. There's enough mineral water, but only ... coke. I'm sorry.
10. Hurry up if you want one of the CDs! There are only ... left.
11. ... people in Austria speak Chinese perfectly.
12. During the school year I have ... time for sport, so I do it in summer.

Additional exercise Seite 175

F ALL – EVERY – EACH – SOME – NONE

Auch diese Wörter richten sich nach Einzahl und Mehrzahl.

1 all

- heißt **„alle"** und meint die **Gesamtmenge**; das Hauptwort steht im **Plural**:

  *At night, **all cats** are grey.*
  ***All boys** like football.*

- heißt **„ganz"** und meint eine **Zeitdauer**; das Hauptwort steht im **Singular**.

  *You can't stay out **all night**.* (die ganze Nacht)
  *The hotel stays open **all winter**.* (den ganzen Winter)

- mit ***"all the"*** oder ***"all of the"*** meint man **alle aus einer Gruppe**; das Hauptwort steht im **Plural**:

  *You can ask **all the girls** in my class.*
  ***All of the people** at your party wanted to speak with me.*

2 every – each

- ***"every"*** heißt **„jeder"** und bezieht sich auf die **Gesamtmenge**; das Hauptwort steht im **Singular**:

  *At night, **every cat** is grey.*
  ***Every boy** wants to play football like Ronaldinho.*

- ***"each"*** oder ***"each of"*** heißt **„jeder (einzelne)"** und bezieht sich auf eine **Teilmenge**; das Hauptwort steht im **Singular**:

  ***Each day of the week** has 24 hours.*
  *The police talked to **each of the people in the house**.*

3 some

- heißt **„einige"** aus einer **Gesamtmenge** und bezeichnet **zählbare** Sachen:

  ***Some boys** hate football.*
  *We saw **some** interesting **pictures** at the gallery.*

- heißt **„etwas"** von einer **Gesamtmenge** und bezeichnet **nicht zählbare** Sachen:

  *We need **some time** to finish the project.*
  *I've got **some orange juice**, but there's nothing to eat in the fridge.*

4 none of

- heißt **„keine"**, meist aus einer **Teilmenge**; das Hauptwort steht im **Plural**:

  ***None of the men** could help us.*
  ***None of these things** is true.*

F 164 **Setze die passenden Wörter ein:**

1. My friends go to the sports center ... Saturday. They stay there ... morning.
2. ... year has 365 days, but a leap year has 366.
3. I've asked ... people in my class, but ... them has seen my mobile phone.
4. My dad likes books by Donna Leon, but he says ... are better than others.
5. Can I have ... money, Dad? I have to buy lunch at school today.
6. Jack gets his pocket money ... Sunday for the following week.
7. My mum has painted ... the pictures in this room.
8. Sometimes, when she feels like it, she paints ... day.
9. ... my friends know where Emma lives. I've asked them ... .
10. Look, Grandma has taken ... her pills. We have to get her new ones.
11. We've waited for you ... afternoon, Joe. Where have you been?
12. I think I need ... sugar and flour and ... eggs for this cake.
13. ... bottle of wine on this shelf costs more than 50 £.
14. ... football matches last 90 minutes.
15. Judy watches the news on TV ... evening.
16. I've sent Sylvia five emails, but she has answered ... them.
17. Dad brought me a souvenir from ... of the cities he visited.
18. ... of the people in our street have pets and ... don't.
19. Norman has asked ... the girls in his class for a date, but ... them wants to go out with him.
20. ... day has 24 hours, and ... hour has 60 minutes.
21. James Dean made only three films, but ... of them was great.
22. What a mess! ... the CDs is where it should be!
23. Charlie says he has danced with ... girl at the party.
24. Dad is very tired. He's worked very hard ... week.
25. We waited for ... time, but nobody came, so ... of us wanted to go home.
26. The test was quite difficult, but I think I've answered ... the questions.
27. Can I have ... apple juice, Mum? – I'm sorry, Dora, but ... the bottles are empty. I think your friends drank ... the juice last night.
28. Have you really spoken with ... people on your team? – Yes, I have, but ... them can play tomorrow.
29. There were lots of presents under the Christmas tree, and ... of them were for me.
30. Patrick has three brothers, and ... of them play hockey.

Additional exercise Seite 175

25. KAPITEL *"SOME" & "ANY"*

Die beiden Wörter bedeuten das Gleiche: „etwas" oder „einige". Man darf sie aber nicht nach Belieben verwenden, denn es gibt wieder ein paar wichtige „Regeln".
Das Gleiche gilt auch für die **Zusammensetzungen mit *"some"* und *"any"***:

something/anything
somebody/anybody
someone/anyone
somewhere/anywhere

A *"SOME"*

Du verwendest ***"some"*** und die Zusammensetzungen mit *"some"* in den folgenden Fällen:

- **Aussagen ohne Verneinung**

  *I've seen **some** interesting films this month.*
  ***Something** smells funny in this room!*
  *I can't find my glasses, but they must be here **somewhere**.*

- **Fragen mit erwarteter positiver Antwort**

  *Mum, can I have **something** to drink, please**?***
  *Can I see **some** of your new pictures, Joe**?***
  *Has **somebody** seen the new King Kong movie**?***

B *"ANY"*

Du verwendest ***"any"*** und die Zusammensetzungen mit *"any"* in den folgenden Fällen:

- **Aussagen mit Verneinung**

  *We have**n't** seen **any** interesting films this month.*
  *I **can't** smell **anything** strange.*
  *Dad did**n't** stop **anywhere** between London and Glasgow.*

- **Fragen mit jeder möglichen Antwort**

  *Is there **anything** to drink in the fridge, Mum**?***
  *Were there **any** of your friends at the party**?***

- ***"if-clauses"***

  ***If** you find my glasses **anywhere**, please let me know.*
  *I'll help you with your homework **if** you've got **any**.*

- **Aussagen, in denen *"any"* „beliebig" bedeutet**

  *You can look at **any** room in the house except my room.*
  *Grandma said she would cook us **anything** we liked.*

A B 165 **Bilde die Entscheidungsfragen *(general questions)* und die Verneinung *(negation)* mit den folgenden Sätzen.**

1. I've got some news from Edwin. (Bilde die Frage mit *"you"*.)
2. Joe has told us something about an old mine in the woods. (... *"you"*.)
3. There were some interesting people at the party.
4. I need some help with this exercise. (Bilde die Frage mit *"you"*.)
5. We know someone who can show us the way.
6. I can tell you something about Mary that nobody else knows. (... *"you"*.)
7. They left the letter somewhere in this room.
8. There is some coffee left in the thermos.
9. Mr. Smith said something about the exam next week.
10. They will ask us some silly questions.
11. Tony has written some books about famous people.
12. There is somebody at the door.

A B 166 **Setze *"some"* oder *"any"* ein.**

1. Terry is not in his room, but he must be ...where in the house.
2. I tried to get Mum ... flowers on Valentine's Day, but they didn't have ... .
3. The Rocky Mountains are wonderful. I've never seen ...thing like them.
4. Can ...body help me with this text? I don't know ... of the new words.
5. ...thing must be wrong with Mike. I haven't seen him for days.
6. If ...one wants to leave before the end of the game, now is the time.
7. You can ask Kevin ...thing you like about physics, he will know the answer.
8. You can call me ... time you like if you need ... help.
9. If you have enough money, you can buy ...thing you like.
10. For this cake, you need ... hazelnuts, but don't put ... raisins in it.
11. It took me ... time to finish the project, but it was very good.
12. Do you take ... sugar with your tea, Mrs. Jones?
13. I need ... paper for the printer, Dad. Have you got ... at your office?
14. I have ... orange sweaters and ... blue ones, but I haven't got ... black ones.
15. If I had ... black sweaters, I would take them with me on the trip.
16. This moped is okay, but I want ...thing different, ...thing more powerful!
17. Listen, ...one is knocking at the door! – Really? I can't hear ...thing.
18. They didn't have ... fishburgers, so I bought ... chickenburgers.
19. There were ... interesting people at the conference, but I did not really speak with ... of them.
20. There's ...one on the phone for you, Dad. He says he is calling from ...where in the USA.

Additional exercise Seite 175

26. KAPITEL | *THE WORD ORDER* – DIE WORTSTELLUNG

Die Grundformel für die englische ***word order*** lautet:

A S A P O A

A DIE „ERSTE REGEL" DER *WORD ORDER*

- Das **Subjekt** steht immer **vor** dem **Prädikat.**
- Das **Objekt** steht immer **sofort nach** dem **Prädikat.**
- **Niemals** steht ein Wort **zwischen Prädikat und Objekt.**

S	P	O
Max	*likes*	*basketball.*
We	*found*	*the books.*
Joe	*has opened*	*the windows.*

B DIE „ZWEITE REGEL" DER *WORD ORDER*

- **Orts- und Zeitangaben** stehen normalerweise **am Satzende**, und zwar in der Reihenfolge **Ort vor Zeit** (*place before time*).
- Bei **zwei Zeitangaben** am Satzende steht **die genauere vor der allgemeinen.**
- Wenn man Ort und/oder Zeit des Geschehens **hervorheben** will, kann man die Angaben auch **an den Satzanfang** stellen.

	Dad	***studies***	***documents***	***in his office***	***every morning.***
	Dad	***studies***	***documents***	***at 10 a.m.***	***every morning.***
Every morning	***Dad***	***studies***	***documents***	***in his office.***	

C DIE „DRITTE REGEL" DER *WORD ORDER*

Das **Häufigkeitsadverb** ***(adverb of frequency)*** steht:

- **zwischen Subjekt und** einteiligem **Prädikat**;
- **nach dem ersten Prädikatsteil** bei mehrteiligen Prädikaten;
- **nach** der Form von ***to be***.

Max		*often*	*plays*	*basketball.*
You	*have*	*never*	*seen*	*this film.*
Joe	*is*	*always*		*in trouble.*

A B 167 **Bilde sinnvolle Sätze mit den vorhandenen Satzteilen. Überlege, ob du irgendetwas besonders hervorheben willst.**

1. Victor – in – is playing – the school orchestra – the trumpet – today
2. on Sunday – have – we – no school
3. € 5 – sends – me – Grandma – every week
4. Sheila – lots of – in her room – posters – has got
5. every autumn – burns – our neighbour – the dead leaves – in the garden
6. watch – at 4 p.m. – Gina and Jenny – every day – their favourite TV show
7. the books – can – you – put – on the shelves
8. every evening – watch – my parents – on TV – the news
9. a wallet – has – Joe – found – in the park
10. every afternoon – plays – David – in his room – computer games
11. in Paris – last summer – Mum – a beautiful blouse – bought
12. in the park – are playing – football – the boys

C 168 **Setze die *frequency adverbs* an die richtige Stelle.**

1. Children are afraid of the dark. (*often*)
2. I read the sports pages of the newspaper. (*always*)
3. You will see these people again. (*never*)
4. Mum takes the bus to work. (*usually*)
5. Dad helps me with my homework. (*sometimes*)
6. We play games in our English lessons. (*hardly ever*)
7. It rains in the Sahara. (*seldom*)
8. My bus is late. (*often*)
9. Grandpa has been to America. (*never*)
10. Julie goes to the disco on Saturday. (*sometimes*)
11. You should be polite to older people. (*always*)
12. We go to the mountains in summer. (*usually*)

ABC 169 **Bilde sinnvolle Sätze aus den durcheinander geratenen „Worthaufen". Du musst dabei alle Regeln – von A bis C – beachten.**

1. when – I – there – need – there – is – him – Dad – always
2. we – on – no – Friday – have – English
3. every – has – tea – Mum – for – morning – breakfast
4. milk – there – bottle – is – the – hardly – in – any – left
5. girl – this – from – know – school – I
6. our – meet – friends – at – often – we – the – weekend
7. by himself – Joe – homework – usually – his – does
8. has got – computers – in his room – three – Jack
9. Dad – breakfast – always – at – reads – newspaper – the
10. garden – in – our – summer – in – we – parties – sometimes – have
11. tired – Grandpa – evening – often – in – is – the
12. often – been – have – to Rome – in spring – Jill and Jody

ADDITIONAL EXERCISES – ZUSÄTZLICHE ÜBUNGSSÄTZE

1. KAPITEL – *ADJECTIVE*

C 1

Setze ein: *"one"* oder *"ones"* statt eines Nomens.

1. The old house was okay, but the new ... is much better.
2. Can I have a hammer, please? – Do you want the big ... or the small ...?
3. Oh, I see you've got new skis! What did you do with the old ...?
4. We'll have to get a better PC. This ... is too slow.
5. Bob is a fantastic dancer. I've never danced with a better ... .
6. Peter's dad has got a wine cellar with lots of red wines and a few white ... .
7. Look at these shoes! Aren't they fantastic? I like the ... on the right best.
8. Cinderella put the good peas in the pot and she fed the bad ... to the birds.
9. There are two more buses tonight. You can take the next ... or the last ... .
10. Which group won the first prize? – We did. We were the lucky ... .
11. Put the heavy books on the desk and the smaller ... on the shelf, please.
12. Shall we take the big room on the ground floor or the small ... on the first?
13. They call Michael "the honest ..." because he never tells lies.
14. Do you know those boys over there? – Oh, yes, I do. The tall ... is my cousin Frank, and the fat ... is his friend Paul.
15. Mum, where are my socks? – The white ... are in your dresser and the black ... are still in the laundry.
16. A clever fisherman keeps the big fish and throws the small ... back into the water.

D 2

Bringe die Adjektive in die richtige Reihenfolge.

1. hair – long, wonderful, black
2. jeans – blue, new, clean
3. some chocolate – Swiss, dark, excellent
4. a chair – old, expensive, wooden
5. a dress – black, old, simple
6. flowers – horrible, plastic, pink
7. a man – friendly, black, old
8. eyes – beautiful, big, blue
9. a mask – old, expensive, wooden, Chinese
10. a car – small, red, Italian
11. operas – modern, interesting
12. a document – Latin, old, important
13. a city – American, fascinating, big
14. a carpet – Turkish, red and green, valuable
15. a composer – famous, modern, Austrian
16. a box – metal, big, black

E 3 **Beende die folgenden Sätze mit passenden Komparativen.**

1. You looked very sad yesterday, but today you look a lot (*happy*) ... .
2. I was late for school this morning. Tomorrow I have to get up (*early*) ... .
3. Aunt Jane takes her tea without sugar. I like it a little (*sweet*) ... .
4. The car was quite cheap. We thought it would be (*expensive*) ... .
5. It was very hot in Kenya. I like places (*good*) ... where it's (*cool*) ... .
6. You are here already? We thought you would come (*late*) ... .
7. I don't like sitting next to the window. Let's find a table (*far*) ... away.
8. This book is boring! I hope the next one will be (*exciting*) ... .
9. You look horrible in this dress! Haven't you got anything (*pretty*) ...?
10. You did quite well this time, Joe. Your first game was a lot (*bad*) ... .
11. Don't give up hope, Michael. Things can only get (*good*) ... from now on.
12. Did you have enough to eat or would you like (*much*) ...?
13. Which is (*near*) ..., the bus stop or the train station?
14. This is too much homework, Mr. Smith! Please give us (*little*) ... to do!
15. The exam was rather easy. We had thought it would be (*difficult*) ... .
16. This isn't a very good story. I'm sure you can do (*good*) ... .

E F 4 **Finde passende Formen der angegebenen Adjektive und setze sie ein.**

1. Which do you like (*good*) ..., pizza or spaghetti?
2. All my friends think that French is (*difficult*) ... to learn than English.
3. The (*bad*) ... film of all times was "The Attack of the Killer Tomatoes".
4. This year, I get (*much*) ... money for babysitting than last year.
5. My new PC was (*cheap*) ... than I had thought, so I could buy some CDs, too.
6. Today is the (*happy*) ... of my life – Jessica has kissed me!
7. I've read that the (*dangerous*) ... animal on earth is a spider.
8. "Psycho" was one of the (*exciting*) ... films that I've ever seen.
9. Old cars aren't as (*fast*) ... as new ones, but they look much (*good*) ... .
10. You are lucky! Your exam was not as (*hard*) ... as ours. That's unfair!
11. Joe says he has (*many*) ... CDs than I, but that's not true.
12. "The Rolling Stones" are the (*successful*) ... rock band of all times.
13. Is Rome (*far*) ... from here than Munich?
14. Which is (*comfortable*) ..., the TV chair or the couch?
15. In the fourth form you will have (*little*) ... time for you hobbies than in the years before.
16. My mum is four years (*young*) ... my dad. Dad is the (*old*) ... in the family.

G 5 **Bilde die „zunehmende" Steigerung.**

1. Finding a good job is getting (*hard*) ... .
2. It's becoming (*dangerous*) ... to drive at night.
3. Congratulations, Jenny! Your German is getting (*good*) ...!
4. They say that every year (*many*) ... people decide to learn German.
5. Mum, look at my sweater! The hole on the elbow is getting (*big*) ...!
6. As the day of the exam came near, Fred had (*little*) ... time for us.
7. Since I came to London, my English has got (*good*) ... .
8. People say that skiing is becoming (*expensive*) ... .
9. We hoped the weather would get better, but it got (*bad*) ... .
10. Gina became (*excited*) ... while she was waiting for Jack.
11. There was no lift to the fourth floor, and my bags got (*heavy*) ... .
12. When Mr. Dalton told us what we had to do, we became (*quiet*) ... .
13. Towards the end, the film got (*violent*) ... .
14. I find it (*difficult*) ... to get a good grade in maths.
15. While Dad was listening to the interview, he was getting (*angry*) ... .
16. When everything is fine, you seem to have (*many*) ... friends every day, but when things go bad, your friends become (*few*) ... .
17. In the beginning the book was okay, but then it got (*boring*) ... .
18. We are (*surprised*) ... at our success.
19. It got (*late*) ..., but the children did not come back.
20. What's wrong with Chuck? He's getting (*crazy*) ... .

H 6 **Verändere diese Sätze so, dass sich „je – desto"-Sätze mit *"the ... the"* ergeben.**

1. If the prices are low, people will buy more.
2. If we leave early, we will get there soon.
3. If you are older, you can stay out longer at weekends.
4. They say that if a hotel is elegant, it is also expensive.
5. If you eat more, the bill will be higher.
6. If you have many friends, it will be easy to get help.
7. If I have a lot of work, I drink a lot of coffee.
8. If there's a lot of ice on the road, driving gets dangerous.
9. If you smoke a lot, you will die soon.
10. If you are older, it's easier to do what you want.
11. If you work hard, you will make a lot of money.
12. If the water is dirty, many people will get ill.
13. It got later and later. We saw fewer and fewer people.
14. We thought a lot about the idea. We did not like it very much.
15. I had to wait a long time. I got colder and colder.
16. It got darker and darker. We could not see much.
17. If you eat so much, you will get fat.
18. If we provoke Mrs. Miller so much, she will get very angry.

B C 7 *Adjective or adverb?* **Setze die richtige Wortart ein.**

1. I'm (*deep*) ... in love with Sally. My feelings for her are very (*deep*) ... .
2. Although Jim lives (*near*) ... the bus stop, he (*near*) ... missed the bus today.
3. I have a very (*friendly*) ... dog. He always wags his tail (*friendly*) ... when he sees someone he knows.
4. Jack is an (*early*) ... riser, but at the weekend he gets up (*late*) ... .
5. (*late*) ... I've had a lot of work, so I get up (early) ... (*near*) ... every day.
6. This is an (*excellent*) ... book. I can (*hard*) ... wait to read it.
7. We get one newspaper (*daily*) ... and one (*monthly*) ... .
8. What I like (*most*) ... about football is the atmosphere in the stadium. I go there (*most*) ... at the weekends or in my holidays.
9. The first fifty visitors get (*free*) ... tickets to the show, but they must tell us (*free*) ... what they liked and did not like about it.
10. I know this is a (*fast*) ... car, but you mustn't drive so (*fast*) ... at night.
11. Bob is not a (*pleasant*) ... person. He often speaks about others (*ugly*) ... .
12. If you ask me a (*direct*) ... question, I will answer it (*direct*) ..., if I can.

A-E 8 *Adjective or adverb?* **Setze die richtige Wortart in der richtigen Form ein.**

1. Your new room looks (*good*) ... . You've decorated it very (*nice*) ... .
2. What's (*wrong*) ... with Stella? – She's (*sad*) ... because her cat is (*ill*) ... .
3. The wind was blowing so (*strong*) ... that we couldn't go sailing.
4. This cake smells (*great*) ...! – That's because it's (*fresh*) ... from the oven.
5. Joe was so (*hungry*) ... that he swallowed everything down (*quick*) ... .
6. Why are you walking so (*slow*) ..., Sarah? – I hurt my ankle, so I can't walk (*fast*) ... than that. – Does it hurt? – It's not so (*bad*) ... .
7. Boys, come here (*quick*) ...! You must do something (*important*) ... for me.
8. Andy left the room (*quiet*) ... because he did not want to disturb us.
9. Andy is a very (*thoughtful*) ... person and a (*wonderful*) ... friend.
10. Gina left the party (*early*) ... because she felt (*sick*) ... .
11. Old Mrs. Jenkins smiled (*sweet*) ... as she (*slow*) ... crossed the street.
12. The sun is shining (*bright*) ..., the birds are singing (*happy*) ... – everything is (*perfect*) ... .
13. Yoshi is from Japan, but he speaks English and German (*real*) ... (*good*) ... .
14. This was (*hard*) ... work. Everybody had to work (*hard*) ... to finish it.
15. Mrs. Thomas is an (*excellent*) ... teacher. We can (*easy*) ... understand her.
16. John was (*terrible*) ... (*sad*) ... after losing the (*important*) ... match of the season.
17. My mum is a (*wonderful*) ... cook. Her goulash is (*simple*) ... the best.
18. Have you spoken with Josie (*late*) ...? How is she? – I have, and she feels much (*good*) ... now than last week.
19. The film was so (*silly*) ... that many people left the cinema (*angry*) ... .
20. Grandma and my mum speak (*daily*) ... on the phone.

F-H 9 ***Word order:*** **Setze die *adverbs* an die richtige Stelle im Satz.**

1. Joe did his homework. (*today, quickly*)
2. Mr. Harrison treats his students. (*unfairly, never*)
3. You will pass the exam. (*easily, tomorrow*)
4. Dad drives. (*fast, usually*)
5. Harry looked at me. (*sweetly, today*)
6. My parents have lived. (*always, here*)
7. Have you seen an alligator? (*here, ever*)
8. The wind blew. (*all night, softly*)
9. Jenny is nervous. (*terribly, often*)
10. We had to stay. (*all day, inside*)
11. I can remember the place. (*now, hardly*)
12. They cook. (*very well, here, usually*)
13. We will call you. (*really, tomorrow*)
14. Dad worked in the garden. (*yesterday, hard*)
15. Willie fails a test. (*completely, hardly ever*)
16. They will visit us again. (*here, never*)

3. KAPITEL – *ARTICLE*

A-G 10 **Füge den Artikel (*a/an, the*) ein oder lasse ihn weg.**

1. We are not allowed to wear ... shoes inside ... school building.
2. I know ... young man who works for ... police, but he's not ... policeman.
3. Danny is not in ... kitchen and he's not in ... garden. He is in ... bed.
4. For this cake you need ... butter, ... flour, ... sugar and ... egg.
5. I can't stand ... noise ... boys are making. It's horrible!
6. Did you like ... apples from ... farmers' market? – Yes, I did. I don't usually like ... apples very much, but these were very tasty.
7. My parents like ... classical music very much, and Mozart is ... composer whose music they like ... best.
8. ... painting that you can see over there is called "... Kiss".
9. This picture is so valuable because of ... gold that was used to paint it.
10. When I leave ... school in four or five years, I want to work in ... office.
11. I think ... lunch we had at ... little restaurant in ... park was really good.
12. Linda is in ... kitchen. She is making ... lunch for ... family.
13. Colin lives in ... England, which is ... part of ... United Kingdom.
14. ... plane which Charles Lindbergh used on ... first transatlantic flight was called "... Spirit of St. Louis".
15. Sam, have you read ... email I sent you this morning? – No; I didn't know that there was ... email, but I'll read it when I get home from ... school.
16. ... DVD in ... player is about ... man who crossed ... Antarctic on skis.
17. There is ... ugly fly in ... soup! I hate ... soup with insects in it!
18. ... last day of ... skiing trip was ... worst – Kevin fell and broke his leg, so we had to call ... mountain patrol, and they called ... helicopter which took Kevin to ... hospital.

4. KAPITEL – *CONDITIONS*

A 11 **Bilde den „Fall der Wirklichkeit" mit den folgenden Sätzen.**

1. If I find your keys, I (*tell*) you.
2. If Uncle Ben offers us a job, we (*take*) it.
3. If we don't catch the 10 o'clock train, we (*have*) to wait until tomorrow.
4. If Fred buys my bike, I (*put*) the money in the bank.
5. If you meet Mary again, what (*you, say*)?
6. If you don't have a passport, they (*not let*) you into the country.
7. Sue will be very upset if you (*forget*) her birthday again.
8. You will feel a lot better if you (*not sit*) at your computer all day.
9. Mark will leave without us if we (*not hurry*).
10. You won't hear a thing if you (*not come*) into the room.
11. Simon will take the job if you (*not take*) it.
12. I'll go to your party if you (*come*) to mine.

A 12 **Bilde auch hier wieder den „Fall der Wirklichkeit".**

1. If Samantha (*ask*) me, I (*help*) her.
2. If Dad (*come*) home in time, we (*play*) a game of chess together.
3. If I (*throw*) the ball, (*you, catch*) it?
4. If you (*tell*) my parents, I (*not speak*) with you again.
5. If we (*not run*), the bus (*leave*) without us.
6. If the rain (*not stop*) soon, we (*not go*) camping tomorrow.
7. We (*come*) to the concert with you if we (*finish*) our project in time.
8. Bill (*sing*) a song if you (*dance*) with him.
9. I (*make*) some tea if the children (*be*) thirsty.
10. You (*not notice*) the pain if you (*take*) a pill.
11. The neighbours (*call*) the police if we (*not turn*) off the radio.
12. We (*visit*) a museum if the sun (*not shine*) this afternoon.

B 13 **Bilde den „Fall der Möglichkeit".**

1. If the CDs were cheaper, I (*buy*) them.
2. If someone saw us here, we (*be*) in deep trouble.
3. If my parents could sell the house, they (*have*) a lot of money.
4. If it didn't snow, I (*go*) shopping now.
5. If you worked harder, you (*not get*) bad marks all the time.
6. If you weren't my friend, I (*not ask*) you to come to my party.
7. If Dad found the tickets, we (*go*) to the concert.
8. Gina would look like a clown if she (*dye*) her hair orange.
9. You would feel a lot better if you (*do*) more sport.
10. Mum wouldn't smile if she (*knew*) about my exam.
11. We would go to the cinema tonight if we (*not have*) so much to do.
12. I wouldn't be here if I (*not like*) you.
13. I would walk to school in the morning if I (*can*) get up more easily.
14. We wouldn't buy the car if we (*not have*) the money.

C 14 **Bilde den „Fall der Unmöglichkeit".**

1. If the band had stopped playing, the people (*go*) home.
2. If I had not left my camera at home, I (*take*) lots of good pictures.
3. If the bus had been on time, we (*not miss*) the beginning of the film.
4. Grandma would have found her glasses if she (*look*) into the drawer.
5. We would not have waited so long if you (*tell*) us about the delay.
6. I would not have come with you if you (*not ask*) me so nicely.
7. If Amanda (*stay*) longer, she (*meet*) some interesting people.
8. If Dad (*have*) more time, he (*come*) to the concert with us.
9. If I (*know*) the correct answers, I (*win*) the first prize.
10. Julia (*throw*) the letter away if she (*know*) that it was from Simon.
11. We (*finish*) the project in time if we (*have*) more help from you.
12. I (*speak*) with Betty if I (*see*) her at the party.
13. Mum (*not be*) so angry if we (*not lie*) to her.
14. If you (*tell*) me about Lucy's birthday sooner, I (*buy*) her a present.
15. If James (*not break*) his leg, we (*go*) skiing together.
16. Joe (*not ask*) me for help if he (*not be*) desperate.

5. KAPITEL – *FUTURE*

A-E 15 **Verwende die passende Form für *future*: *"will", "going to", present progressive, present simple.***

1. Joanne is sure that one day she (*be*) a doctor.
2. Look at these clouds. It (*rain*) very soon.
3. Hi, Helen. Let's go to a café, shall we? – Okay, I (*come*) with you.
4. Paula and I (*go*) to the cinema tonight. They (*show*) "The Hand of God".
5. The film (*begin*) at 7.45
6. [At the restaurant] I think I (*have*) steak and chips. What (*you, have*)? – I can't decide. I (*probably, have*) steak, too.
7. We could need a fourth person for our game of poker! – I (*call*) Joe, okay?
8. Mum is so busy she has no time for shopping. – No problem. We (*do*) it!
9. What are you doing with that axe, Fred? – Dad and I (*chop*) some wood.
10. Grandma (*visit*) us again next weekend. Her bus (*arrive*) at 1.30. Who (*fetch*) her from the bus station? – I think Dad (*pick*) her up in his car.
11. When the girls are older, they (*have*) better chances of finding good jobs.
12. Look, it's raining! Your hair (*get*) wet, and if you don't wear a hat, you (*catch*) cold.
13. How (*you, get*) around in America? – I don't know yet. We (*probably, drive*).
14. Julia and Brian (*leave*) for London next Monday. They (*stay*) at a hotel near Victoria Station, but they haven't booked it yet.
15. I (*meet*) Evie later tonight. – Tell her I (*call*) her next week.
16. Look, Johnny (*play*) something on the piano for us.

6. KAPITEL – *GERUND*

A-G 16 **Übersetze mit Hilfe des Gerunds in gutes Englisch.**

1. Schwimmen macht Spaß.
2. Ich übersetze nicht gerne englische Texte.
3. Das Fischen ist hier nicht erlaubt.
4. Wir hörten das Klappern (*clatter*) unserer Zähne.
5. Jede Frage richtig zu beantworten, war nicht leicht.
6. Elsie genießt es, in der Sonne zu liegen und nichts zu tun.
7. Es hat schon vor einer Weile zu schneien aufgehört.
8. Ich hasse es, im Regen mit dem Hund spazieren zu gehen.
9. Das Warten auf den Weihnachtsmann kann sehr aufregend sein.
10. Computerspiele zu spielen macht mehr Spaß als die Hausübung auf dem Computer zu schreiben.
11. Ich glaube, Joe ist in der Lage, das Problem zu lösen (*solve the problem*).
12. Wer ist für das Abwaschen verantwortlich?
13. Ich glaube, du bist müde vom vielen Schlafen!
14. Wer hat Angst davor, in den Keller zu gehen?
15. Wir haben es satt, immer auf euch zu warten.
16. Rita war überrascht, ein „A" auf die Prüfung zu bekommen.
17. Wer hat Interesse daran, auf den Schulball zu gehen?
18. Gina spielt ihren Freundinnen gerne einen Streich (*play a trick*).
19. Ich bin stolz darauf, dich zum Freund zu haben.
20. Max ist sehr gut darin, anderen Menschen zuzuhören.
21. Joe gab zu, mein Handy verwendet zu haben.
22. Ich kann mir gut (*well*) vorstellen, später hier zu arbeiten.
23. Mach dir keine Sorgen, ich bin es gewöhnt zu warten.
24. Habe ich erwähnt, dass ich Gina getroffen habe?
25. Ich hoffe, es macht euch nichts aus, neben uns zu sitzen.
26. Du riskierst einen Sturz, wenn du so schnell fährst (*ride*).
27. Liza vermeidet es immer, mit Peter zu tanzen.
28. Ich vermisse es, mit meinem Opa Schach zu spielen.
29. Macht es dir etwas aus, das Fenster zu schließen?
30. Hast du dir je (*ever*) überlegt, dein Zimmer auszumalen?
31. Ich schlage vor, wir fahren mit dem Bus (*take the bus*).
32. Joe entschuldigte sich dafür, dass er mein Handy verwendet hatte.
33. Danny fuhr weg, ohne uns zu fragen.
34. Ich kann nicht aufhören, an Alex zu denken.
35. Wir freuen uns darauf, Linkin Park kennenzulernen (*meet*).
36. Ich hoffe, sie verschieben nicht schon wieder die Eröffnung der Show.
37. Julia besteht darauf, Jeans in die Schule anzuziehen (*wear ... for school*).
38. Dem Roten Kreuz ist es wichtig, Menschen in Not (*in distress*) zu helfen.
39. Niemand kann mich davon abhalten, mit dir zu reden.
40. „Durchstarten" ist lesenswert.

H 17 **Verkürze diese Temporalsätze mit Hilfe des Gerunds. (Achtung – nur der Gliedsatz darf verändert werden!)**

1. Grandma always asks who's there before she opens the door.
2. Before I take the dog for a walk, I feed her.
3. I always tidy my desk before I go to bed.
4. Before Mum leaves the house, she checks all the lights.
5. Dad usually studies the facts before he makes a decision.
6. When Joe heard about the concert, he bought five tickets.
7. We called the police after we had read the article about the runaway dog.
8. After we had found the hotel, we parked the car and went to our rooms.
9. Gabriel quit his job after he had won in the lottery.
10. After Mum had washed the curtains, she ironed them.
11. Mehmet left the room after he had handed in his test paper.
12. After we had watched the ski race on TV, we went out to celebrate.

I 18 **Verbinde oder verkürze die folgenden Sätze mit *"by + gerund"*.**

1. If you use natural products instead of plastic, you can protect nature.
2. I think we will get to the airport faster if we take a taxi.
3. If we answer eight of the ten questions correctly, we may win the quiz.
4. You can make your teachers very happy if you get a haircut.
5. If you save all your money, you will be able to afford a laptop soon.
6. We won't solve the problem if we look the other way.
7. I got to the sports centre first. I took a shortcut through the park.
8. The terrorists got into the country. They showed false passports.
9. My parents sometimes punish me. They take away my computer.
10. Fred ran the 100 m in 12.3 seconds. He set a new school record.
11. Jackie surprised everybody. She finished the maths contest first.
12. My team qualified for the next round. We beat our opponents 3 : 1.

J 19 **Bilde jeweils zwei Gerund-Sätze, einen mit Fürwort *(personal or possessive pronoun)*, einen ohne.**

1. Joe – looking forward – visit London – this summer – (*we*)
2. they – not interested – know the whole story – (*I*)
3. Mum – apologised – forget the appointment – (*you*)
4. I really enjoy – be here – (*you*)
5. the police – surprised – find the stolen car so soon – (*I*)
6. you cannot – take my books – without – notice it – (*I*)
7. Dad – doesn't mind – watch TV – late at night – (*we*)
8. Mum – worries about – get lost at night – (*I*)
9. do you mind – stay overnight – (*he*)
10. I – miss – play the piano – (*you*)
11. we – don't mind – watch this film – (*she*)
12. I – tired of – sit – in front of the computer – all day – (*you*)

7. KAPITEL – *REPORTED SPEECH*

A-F 20 **Setze die folgenden Sätze in *reported speech*. Das einleitende Verb soll dabei in *past tense* stehen.**

example: *"I'm going to buy a CD today." (Joe, say)* ▶
Joe said that he was going to buy a CD that day.

1. "My mum and her best friend work for the same boss." *(Martin, tell)*
2. "I bought this bicycle from your brother." *(Frank, inform)*
3. "Nobody has noticed my new glasses." *(Jenny, complain)*
4. "Take this book to the library tomorrow!" *(Mum, tell)*
5. "My sister and I will get flowers for our mum." *(Sarah, say)*
6. "Call me again next week!" *(the doctor, tell)*
7. "We'll wait for you in our car." *(my friends, say)*
8. "I've left my English books at school." *(Tim, say)*
9. "My wife and I have always wanted to see Paris." *(Mr. Jones, say)*
10. "Emily doesn't like her new teachers." *(Sue, tell)*
11. "I was not talking about my problems, but yours." *(Tony, say)*
12. "We can't help you; we are in a hurry." *(my friends, say)*
13. "I'll meet you here after the concert next Saturday." *(Tim, suggest)*
14. "Show me your homework at once!" *(Mrs. Smith, order)*
15. "We bought this house two years ago." *(our neighbours, tell)*
16. "Mike wants to talk to you." *(Max, inform)*
17. "Somebody is watching our house." *(Dora, think)*
18. "Don't call me again!" *(Sue, tell)*
19. "I'm not very good at skiing but I can dance very well." *(Robert, say)*
20. "We will return the books by next weekend." *(Phil, promise)*
21. "Please write your name on this piece of paper!" *(Mr. Brown, ask)*
22. "I've been waiting for an answer since last week." *(Joe, complain)*
23. "Have you seen my car keys anywhere?" *(Dad, ask)*
24. "Do you like this song?" *(Kevin, want to know)*
25. "Will they keep us waiting long?" *(I, wonder)*
26. "Did you unterstand my question?" *(the policeman, want to know)*
27. "Can I go home now?" *(the man, ask)*
28. "Are you speaking with us?" *(the girls, want to know)*
29. "Has Charlie been to one of your parties?" *(Gina, ask)*
30. "Is everybody here?" *(Tom, want to know)*
31. "What do you think of my new trainers?" *(Alex, want to know)*
32. "What have you done to your hair?" *(Mum, ask)*
33. "When does Dad's plane arrive?" *(Joe, want to know)*
34. "Where did I put my books yesterday?" *(Dad, wonder)*
35. "How will we find the right street?" *(the tourists, wonder)*
36. "Why is nobody here yet?" *(Max, want to know)*
37. "Who can tell me the name of this building?" *(the guide, ask)*
38. "What shall I tell my parents?" *(Fred, wonder)*

8. KAPITEL – *INFINITIVE*

ABEH 21 Übersetze die folgenden Sätze mit Hilfe des Infinitivs in gutes Englisch.

1. Ich hörte zufällig von deinen Abenteuern in Indien.
2. Wir weigern uns, mit diesen Menschen zu sprechen.
3. Du musst lernen, deine Probleme selbst zu lösen.
4. Joe sollte lieber zum Arzt gehen.
5. Wir können es uns leisten, in diesem Hotel zu wohnen.
6. Frank möchte mehr über dich wissen.
7. Sie ließen mich nicht mitspielen.
8. Das ist eine gute Gelegenheit, deine Englischkenntnisse zu verwenden.
9. Larry bot an, uns zu helfen.
10. Ich musste meinen Eltern versprechen, vor Mitternacht zu Hause zu sein.
11. Bitte zögere nicht, mir die Wahrheit zu sagen.
12. Wir beschlossen, uns den Film noch einmal anzuschauen.
13. Ich würde heute abend lieber ausgehen.
14. Es gelang uns, die Schatztruhe (*treasure box*) zu öffnen.
15. Die Fähigkeit zum Zuhören ist besonders (*particularly*) wichtig.
16. Niemand hat das Recht zu töten.
17. Es war meine Entscheidung, Bill um Rat (*advice*) zu fragen.
18. Der Bauer gab uns die Erlaubnis, neben seinem Haus zu campieren.
19. Lenny war der erste, der alle Aufgaben löste.
20. Wir erwarten, bald wieder von euch zu hören.
21. Es scheint heute sehr kalt zu sein.
22. Sie waren einverstanden (= sie stimmten zu), uns das Haus zu zeigen.

D 22 Verkürze mit Hilfe der Fügung *question word + infinitive*.

1. Nobody could tell us how we should do this exercise.
2. Do you know where we should take these books?
3. The boys have no idea when they should be at the sports centre.
4. Can you tell me what I should get Mum for Christmas?
5. You should know who you can trust in a difficult situation.
6. I'd like to know how I can end this silly quarrel.
7. I hope everybody knows what they should do during an earthquake.
8. This brochure tells you where you can find a cheap place to eat and sleep.

G 23 Übersetze mit Hilfe der Fügung *verb + object + infinitive*.

1. Ich möchte, dass du mir die Wahrheit sagst.
2. Wir können euch helfen, die Sachen wieder zu finden.
3. Sie luden mich ein, in ihrem Chor (*choir*) zu singen.
4. Charlie möchte, dass du ihm verzeihst (*forgive*).
5. Kannst du mir beibringen (= mich lehren), wie man gewinnt?
6. Sie befahlen uns, die Schuhe auszuziehen.
7. Ich rate dir, deinen alten Computer zu verkaufen.
8. Sie erwarteten, dass wir ihnen helfen.

9. KAPITEL – *INFINITIVE OR "ING-FORM"*

24 ***Infinitive or "ing-form"?* Entscheide und setze die richtige Form ein.**

1. Frank was only three years old when he learnt (*ride*) the bike.
2. I really don't mind (*wait*) for you, but I'd rather (*wait*) inside if it's cold.
3. Chris is so stubborn! When he decides (*do*) something, he refuses (*listen*).
4. The party was great. We all enjoyed (*see*) you again.
5. Who told you (*read*) this story? I can't remember (*say*) anything about it.
6. Tomorrow is Joe's big day. Don't forget (*get*) him a nice present.
7. In Mexico, you should avoid (*drink*) water and (*eat*) ice cream.
8. Mary pretended (*listen*) to me, but her thoughts were somewhere else.
9. I'd like (*know*) how you managed (*finish*) the project without (*ask*) for help.
10. Betty likes (*make*) her own dresses. She's quite good at (*do*) it, too.
11. Matt used (*play*) the violin and he seemed (*like*) it, but then he stopped.
12. What made you (*tell*) my parents about the exam? You know I hate (*quarrel*) with them.
13. The train station is very close. It's not worth (*take*) the bus.
14. Harry is tired from (*play*) tennis all day, so he doesn't feel like (*go*) out.
15. We happened (*meet*) Sue in town yesterday. She seemed (*be*) rather sad.
16. I've got a cold. Do you mind (*shut*) the window, please?
17. Our house is getting too small, so we are thinking of (*buy*) a larger one.
18. Can you (*come*) with me? I'm afraid of (*walk*) home all by myself.
19. I would never (*go*) to an open air concert. I can't stand (*be*) in a crowd.
20. Grandma is tired. She's not used to (*walk*) so far any more.
21. Mark has moved to England, and he seems (*enjoy*) (*live and work*) there.
22. I don't want (*speak*) with Mr. Gordon. I'd rather (*keep*) my mouth shut.
23. Harry is proud of (*play*) for the team, but he did not expect them (*win*).
24. What a boring evening! Fred insisted on (*tell*) us everything about his time in hospital. I felt like (*fall*) asleep once or twice.
25. After (*read*) the book, I began (*understand*) why it is so famous.
26. Where have you been? You promised (*be*) here in time. I'm tired of (*wait*).
27. I must remember (*call*) Judy today. I want (*apologise*) for (*be*) so rude.
28. After (*lose*) our way in the old town, we stopped (*ask*) for help.
29. Who suggested (*go*) to "Gino's" for lunch?
30. Girls, have you finished (*do*) your make up? We have (*leave*) now.
31. I'd like (*take*) a shower now. Would you mind (*close*) the door?
32. Nick managed (*answer*) all the questions. I can't imagine (*do*) that.
33. Detective: Sir, do you admit (*speak*) to this man before (*leave*) the room?
34. We expect (*hear*) great things about you in future.
35. Have you ever considered (*become*) a professional photographer?
36. Remember (*visit*) the Eiffel Tower before (*leave*) Paris.
37. I'm interested in (*know*) more about China, so I've decided (*go*) there.
38. We tried (*pay*) with dollars, but they refused (*accept*) them.
39. We're hoping (*hear*) everything about your trip, so please go on (*talk*).
40. You can't put off (*speak*) with Jane, you know? You'd better (*call*) her now.

10. KAPITEL – *MODAL VERBS*

A-C 25 **Setze die passenden Formen oder Ersatzformen der angegebenen *modal verbs* ein.**

1. We bought the necessary things for the model plane. (*können*)
2. You will drive a car when you are eighteen. (*dürfen*)
3. Mr. Hopkins did not like my pictures, so I drew them again. (*müssen*)
4. I remember your name, but I don't remember your address. (*können*)
5. We did not watch the secret ceremony. (*dürfen*)
6. If Gloria does not answer our emails, we will go and see her. (*müssen*)
7. They have not read the writing on this stone since it was found. (*können*)
8. Is Dennis here? – No, he isn't. He has left. (*müssen*)
9. Before the roof collapsed, most people got out safely. (*können*)
10. Alice has never stayed overnight at a friend's house. (*dürfen*)
11. Good children always do their homework by themselves. (*müssen*)
12. If my hair was as long as yours, I would get a haircut. (*müssen*)

D 26 **Setze passenden Formen von „sollen" ein; Mehrfachlösungen möglich!**

1. You don't look too good, Mary. ... I call the doctor?
2. Is it safe to walk home at night? – I don't think so. You ... take a taxi.
3. I don't know where Tommy can be. He ... be home by now.
4. Dad, Mum said I ... ask you if you can help me with geometry.
5. What are you doing in this room, children? You know you ... not ... to come in.
6. I think you ... keep this wallet. You ... take it to the "lost and found office".
7. You ... ask your parents if you can come on the school trip or not.
8. I really fancy Eric. What ... I do so that he will notice me?
9. Turn off the lights, boys! You ... sleep at this time of the night!
10. We can't really tell you the answer because we ... not ... to know anything.

E 27 **In den folgenden Sätzen hat sich jemand etwas machen lassen. Drücke das mit *have* + (*something*) + *3rd form* aus.**

1. What have you done with your hair, Jane? – I (*dye, it*) yesterday.
2. How do you like my bike? I (*paint, it*) orange and black. I think it looks cool.
3. My grandpa always (*mow, the lawn in his garden*) by the neighbours' boy.
4. The engine makes funny noises. Can we (*check, it*) in this garage?
5. I must (*wash and iron, these shirts*) soon. I need them at the weekend.
6. That painting shows my grandmother. She (*paint, it*) when she was 20.
7. We can't take the things with us now, so we (*send, them*) to our address.
8. Look at Mike! He (*tattoo, his girlfriend's name*) on his arm!
9. Before her wedding, Debbie (*do, hair and fingernails*) by her best friend.
10. If you want to know more about the future, you can (*tell, your fortune*) here.

11. KAPITEL – *PASSIVE*

B-D 28 **Bilde *passive voice* mit den angegebenen Verben.**

1. Footballs (*usually, make*) of leather, but mine (*make*) of plastic.
2. VWs (*build*) in several countries all over the world.
3. There was a terrible crash on the highway, but luckily nobody (*kill*).
4. Look at these rocks. They (*bring*) back from the moon by astronauts.
5. They have just finished building the bridge. It (*open*) next month.
6. Thank you for buying the books here. They (*send*) to you tomorrow.
7. The missing children (*find*) at last, and they are okay.
8. I'm sure the door (*open*) while we were gone!
9. The test papers must (*hand*) in at the end of the lesson.
10. Tickets can (*buy*) between 8 a.m. and 5 p.m.
11. Don't forget, the paintings must not (*touch*) or the alarm will go off.
12. When the fire engine arrived, the fire (*put*) out by the neighbours.
13. A secret is something that should not (*tell*).
14. We did not go to the cinema yesterday because the show (*cancel*).
15. Thank God, my TV (*repair*), so we can watch the Olympic Games again.
16. I can't use my room for a week because it (*decorate*).
17. Julia Robert's latest film (*believe*) to win an Oscar this year.
18. Kurt learnt to play the piano when he was five. He (*teach*) by his uncle.
19. Your texts must (*write*) on a computer and then (*print*).
20. Your drinks will arrive in a minute. They (*prepare*) at the moment.
21. The house next to ours (*sell*) at last. I hope the new owners are nice.
22. Sometimes mistakes (*make*). That's part of life.
23. These pills must not (*take*) all at once, but one at a time.
24. We (*tell*) to ask for more information. Can you help us?
25. Hey, look! Your car (*load*) onto a lorry!
26. This is a bad part of the town. If you don't lock your car, it (*steal*).
27. After the Great Fire of London, almost a hundred churches had to (*build*).
28. Most of these churches (*design*) by Sir Christopher Wren.
29. They say Disney World (*visit*) by more than 200,000 people every day.
30. After the doors (*shut*) behind us, we (*take*) to a very large room.

F 29 **Verwandle von Aktiv zu Passiv (1–6) und von Passiv zu Aktiv (7–10).**

1. You cannot answer these questions.
2. They scored four goals in ten minutes.
3. They will throw away the empty bottles.
4. We have switched off all the lights in the house.
5. Don't use the copier! They are servicing it at the moment.
6. They gave us the worst seats in the room.
7. These trees were planted by the first settlers.
8. The road across the pass has been closed.
9. The doors had been locked when we arrived.
10. You will be told when to come back.

12. KAPITEL – *PAST PERFECT TENSE*

B C 30 **Verwende *past perfect tense* für die <u>frühere</u> Handlung und *past tense* für die <u>spätere</u> Handlung.**

1. After I (*leave*) the house this morning, I (*ride*) my bike to school.
2. We (*cannot*) open the door because somebody (*leave*) the key in the lock.
3. Elsie (*be*) very happy after Malcolm (*ask*) her to be his girlfriend.
4. Two months after the Browns (*bought*) the house, they (*move*) in.
5. When we (*come*) to the stadium, the match (*already, begin*).
6. After the children (*go*) to their rooms, the grown-ups (*play*) poker.
7. Camilla (*hear*) strange noises after she (*enter*) the big room.
8. We (*have*) to go back to the house because we (*forget*) the shopping list.
9. After Erica (*feed*) the dog, she (*start*) to prepare dinner.
10. I (*not recognise*) the man because I (*never, see*) his picture before.
11. Mark (*not sleep*) well because he (*eat*) too much the night before.
12. All the newspapers (*write*) about Joe after he (*save*) a drowning child.

E 31 **Verwende *past perfect progressive* (für Handlungen, die „schon seit …" andauerten) und *past simple* (für Handlungen, die „dann" geschahen).**

example: *Mum was watching TV. After a short time she fell asleep.* ▶
Mum had been watching TV for some time when she fell asleep.

1. I was riding my bike. After an hour or so I noticed that I had a flat tyre.
2. The children were waiting for Santa Claus. After a long time they heard a bell from the living room.
3. It was snowing heavily. After three days the first avalanches came down.
4. Joe was looking for his stamp album. After an hour he found it in his drawer.
5. We were sleeping. After half an hour the phone rang.
6. We were travelling through China. After a week we met our friends.
7. Mike was leading the race. After 20 minutes he was overtaken by Arthur.
8. We were watching the fight. After only a few seconds the champion knocked out his opponent.

E 32 **Gleichzeitige Handlungen *(past progressive)* oder eine Handlung vor der anderen *(past perfect?)*.**

1. Joe was quite hungry because he (*not eaten*) for two days.
2. When I came into the room, everyone (*watch*) the Olympic Games on TV.
3. I saw you at the concert on Saturday. You (*talk*) to a stranger.
4. We (*wait*) for the beginning of the show for hours when the curtains finally opened and the show began.
5. I (*work*) for school for some time when my friends called.
6. The boys were very depressed because their team (*lost*) the championship.
7. Mona and Chris (*be*) together for six months when Chris gave her a ring.
8. Luke (*run*) down the stairs when he slipped and fell.

13. KAPITEL – *PAST TENSE*

B 33 **Bilde die Entscheidungsfrage und die Verneinung (1–8) und frage nach den unterstrichenen Satzteilen.**

1. Peter was watching TV from 5 to 10.
2. My friends were playing cards in the living room.
3. We could see the play very well from our seats.
4. Everybody had to leave the theatre after the show.
5. Mr. Smith needed a taxi because his car was at the garage.
6. Gina sent her grandma a postcard from Florida.
7. Charlie and Fiona got married in Las Vegas last summer.
8. The Jacksons stayed at a campground because it was cheaper.
9. The telephone was not working when we rented the house.
10. The girls were not able to open the door because they had no key.

C D 34 **Wähle aus: *past simple or past progressive?* Streiche die falsche Variante durch, so dass ein richtiger Satz übrig bleibt.**

1. Everybody *thought/was thinking* about the problem when Joe *had/was having* an idea.
2. When Judy *came/was coming* to the bus stop, Fred *already waited/was already waiting* for her.
3. It *rained/was raining* heavily while they *waited/were waiting* for the train.
4. Nobody *entered or left/was entering or leaving* the room as long as I *watched/was watching* the door.
5. When Erin *got/was getting* the telegram, she *knew/was knowing* that Ian would come home soon.
6. While Joe *packed/was packing* his bags, Marion *packed/was packing* hers.
7. We *tried/were trying* to call you all day yesterday, but we *did not get through/were not getting* through.
8. Jack *walked/was walking* home from school when he *found/was finding* a ring that *belonged/was belonging* to his friend Claudia.
9. In 1999, Helen *saw/was seeing* Charlie for the first time. She *lived/was living* in London at that time. He *did not impress/was not impressing* her very much then. But while they *worked/were working* in the same office, she *began/was beginning* to like him more and more.
10. The band *still played/was still playing* when the "Titanic" *sank/was sinking* beneath the waves.
11. When Jessica *opened/was opening* the front door, she *heard/was hearing* loud voices from the living room.
12. When Clarissa *arrived/was arriving*, a car *waited/was waiting* for her.
13. As Linda *rode/was riding* her bike home from the sports club, she *noticed/was noticing* Tommy at the corner of the street. He *talked/was talking* to a very pretty dark-haired girl. Linda *did not know/was not knowing* her.
14. Leslie *wanted/was wanting* to go jogging, but it *rained/was raining*, and so he *decided/was deciding* to stay at home and watch a DVD.

14. KAPITEL – *POSSESSIVE CASE*

AB 35 **Bilde von allen Beispielen den zweiten Fall. Wo es möglich ist, wende *Saxon Genitive* an.**

1. atlas – pages
2. birds – nests
3. Conny – new job
4. DVD player – quality
5. fish – taste
6. my grandfather – car
7. hurricane – eye
8. Judy – phone number
9. Luxemburg – capital
10. man – clothes
11. The Netherlands – queen
12. Oliver – room
13. petrol – price
14. Rosie – boss
15. shop – opening hours
16. Teresa – scooter
17. umbrella - colour
18. Victoria – mother
19. winter – beginning
20. Zurich – airport

15. KAPITEL – *PRESENT PARTICIPLE*

EF 36 **Baue in die folgenden Sätze mindestens ein *present participle* ein. Bei gleichzeitig ablaufenden Handlungen sind auch zwei Mittelwort-Konstruktionen möglich.**

1. Jennifer walked home from school. She thought about Joe's letter.
2. Mum looked out of the window. She noticed smoke coming from the house next door.
3. Max made himself a sandwich. He listened to the news on the radio.
4. Jack skied down the slope. He almost hit a snowboarder.
5. Jack skied down the slope. He listened to his favourite music on his iPod.
6. They looked for oil or gas. They found thermal water instead.
7. The boys tried to climb into the house through the window. They cut their hands badly on broken glass.
8. Grandpa sat in his favourite chair. He watched his favourite TV show.
9. I read the text carefully. I noticed three mistakes in it.
10. Charlie ran faster than ever before. He won the race.
11. The old lady did not know what to do. She called the police.
12. Sandra walked slowly through the park. She looked at all the lovely flowers.
13. Mum rode the bus to work. She read a book.
14. Greg looked at the finished painting. He felt very proud of himself.
15. The girls were sitting in a café. They were discussing boys.
16. Mike has enough money left. He will have lunch at a restaurant.
17. Mark forgot to lock the front door. He got into his car and drove off.
18. I knew lots of people at the party. I had a great time.
19. Robert was snorkelling in the Red Sea. He enjoyed the colourful coral reefs.
20. Sarah shut the book and turned off the lights.

16. KAPITEL – *PRESENT PERFECT TENSE*

A 37 **Bilde *present perfect simple* und *present perfect progressive*. Bilde beide Formen mit den folgenden Personen und Verben.**

1. we – answer
2. Mum – bake
3. Ian – cut
4. Dad – drive
5. I – entertain
6. we – fly
7. they – get
8. the girls – help
9. Laura – illustrate
10. I – jog
11. Tina – learn
12. you – meet
13. Jack – open
14. the boys – push
15. you – ride
16. I – shop
17. Liza – stare
18. Joe – take
19. you – think
20. we – wash

A 38 **Setze *present perfect simple* (1 bis 6) und *present perfect progressive* (7 bis 12) ein.**

1. The bell (*ring*) …, the lesson is over.
2. Peter is angry. He (*have*) … bad news.
3. I (*not speak*) … with Martha yet, but I will do it this afternoon.
4. (*you, see*) … your sister this week? – No, I haven't.
5. (*Gina, finish*) … the book? – I really don't know, but I can ask her.
6. It (*snow*) … again, and everything is white.
7. Mark (*listen*) … to rap music since his trip to Los Angeles.
8. This egg (*boil*) … for ten minutes. Isn't this too long?
9. Linda and I (*go*) … out together since her birthday party.
10. It's past midnight! What (*you, do*) … all this time?
11. They (*repair*) … this bridge for half a year. They will never finish!
12. I (*listen*) … to your excuses for years! I don't believe you any more!

B 39 **Wie ist es dazu gekommen? Setze *present perfect simple* ein.**

1. I'm really sorry, Mum. *(I – forget – feed the dog)*
2. You can't call Sue at this time of the night. *(she – go – to bed)*
3. I'm going home now. *(I – be here – long enough)*
4. Harry and Sally are good friends. *(they – know each other – long time)*
5. Sally is quite happy. *(she – get an "A" – English test)*
6. We're sorry we can't lend you the lawn mower. *(we – sell – it)*
7. Helen looks different, doesn't she? *(she – cut – her hair)*
8. Jim won't play football for weeks. *(he – break – his leg)*
9. I think we have to go now. *(we – spend – all our money)*
10. Quick, call the police! *(they – steal – our car)*
11. You can come out of your hiding place now, Tony. *(Max – leave)*
12. Why is it so hot in this room? *(someone – turn up – the heating)*
13. I can't read this text. *(I – leave – my glasses – at home)*
14. Simon is the absolute favourite. *(he – win the race – three times)*

D 40 **Setze ein: *present perfect simple* oder *present perfect progressive*?**

1. My friend's parents (*go*) … to Italy every summer since 1980.
2. Brian (*sleep*) … for ten hours. I think he (*take*) … a sleeping pill.
3. We (*try*) … to get in touch with Albert, but he (*not answer*) … yet.
4. I (*take*) … Spanish lessons for three years, and I (*already, learn*) … a lot.
5. Martin, (*you, hide*) … my trainers? I (*look*) … for them everywhere, but I can't find them.
6. (*Joe, call*) … today? – No, he hasn't. I (*not hear*) … from him for weeks.
7. Who (*make*) … this mess in the living room? – It wasn't me, Mum. I (*not be*) … in the room since the weekend.
8. Esther (*work*) … as a tourist guide for many years, and she (*meet*) … many interesting people from all over the world.
9. Look, it (*stop*) … raining! Now we can go out again.
10. Joe, switch off the TV and go to bed! (*You, watch*) … long enough today!
11. One of my teeth (*ache*) … since last night. I think it's time to go to the dentist! I (*not have*) … a check-up for two years.
12. (*anyone, read*) … the French text for tomorrow? – I have. It's really easy.
13. Look at your hands, Alice! What (*you, do*) …? – I (*pick*) … blackberries!
14. We (*wait*) … for Dad's train for half an hour, but it (*not arrive*) … yet.
15. Olivia! What a surprise to see you! – (*anybody, not tell*) … you that I was coming? – No, they haven't!
16. (*you, ever, try*) … "black pudding"? – No, I haven't. What is it? – It's something like "Blutwurst". The English (*make*) … it for centuries.
17. Harry, (*you, throw*) … away the papers that were lying on my desk?
18. These clothes (*lie*) … around for days! Are they yours, Bill? – No, they aren't. I (*never, see*) … them before.
19. How long (*you, have*) … this car? – For over six years, and I (*never, have*) … any problems with it.
20. Where's Mr. Green? – Don't you know? They (*take*) … him to hospital.
21. Miriam (*study*) … Chinese for three years now, but she (*not visit*) … the country yet.
22. In the last few days, I (*often, think*) … of Mary. I hope she is alright.
23. Jules (*take*) … piano lessons for six years. He (*already, play*) … with some very good orchestras.
24. This is Jim. I (*know*) … him since kindergarten.
25. Uncle Fred (*drive*) … Toyotas for more than 30 years. He (*never, have*) … a different type of car.
26. Since we moved to this town, we (*live*) … in the same house, but we (*often, think*) … of buying or renting a bigger one.
27. Alex (*play*) … for the "Tigers" for a year, and he (*win*) … all his games so far.
28. Susanne, you (*study*) … for four hours now. Aren't you tired?
29. Norbert (*collect*) … stamps since he was a boy. I (*never, understand*) … why he is so fascinated with stamps!
30. I (*always, want*) … to see the Tadj Mahal, but so far I (*not, be*) … able to afford a journey to India.

E 41 **Setze ein: *past simple* oder *present perfect simple.***

1. (*you, see*) … the documentary on Siberia on TV yesterday? – No, I didn't. I (*not, watch*) … TV for several days.
2. My parents (*go*) … to Africa last winter, and they (*like*) … it very much.
3. I (*never, be*) … outside of Europe, but I (*already, travel*) … to 26 European countries.
4. Look what Aunt Margaret (*send*) … you! A £ 5 note!
5. Thomas (*save*) … all his pocket money. Now he wants to buy a better bike.
6. Danny and Tim (*go*) … to the cinema last night. They (*see*) … "Matrix". – That's a great film. I (*see*) … it four times already.
7. Dora (*have*) … horses for many years, and no horse (*ever, kick*) … her.
8. Ah, here you are! I (*want*) … to talk to you for days! Where (*you, be*) …?
9. (*the dog, have*) … his food yet? – Oh yes. Joe (*already, feed*) … him.
10. Walter, (*you, close*) … the window yet? – Why? I (*just, open*) … it.
11. I (*speak*) … to Walter last Sunday, but I (*not see*) … him since then.
12. Where (*you, go*) … on your skiing holiday last year? – To Saalbach, as usual. We (*be*) … there four times so far.
13. Look, there's a postcard for you. – I (*already, see*) … it. It's from Jackie. She (*write*) … it a few days ago, when she (*be*) … in Venice.
14. (*you, ever, have*) … fish for breakfast? – Yes, last year in London. They (*serve*) … us kippers in the morning, which is a kind of smoked herring.
15. I first (*travel*) … to the USA six years ago, and I (*like*) … it very much. Since then I (*visit*) … the country four more times.
16. Someone (*be*) … in the house while we (*be*) … gone. They (*leave*) … footprints everywhere.
17. Peter, (*you, lock*) … the front door last night? – No, I didn't.
18. Lucy (*come*) … back from her holiday yesterday, but I (*not be*) … able to speak with her yet. I hope she (*have*) … a good time.
19. Andrew Lloyd Webber (*write*) … more than ten musicals so far, and I (*see*) … them all.
20. As a young man, Dad often (*go*) … to discos with his friends. One evening, sixteen years ago, he (*meet*) … a pretty girl and (*fall*) … in love with her – and she with him. A year later, they (*get*) … married, and they (*be*) … married ever since. The pretty girl is my mum, of course.
21. We (*spend*) … too much money this month. Last month (*be*) … a lot cheaper.
22. Who (*eat*) … the last piece of cake? – George! I (*see*) … him!
23. (*anybody, call*) … for me? – Yes. About ten minutes ago, somebody (*want*) … to know your private phone number, but I (*not give*) … it to him.
24. (*you, hear*) … the latest news? Jim (*ask*) … Caroline to marry him, and she (*say*) … no!
25. Give me your test papers, boys! I hope you (*all, finish*) …!
26. Last week, I (*send*) … you an email, but you (*not answer*) … . Why not? – I'm sorry, but I (*not have*) … any time. It (*be*) … a very busy week so far.
27. Look, the lights (*change*) … . We can cross the street now.

17. KAPITEL – *PRESENT TENSE*

A 42 **Setze die Beispiele in *present simple* (1–8) und *present progressive* (9–14). Achte dabei auf die vorgegebene Person.**

1. My sister and I (*make*) ... our own dresses.
2. Julia (*speak*) ... Chinese and Korean.
3. Many people still (*believe*) ... that the sun (*turn*) ... around the earth.
4. The British Prime Minister (*live*) ... and (*work*) ... at number 10, Downing Street.
5. Jeremy (*like*) ... pizza, but he (*not like*) ... pasta.
6. Uncle Bob and Aunt Sue (*operate*) ... a farm. They (*grow*) ... mainly potatoes.
7. Wine (*not grow*) ... in cold climates.
8. In Vienna, seven bridges (*lead*) ... across the Danube.
9. At the moment, Mum (*speak*) ... with her friend Emily.
10. Don't disturb me, please! I (*think*)...!
11. Look at the people! They (*all, go*)... to the concert.
12. Listen, somebody (*call*) ... your name.
13. Slow down, Jackie. You (*go*) ... too fast for me.
14. I (*leave*) ...! (*anybody, come*) ... with me?

B 43 **Bilde die Entscheidungsfrage und die Verneinung und frage nach den unterstrichenen Satzteilen.**

1. <u>Many people</u> spend <u>their spare time</u> <u>outdoors</u>.
2. <u>We</u> are going <u>home</u> <u>in ten minutes</u>.
3. Oliver leaves <u>the office</u> <u>at five p.m.</u>
4. Gina is crying <u>because she is sad</u>.
5. <u>Alicia and Rudy</u> dance <u>excellently</u>.
6. Every year, the Coopers invite <u>all their neighbours</u> to a garden party.

CD 44 ***Present simple or progressive?***

1. Who (*speak*) ...? Who? I (*not understand*) ... you!
2. Charlie (*be*) ... an honest person. He never (*lie*) ... .
3. I usually (*come*) ... home from school between 3 and 3.30.
4. Today, my class (*go*) ... to the cinema to see the latest Harry Potter film.
5. Claudia always (*talk*) ... about herself. This (*get*) ... quite boring!
6. Gina (*want*) ... to go home now. She (*not feel*) ... well.
7. Why (*you, laugh*) ...? – Because Nick always (*tell*) ... funny stories.
8. What (*the boys, do*) ... in the garden? – They (*build*) ... a snow castle.
9. Most restaurants (*open*) ... at noon and in the evening.
10. Run! They (*close*) ... the doors!
11. (*you, always, walk*) ... to school? – No, Mum usually (*drive*) ... me.
12. This was my grandpa's watch, but now it (*belong*) ... to me.
13. Sue can't come to the phone right now. She (*take*) ... a shower.
14. Sue (*shower*) ... every evening, and twice a week she (*wash*) ... her hair.

18. KAPITEL – *PRONOUNS*

A 45 Setze die passenden persönlichen Fürwörter ein.

1. Where are ..., Silvia? I can't see ...!
2. Is Michael here? Somebody has brought a letter for ... .
3. Sarah is only three years old, but ... can count to 20.
4. Please tell the boys that ... must be back before dark.
5. Joe, come here! I must speak with ...! – ...'m coming, Dad!
6. Jim and I often go to the cinema, and sometimes Tom comes with ... .
7. Jim and I love films. ... go to the cinema every weekend.
8. Girls, have ... seen Jenny? – Yes. ... is in the schoolyard with the boys.
9. When you see the girls, tell ... I want to see ..., please.
10. The girls are in the music room. ... are practising for the concert.
11. Don't take this umbrella. ... doesn't work.
12. Simon has got a new bike. – I know. ... always talks about ...!
13. Look, there are Lisa and Jill. Let's walk over to ... .
14. Bob, ... know Veronica, don't ...? – Yes, ... is my cousin.

A 46 Ersetze die unterstrichenen Wörter durch passende Fürwörter.

1. The boys are okay. Let's invite the boys to the party.
2. Please don't tell my mum about the accident.
3. The car was expensive, but Dad wanted the car.
4. Sometimes my sister and I visit Uncle Albert.
5. Helen often quarrels with me and my sister.
6. The new dress looks very good on you.
7. You can put the books on the shelf.
8. Oscar liked the new song very much.

B 47 Setze das passende *possessive pronoun* ein.

1. I like Joe, but ... brothers are silly.
2. Me and ... sister often do things together with ... parents.
3. Julia, can I come to ... place after school? ... mum says it's okay.
4. I could see the car, but I could not see ... driver.
5. Look, there are Sabrina and ... new boyfriend. I think ... name is Justin.
6. Boys, you can't race ... model cars here. There is too much traffic!
7. Dad thinks ... next motorbike will be a Harley-Davidson; he likes ... sound.
8. Nobody in my class likes ... new history teacher.
9. I've found a bunch of keys in the corridor. Are they ..., Martina?
10. This is not my sweatshirt. It is blue, and ... is red and white.
11. This looks like Helen's scarf, doesn't it? – Yes, it's ... . I've seen her wear it.
12. Girls, you can't wear these uniforms. They are not ...!
13. Let me use the PC now! It's ... and I can use it whenever I want to!
14. Tim and Sue live in a big old house, but it isn't ...; it belongs to Sue's dad.
15. Whose trainers are these, Joe? ... or your brother's? – They are ..., because my trainers are smaller.

E 48 Setze die passenden *reflexive pronouns* ein.

1. Babies cannot take care of ..., so they need their parents.
2. Can you do it ... or shall I help you?
3. Believe me, the story is true. I've heard it from Mr. Smith ...!
4. When I have a lot to do, I really enjoy being all ... for a few minutes.
5. Monica is strange, isn't she? She always speaks with ... during the lesson.
6. The Queen ... will be at the opening of the Edinburgh Festival.
7. Nobody was there, so the boys had the whole place to ... . That was fun!
8. This computer will shut ... off after two minutes.
9. Children, you can't stay here ...! It's too dangerous.
10. Sometimes I have to remind ... to work a little harder.
11. Money ... is not important, but it makes life a lot easier.
12. When Sue gets nervous, she tells ... that everything will be alright.
13. Benny is very proud of ... because he finished the project all ... .
14. Did you make these decorations ..., girls, or did somebody help you?

E 49 *"self-pronouns"* oder *"each other"/"one another"*?

1. Boys, you have to work together and help *yourselves/each other*.
2. The two groups should speak with *themselves/each other* and not fight.
3. Tim and I are proud of *ourselves/each other* because we finished the game.
4. Since Betty moved to Canada, we often write to *ourselves/each other*.
5. Since Betty moved to Canada, she and Tom have not seen *themselves/each other* very often.
6. You should ask *yourselves/each other* why your results are not better.
7. The day on the beach was great fun, and we enjoyed *ourselves/each other* very much.
8. The Coopers and the Browns have not visited *themselves/each other* for some time, although they are good friends.

E 50 Übersetze die folgenden Sätze ins Englische.

1. Ich mache mir oft Sorgen, ob ich die Prüfung schaffe (*make*).
2. Du denkst immer nur an dich selbst!
3. Joe war so müde, dass er sich nicht bewegen konnte.
4. Mary ist wieder gesund (*well*). Der Arzt hat es ihr selbst gesagt.
5. Oma hat den Kuchen für uns gebacken, nicht für sich selbst.
6. Tom und Tina trafen sich nach der Schule im Park.
7. Ich fühle mich hier nicht wohl (*comfortable*).
8. Möchtest du alleine sein?
9. Ich hoffe, du hast dir nicht den Finger gebrochen!
10. Der Mann setzte sich neben uns und begann, mit sich selbst zu reden.
11. Du wirst dich verletzen, wenn du so unvorsichtig (*careless*) bist.
12. Wir fragen uns oft, warum du nicht hier bist.
13. Du musst dich beeilen! Der Bus wartet nicht.
14. Ich kann mich wirklich nicht an dich erinnern.

19. KAPITEL – *QUESTION AND NEGATION*

AB 51 **Bilde zuerst die die Entscheidungsfrage und die Verneinung und anschließend so viele Ergänzungsfragen wie möglich.**

1. Everybody is happy.
2. The children are playing hide and seek in the garden.
3. I was your best friend in kindergarten.
4. Norah has answered all the questions correctly.
5. The ambulance will be here in five minutes.
6. You can hear me from here.
7. I can stay up late tonight.
8. We must do these exercises again because we've made many mistakes.
9. The girls want to go home in half an hour.
10. Stephen lives with his parents.
11. You went to bed late last night.
12. The people came to hear the President speak.
13. Manuel played the drums in a rock band when he was younger.
14. Olivia works as a skiing instructor in the Tyrol.
15. It rains most in June and July.
16. They close the shop over the weekend.

C 52 **Bilde mit den folgenden Sätzen die „Nicht wahr"-Frage (*tag question*, Frage-Anhängsel) und beantworte sie in Form von Kurzantworten (soweit vorgesehen).**

1. Bill is an excellent skier, ...? – Yes, ...
2. I'm on the list, ...? – No, ...
3. You aren't angry at us, ...? – Oh yes, we ...!
4. Gina was not on the train, ...? – No, ...
5. You weren't in the room when the lights went out, ...? – Yes, I ... .
6. I haven't done anything wrong, ...? – No, ...
7. Your dad has sold his motorbike, ...? – Yes, ...
8. There will be music and dancing, ...? – Yes, ...
9. You won't call the police now, ...? – Oh yes, ...!
10. Soon you will forget the whole thing, ...? – No, ...
11. We can do it tomorrow, ...? – No, you ... . You must do it now!
12. You can't help me, ...? – Yes, ...
13. You don't know my name, ...? – No, I'm sorry ... .
14. Alice lives in London now, ...? - Yes, ...
15. Doris drives a Renault, ...? – No, ... She drives a Peugeot.
16. Children like chocolate, ...? – Of course ... .
17. It doesn't rain any more, ...? – Yes, ... Look for yourself.
18. Mozart wrote many operas, ...? – Yes, ...
19. You didn't miss the train again, ...? – I'm sorry, but ... .
20. Let's talk about something else, ...? – Okay, fine with me.

20. KAPITEL – *RELATIVE CLAUSES*

AG 53 **Setze ein Relativpronomen ein, wo es sein muss, und lasse es weg, wo es möglich ist.**

1. I have no idea ... you want me to do, Dad.
2. My grandfather is the person ... I respect most.
3. The people ... live across the street are from Scotland.
4. This is the film ... won the "Golden Globe" last year.
5. Did you like the music ... they were playing at the party?
6. We are looking for the person ... car is blocking the exit.
7. Bob broke his arm when he crashed into the tree, ... must have hurt a lot.
8. I'd like to visit the town ... my dad was born.
9. Can you tell me ... we have to go to this meeting?
10. Do you know the people ... we are waiting for?
11. Light travels at about 300,000 km per second, ... is very, very fast.
12. The shirt ... you are wearing today is very elegant.
13. All the foxes ... were kept on the farm ran away during the night.
14. Alan, ... sister you will meet tonight, is one of my new friends.

G 54 **Verbinde die folgenden Sätze mit Hilfe von Relativsätzen miteinander.**

1. Have you seen the cake? Mum has baked it for the party tomorrow.
2. This is the man. He has bought the pizzeria on the corner.
3. The film was quite shocking. We saw it in biology today.
4. Do you know the people? Their car is for sale.
5. Mum? There's a man on the phone. He wants to speak with you.
6. We stayed at the hotel. You had told us about it.
7. Kevin's temperature is normal again. This is a good sign.
8. Tanya is interested in clothes. This is quite normal for a girl her age.

H 55 **Einschränkende und erweiternde Relativsätze: Setze Relativpronomen und Beistriche dort ein, wo es sein muss, und lasse sie dort weg, wo es sein kann oder muss.**

1. Mr. Morris ... was my dad's boss for many years has died.
2. I like talking to people ... come from all corners of the world.
3. Lance Armstrong ... is American won the Tour de France seven times.
4. The man ... sold us the DVD player was not very competent.
5. Sandra has hurt her elbow ... means she can't play tennis this week.
6. We were shown around Rome by a tour guide ... English was excellent.
7. Look, Joe! This is the man ... you have to ask if you want to know more.
8. The London Eye ... is the city's latest attraction is near the Parliament.
9. Everybody wanted to interview John Smith ... horse had won the race.
10. The factory ... my grandfather used to work has been shut down.
11. Police are looking for the paintings ... have been taken from the museum.
12. Santa Fe ... is the capital of New Mexico is famous for its architecture.
13. Ms. Jones did not like ... I had written, so I had to write it again.

21. KAPITEL – *SINGULAR AND PLURAL*

E 56 **Setze *"much, many, a lot of, lots of"* (1–7) und *"little/(a) few"* (8–10) ein.**

1. Do you know how ... people came to hear U2?
2. That's too ... work for today. I'll do the rest tomorrow.
3. Our new car cost £ 35,000. – Wow! That's ... money!
4. Are there ... girls in your class, Joe? – No, not ..., but we have ... of fun.
5. There are too ... cars in the streets and there is too ... pollution.
6. I like these jeans! How ... are they? – 15 £. – That's not ... . I'll take them.
7. Gerald's uncle moved to New York ... years ago.
8. Dad's favourite hobby is climbing, but he has ... time for it.
9. I love fishing, but only ... of my friends like it, too.
10. Hurry up, there's only ... time left before the game starts.

F 57 **Setze *all, every, each, some* oder *none* (oder Zusammensetzungen) ein:**

1. It rained ... day yesterday, so ... of us could do much outside.
2. Mrs. Jenkins asked ... of us to write an essay, but ... of us did it.
3. ... girls in my class like science fiction, and ... don't.
4. ... school day starts at 8 a.m., which is too early for me.
5. Grandma, can you tell me ...thing about Dad when he was young?
6. Maria goes to church ... Sunday.
7. ... the women in my family have the same hair colour – they are ... blond.
8. The museum is open ... year, except on December 24.
9. You can ask ... of my friends, and they will tell you the same thing.
10. Do you know these girls? – Only ... of them.

22. KAPITEL – *SOME & ANY*

A B 58 **Setze *"some"* oder *"any"* ein.**

1. There's ... milk in the fridge, but there isn't ... juice.
2. I need ...thing to write on. Is there ... paper in the drawer?
3. If you need ... information, I can give you ... .
4. Jill says she saw ...one entering the house a while ago, but she didn't see ...body coming out again.
5. You know, Lucy, you can tell me if ...thing's wrong! I'm your friend.
6. Do you know ...body who could repair this lock?
7. I know my keys are ...where on my desk, but I can't see them ...where.
8. Let's ask the people over there. I'm sure ... of them can tell us the way.
9. I think the post office is ...where near the church, but I'm not sure.
10. Mum wanted to buy ... mushrooms, but they didn't have ... at the shop.
11. Would you like a drink? I can mix you ...thing you like.
12. ... people asked me about the accident, but I didn't tell them ...thing.

STICHWORTVERZEICHNIS